2.23.73

*Hawaiian
Land
Mammals*

Hawaiian Land Mammals

by Raymond J. Kramer

With illustrations
by Khan Pannell

Charles E. Tuttle Company

Representatives

FOR CONTINENTAL EUROPE
Boxerbooks, Inc., Zurich
FOR THE BRITISH ISLES
Prentice-Hall International, Inc., London
FOR AUSTRALASIA
Paul Flesch & Co., Pty. Ltd., Melbourne
FOR CANADA
M. G. Hurtig Ltd., Edmonton

Published by the Charles E. Tuttle Company, Inc.
of Rutland, Vermont & Tokyo, Japan
with editorial offices at
Suido 1-chome, 2-6, Bunkyo-ku, Tokyo

Library of Congress Catalog Card No. 74-134030
International Standard Book No. 0-8048-0743-4

First printing, 1971

PRINTED IN JAPAN

For my Parents
and
Carolyn & Mike

1741795

Table of Contents

7

List of Illustrations

Acknowledgments

I first started compiling information for this book in late 1959. In my haste to record what I felt were pertinent data, I made the very serious error of recording many of my sources only by their Dewey Decimal System library code number; I had, at that time, the notion that I would shortly begin writing, and that I could refer back to these numbers at a later date for the exact bibliographic reference. In late 1967, when I finally returned to the University of Hawaii library to begin examining these data in detail, I was dismayed to find that the library had converted its book code to the Library of Congress numbering system, and that my entire searching code was valueless. I am therefore grateful beyond words to Dr. P. Quentin Tomich, who, in understanding the many hundreds of hours it would have taken to relocate these articles, very kindly allowed me to use a prepublication copy of the annotated bibliography which forms an invaluable section of his book *Mammals in Hawaii: A Synopsis and Notational Bibliography.*

I am much indebted to Mr. Khan Pannell for his very fine pencil sketches which are quite representative of the species discussed.

I am also under grateful obligation to Messrs. Gerald Swedberg, Ronald Walker, and David Woodside, biologists with the State Division of Fish and Game, for the considerable time, effort, and counsel that they devoted to discussion and review of the various chapters; I am also grateful to Mr. Swedberg for his editing skill. I also appreciate the help and information given me by Messrs. Nelson Rice and William Kwon of this same agency.

Mr. Noah Pekelo, Jr., with his intimate knowledge of the Molokai flora and fauna, was of great help in regard to questions about that island, and Mr. Norman Llewellyn gave me some excellent information and insights into the habits of the Kalihi Valley wallabies.

Mr. Edward H. Bryan, Jr., kindly showed me much of the Bishop Museum materials; Dr. Frederick Lynd discussed a number of questions concerning parasites and disease with me; Dr. Allen Miyahara did parasitological work on the wallaby, and Mr. Herbert Kikukawa was an excellent source of information concerning feral animals on the island of Hawaii.

I am also indebted to Mr. Paul Breese, not only for the considerable information he gave me concerning the wallaby but for his general enthusiasm and information imparted me about all of Hawaii's animals.

Drs. Andrew Berger and Stuart Gerry Brown very kindly read portions of the manuscript and made valuable comments. Particular acknowledgment is due Dr. William Graf and Mr. Lyman Nichols, Jr., for not only the instruction and information they have given me over the years but for the many pleasant and memorable field outings I have had with them in the study of Hawaiian mammals.

It should be noted here that the several photographs not credited are my own.

Lastly, I wish to acknowledge a great debt to Miss Sally Bright, whom, it seems in retrospect, was often the only force, through her optimistic cheer and encouragement, that finally allowed me to bring this book to completion.

Introduction

The Hawaiian archipelago is comprised of 73 islands, islets, pinnacles, and atolls stretching some 1,600 miles across the north Pacific Ocean. With the exception of Midway Atoll—which is under the jurisdiction of the federal government—all of these islands belong to the state of Hawaii. Today, ten of these islands or atolls are inhabited by man; these include seven of the eight large islands (Kahoolawe is presently uninhabited), Tern Island of the French Frigates Shoal group, Midway, and Kure atolls. Although Kahoolawe, Laysan, and Lisianski islands were inhabited in historical times, and Nihoa and Necker islands were once the home of an as-yet-unidentified group of Polynesian migrants, the other 58 islands were probably never used as places of permanent residence.

Prior to the arrival of the early Polynesians the only mammals living on this island chain were a rare seal and an even rarer subspecies of American bat. Sometime during the early migration of Polynesian people to Hawaii the dog, the pig, a rat, and perhaps a mouse, were introduced to some of the larger islands, but it was not until sometime after the discovery of Hawaii, in 1778, by Capt. James Cook, that the other species discussed in this book were introduced.

Today, 22 species of animals live under either wild, feral, or free-ranging conditions; two other species, the guinea-pig and the water buffalo, lived in a feral state for a few years but are

17

now entirely under man's control, and the Chinese ox, though commonly used on many islands in the late 1800s, was never known to have become feral or free-ranging. A number of pet animals have escaped into the wilds of Hawaii at one time or another but none are known to be extant today.*

In this book the word "feral" will be used in its broadest meaning: an animal that was once domesticated, or one that was born of domesticated ancestors, but which subsequently lived, or is now living as a wild creature. If we were to try to define ferality in any stricter sense it would be necessary to ask a number of questions for which, to my knowledge, no answer has ever been satisfactorily given. Perhaps it would be more proper to call the mules that live in the wilds of Hawaii "loose" rather than feral, since they cannot reproduce their kind; similarly, we should perhaps refer to the dogs and cats who succumb to "the call of the wild" for a few days or weeks as being "temporarily feral" or "free-ranging," but because the primary purpose of the following chapters is to give a simply understood overview of the past history and present status of the untamed mammals inhabiting the various islands, we shall not entangle ourselves in the offtimes confusing field of scientific nomenclature.

In the course of my residence in Hawaii I have found that an astounding percentage of the population is not only unaware of

* An American gray squirrel was caught at Schofield Barracks, Oahu, in 1943 and others were reported at large there (*Hono. Star-Bull.*, 12/21/43). An American black bear cub escaped from a private owner on Oahu sometime in the middle 1950s and was seen from time to time in the Koolau mountains; the last known report (tracks only) was June 19, 1966, at the Aiea Heights trail. Numerous pet monkeys have escaped from their owners; most escapes have been on Oahu, but at least one animal (a crab-eating macaque) roamed above Hilo, Hawaii, for a few years, and another unidentifed animal ran loose on Kure Atoll for at least two years. Although no one today knows the disposition of the animal, it is interesting to note that J. T. Waterhouse brought a camel to Hawaii in 1861 on the clipper *Yankee* (*Hawaiian Annual*, 1940, p. 140).

the broad spectrum of mammalian species inhabiting the islands but that many persons are quite uneducated as to the physiological characteristics that link them to such diverse creatures as the bat, the seal, and the diminutive kangaroo known as the rock wallaby. In answer to the casually asked question "What is a mammal?" the average person usually answers, "An animal that gives milk, of course!" While this is quite true, this answer is not, in itself, a sufficiently distinguishing character, and is in fact only about third in importance among some seven broad characters that allow present-day mammals to be separated from their earliest reptilian ancestors and from modern reptiles and birds. These seven characters, in their apparent order of importance, are as follows:

(1) *Homoiothermy.* A tongue-twisting word used by biologists which means that this group of animals has the ability to maintain a constant body temperature. This form of thermoregulation, which also occurs in birds, is probably the single most important attribute responsible for the world-wide success of these two groups. Not only does the maintenance of a constant body temperature allow physical activity under adverse conditions but it is also conducive to the development of mental processes, such as learning, memorization, and retention of information in an ongoing manner. There are two types of exception to a complete homoiothermy among mammals: the hibernators, and the bats, whose body temperature regulation is known as "imperfect." Although there are no hibernating mammals in Hawaii there is one species of bat with an imperfect homoiothermy, which causes a drop in body temperature when at rest. This drop is clearly associated with the tremendous amount of thin surface area in the bat's flight-modified forelegs, which makes the conservation of body heat difficult.

(2) *The possession of hair.* A growth similar in appearance to hair is commonly found on invertebrates, such as some flies or bees, but among the vertebrate animals, only the mammals possess true hair. Hairs are an outgrowth of a substance called

keratin (fingernails and toenails are composed of this same material) which is developed from the outer layer of the skin. The hair of each species of mammal is unique in structure and is often used by zoologists for purposes of identification. The importance of hair in most mammals can best be understood when one combines its presence with that of stable internal heat regulation; animals with both capacities are allowed a much greater range of movement throughout varying environments, thus allowing increased chances for survival of the species. Certain mammals, primarily aquatic or subterranean ones, have over eons of time evolved other means of retaining their body heat, with the subsequent result of a reduction in hair, but the tracts where these hairs once grew can still be found if one examines the skin surface closely, and there are always a few vestigial hairs remaining.

(3) *The possession of mammary glands.* Certain epidermal glands secrete milk directly to the exterior of the mother where the young takes it either from a more or less prominent nipple or merely laps it from a broader, less circumscribed area. The derivation of these glands is in debate by biologists as to whether they evolved from sweat glands or oil glands but it is obvious that they owe their origin to the prior development of hair, which made these original glands necessary.

(4) *The dentary (each half of the lower jaw) consists of a single bone.* All other vertebrates have a lower jaw containing several bones behind the dentary. In mammals, these other bones have re-formed and changed shape to become the tiny bones within the ear, the *malleus* and *incus*. Another component of the primitive lower jaw, the angular bone, has changed to form the tympanic ring, or bulla, in the ear of mammals.

(5) *The skull articulates (is united by a joint) with the first vertebra by means of two occipital condyles.* In mammals, the double condyles allow movement only in a vertical plane, with movement in the horizontal plane, or rotation of the head taking place back at the juncture of the first and second vertebrae; in birds

and most groups of reptiles there is only one single median con-
dyle, which allows movement in all directions.

(6) *The heart has four chambers.* This type of heart is much
more efficient since it keeps the pulmonary and systemic blood
from mixing (as occurs in more primitive hearts). Birds and
some other animals such as crocodiles also have a four-cham-
bered heart but from the arrangement of the arteries leading
into these hearts it is clear that this was due to an independent
type of evolution (a situation referred to as parallelism).

(7) *A muscular diaphragm separates the abdominal cavity from the
thoracic cavity.* In mammals other than humans, arboreal, serial,
and aquatic species, the diaphragm plays the major role in the
function of breathing; in the above-mentioned mammals the
thoracic muscles play the major role in respiration even though
the diaphragm continues to separate these two body areas.

The characters listed above, with the noted exceptions, are
found in all the three surviving groups of today's mammals,
namely the monotremes (spiny anteaters and platypus), the
marsupials (pouched animals), and the eutherians or placentals
(all other mammals). If we were to set aside the monotremes we
could name many additional characters, but it is not the purpose of this book to delve too deeply into technicalities, most of
which have little meaning for the nonprofessional person.

No single book could give a total account of all information
known about any one species. It will be evident, at least to biologists reading this book, that there are considerable gaps in the
life history data, or in discussions of social structure, in many
of the species mentioned. There are several reasons for these
omissions, perhaps the major one being that scientific studies
on all but a few species have been sadly lacking. Although a
great many researchers come to Hawaii to study, it would seem
that they are quite naturally more enchanted with the unique
native birds, the land shells or insects, or the wonderful array
of native plants, than they are with the seemingly dull study of

such commonly feral animals as cattle, sheep, goats, pigs, cats, or dogs. Although these animals have made a tremendous impact on our native ecosystem they are only occasionally mentioned in other studies, and have never, by themselves, been thoroughly and systematically studied.

Since a complete discussion of the rats and mice in Hawaii would have shown such a vast array of conflicting and as yet inconclusive information, and would have at the same time entailed writing chapters of several hundred pages in length, I have accorded only a relatively meager section of the book to these species.

A number of other animals, such as the pronghorn, the black-tailed deer, and the mouflon, have been purposely but recently introduced by the Hawaii State Division of Fish and Game. Although some data have been collected on the habits of these animals in their new environment much more information is needed. This will not only take time but will apparently only be obtained by either increasing that Division's biological staff or by soliciting for independent study grants.

It is my hope that a few years from now, when many of the needed studies are completed, I will be able to draw upon these new resources to present a more complete account of each of our island forms.

Hawaiian
Land
Mammals

The Brush-tailed Rock Wallaby

Petrogale penicillata

The rock wallaby belongs to a primitive order of mammals known as the Marsupialia, a word derived from the Greek language meaning "pouched." The name refers to the fact that in many species in this group the female has an abdominal pouch which encloses the milk-giving nipples; here the very immaturely formed young find their way shortly after birth, attach themselves to a nipple, and continue their physical development. Marsupials are separated into specialized family groups, and the rock wallaby belongs to the kangaroo family known as the Macropodidae, another Greek term, meaning "big foot." The front feet of the Macropodes are much smaller than the hind ones, and always have five toes; the hind feet have the first toe missing, the second and third toes short and small and enclosed in a common skin, and the fourth toe is so large that it provides the major point of support for the animal. The outermost, or fifth toe, is even shorter than the second and third ones and is quite unimportant. As a consequence of this peculiar development of the hind foot, the more typical members of this family normally progress over the ground by a series of enormous leaps. The tail has evolved to either help support the body (as in the larger kangaroos) or to act as a stabilizing rudder as they sail through the air (helpful to all species of kangaroo). The Macropodes are arranged in a number of generic groups, and the species vary in their habitat from the flat open central plains, through the scrub country, and into the dense forest lands. The larger kangaroo-type animals are variously known as kangaroos, wallaroos, and wallabies, and they diminish in size accordingly.

Although closely allied to the true wallabies, the rock wallabies differ distinctly in habits, and can be externally separated from the true wallabies by the fact that the region around their nose is entirely naked, the fur on the back of the neck is directed downward, the central claws of the hind feet are very short (an obvious advantage to a cliff-living animal, where friction, and not sprinting power, is the key to survival), and the tail is long, cylindrical, thinner, and is more thickly haired (including a tuft at the tip) than in the flatland wallabies. The rock wallaby also has another interesting adaptation to its rugged environment: the soles of the feet are "tuberculated," meaning that they are covered with little tubercles or bumps on all the pads. These provide added friction for traversing steep slopes.

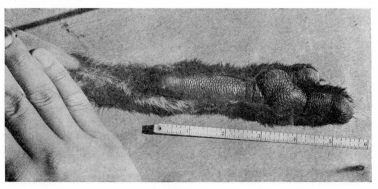

Bumps on the soles of the rock wallaby.

The reason most people in Hawaii never see the wallaby is because of its diminutive size and its coloration, which matches almost perfectly the color of the lava rocks which shelter it. I have been able to measure only one animal and this appeared to be not quite full grown. The comparative measurements are as follows:

Origin and Age	Total Length	Head and Body	Tail	Hindfoot	Ear-Crown
Australia (LeSouef, 1926) Adult	50.2 in. (128 cm.)	28.3 in. (72 cm.)	21.9 in. (56 cm.)	6.1 in. (15.4– 16.4 cm.)	1.9 in. (4.8– 5.1 cm.)
Hawaii, Male, about 1 year	38.9 in. (98.9 cm.)	20.4 in. (51.8 cm.)	18.5 in. (47 cm.)	5.7 in. (14.5 cm.)	2.3 in. (5.9 cm.)

The color is difficult to describe unless we take the animal "piece by piece." The head is a gray-brown with poorly defined whisker marks; there is a gray-cream cheek stripe proceeding from below the eye toward the nose. Below this stripe, and continuing under the jaw the color is blackish gray. The inside and anterior edges of the ears are yellow-rufous; the outside is black at the tip and gray at the base. The crown is gray with a black line running from its center posteriorly a short way down the neck, which is dark gray. The throat and chest are pale gray; the belly region is tinged with yellow down to the anal region where the color becomes a yellow-rufous. The rufous tone then extends around the base of the tail becoming darker, so that from a distance, the major portion of the tail appears rufous-black. Two to three inches of the tail tip may be yellowish (there seems to be no correlation with either age or sex in this character).

The general upper body color is a dull gray-brown but the color on the legs becomes gradually browner until the extremities appear black, with sturdy rufous hairs overlaying the last several inches. There is a blackish patch behind the fore-shoulder, succeeded by a gray one; these are particularly prominent during the cooler months. The young wallaby, or "joey," as it is called in Australia, is markedly darker and does not attain the yellowish or rufous colors until almost full grown.

This beautiful blending and counterpoint of color makes the rock wallaby extremely difficult to locate on the shadowed cliffs, particularly since they are usually seen just sitting quietly in the shadow of a cave.

HISTORY

Spencer Tinker, who wrote of these animals in his book *Animals of Hawaii* (1938), interviewed Richard H. Trent, who purchased the "Adam and Eve" of our present population, and leaves us with some well-documented facts. Add to Tinker's report the news releases of the *Pacific Commercial Advertiser* on August 19 and 20, 1916, and we see the beginning of an extremely unusual biological happening: the establishment, without man's help, of a thriving colony of animals in an alien environment, all springing from only one male and one female; a colony so successful in fact that at least one internal parasite present in the original pair exists today in the present population.

Ellis J. Josephs, an animal collector, purchased a number of Australian animals from the Sydney Zoological Garden and was on his way to the United States mainland to sell them when his ship stopped in Honolulu. Mr. Trent purchased a male and a female, who had a joey in her pouch, for $100, and took them to his home on Alewa Heights, where he also kept a private zoo. This was on August 18, 1916; the next day the wallabies, which were being temporarily housed in a tent until a cage could be built, were harassed by neighborhood dogs and bolted from the tent, with the dogs in hot pursuit. If there had been only the two adults the story might have ended there, as the dogs would probably have caught and killed the both of them. Female kangaroos have a habit of dropping their joey in a bush or clump of grass when being pursued, and returning to retrieve their young after the chase is over. The habit is obviously beneficial since a joey in the pouch is both cumbersome and heavy and certainly impedes the female in her attempts to escape. Whether the female employed this tactic on Alewa Heights, or whether the baby merely fell out of the pouch is unknown; the fact remains that the dogs caught the young one and killed it, while the adult wallabies made good their escape. Mr. Trent offered a reward of $25 for the return of the live wallabies while the *Advertiser* (August 21) offered the prophetic remark that "unless the animals are caught they may become permanent denizens of the mountain districts and . . . may propagate . . . a breed of Hawaiian wallabies."

Little was heard about the wallabies until five years later when the *Pacific Commercial Advertiser,* on March 29, 1921, reported that "the wallaby family has increased in number from the original couple to from 20 to 2,000 according to stories told on the street. While it is admitted that the wallaby multiplies rapidly, it is not believed that there are more than 50 all told on the Island today. The wallaby is now lunching in verdant truck gardens and eating all the ti leaves in sight. For this reason Elmer R. Davis, Bob Lillis, and other expert gunmen are forming a hunting party for Sunday. Mr. Davis also says the wallaby is good eating."

The results of this hunt are unknown and unreported; no further newspaper reports were forthcoming until 1937. Max Landgraf, the late state forester, and former chief of planting parties for the CCC around and above Kalihi Valley, stated that he was offered the opportunity to purchase live wallabies several times in the early 1930s for $25.

In 1937 (July 25) the *Advertiser* terminated a long silence on the subject by entitling a report with the heading "Dogs Mangle Baby Wallaby." The report went on to say, "A young wallaby, an animal similar to the kangaroo, but much smaller, was killed by dogs near Fort Shafter yesterday afternoon. . . .

It is believed the animal was one of many wallabies now roaming the uplands of Kalihi. A number of them were released in this section several years ago." The next *Advertiser* report (February 5, 1939) was entitled "Wallabies at Home in Wilds of Kalihi," and shed no new light on the subject except to estimate a population of about 100; only upper Kalihi Valley was mentioned.

Sometime prior to this report Tinker (*op. cit.*) wrote, "Some Honolulu citizens thought that it might be desirable to protect the wallaby in order to prevent their extermination and, at the same time, give them a chance to increase in number. With this in mind, a bill was introduced into the Territorial legislature, providing a closed season for a period of five years during which time the wallabies might increase in number and better establish themselves. The bill was withdrawn at the suggestion of the Territorial Board of Agriculture and Forestry when it was realized that the wallabies ate only vegetation and might, if they became numerous, do considerable damage to the native forests. Later observations seem to show that this wallaby does not eat trees, but subsists entirely on grass."

From 1939 on, this agile marsupial dropped into anonymity, at least as far as the newspapers were concerned, and the only people who paid any attention to its exploits were residents of Kalihi Valley and passing pig hunters. In 1951, Paul Breese, the former director of the Honolulu Zoo, sent two keepers into Kalihi Valley where they grazed an adult male across the crest of the nose with a single shot, and brought it back to the zoo. It lived there ten days before it succumbed to the injury. Mr. Breese put it in a freezer, where it remained until February 1956, when he shipped it to the Smithsonian Institution. In the next month, Dr. David Johnson of the Smithsonian officially identified the carcass as that of the brush-tailed rock wallaby, *Petrogale penicillata*. The word *Petrogale* is from the Greek language meaning "rock weasel," and *penicillata* is from Latin meaning "brushy-tipped." Both Mr. Breese and Dr. Johnson were quite excited with this identification since it would appear that this particular species is in danger of becoming extinct in its native range. Aside from its native range in southeastern Australia and here in Hawaii, it occurs only on a tiny island called Kawau off the coast of New Zealand, where due to an extermination policy of the New Zealand government, it may be doomed to eventual extinction.*

Our wallaby is so rare in its native land that it has been recorded in Francis Harper's book of endangered wildlife entitled *Extinct and Vanishing Mammals of the Old World*. In Australia in the late 1800s this species was killed in great numbers for its fur, each skin selling at a price varying from threepence to one shilling-and-threepence (Lydekker, 1894). About this same time, the European fox was introduced to Australia; the wallaby had long before adapted to its natural enemies, such as rock pythons, dingoes, and the occasional wedge-tailed eagle, but the fox was something new. Combined with the indiscriminate hunting and trapping pressures of man, and the ravages of the fox, the wallaby began to disappear from its normal haunts. In 1916 it was thought to be extinct in the state of Victoria (Wakefield, 1954) and was not seen there again until 1937. The "rocky," as it is fondly called by the Australians, is still so rare in much of its range that, when I corresponded with Mr. Wakefield in 1961, he asked if I could not arrange to trap a number of the Hawaiian animals and ship them back to Australia, where he was trying to found a protected reserve for them.

* The animal was introduced to Kawau about 1870 (LeSouef, 1930, p. 111) along with two other genera of wallabies, and exhibited after some 60 years a "longer and softer fur and more pronounced coloration. . . ." In view of the rarity of this species I suggested to officials of the New Zealand Forestry Department that they allow the animal to remain unmolested, but they explained that, in view of their government's decision to exterminate all introduced wild mammals, and due to the recognized difficulty of selective poisoning or trapping once the killing program gets under way, it was just not practical to try to save them.

PRESENT STATUS

It would appear that when the original pair raced away from the dogs, they bounded down the north-facing slope of Alewa Heights, passed just above Kamehameha School, and kept going until they reached Kalihi. Here, just above the present Kalihi Elementary School, they stopped and took up residence on this sheer, southerly facing cliff, which is riddled with tiny caves and resembles an area called "Wallaby Rocks" near the Suggan Buggan River in Victoria. After more than 50 years, the major colony is still in these Kalihi cliffs. An estimate of the total number present puts it at less than 100, and in this main colony in Kalihi there are probably not more than 30. The most I have been able to observe in one day with assurance that no individual was counted twice was 14, and this included joeys in the pouch. In the late 1930s and in the early 40s, the total population probably approached 100 animals; with the war and the increasing urbanization, a number of factors combined to force the expanding population back to its original stronghold, where, unless purposely eliminated, a small, but perhaps declining number may continue to exist for many years to come.

DISTRIBUTION AND HABITAT

The brush-tailed rock wallaby lives today in an extremely limited geographic area. The limitations have been imposed by its natural predeliction for relatively dry living accommodations, by its aversion to traveling any distance from steep cliff areas, by its apparent loosely grouped social structure, and probably most important, by man's encroachment upon and through areas which would have provided suitable habitat for a larger population.

When I first began a study of the wallaby in 1960, the first problem was to locate a colony which was not only relatively accessible but would also provide clues to the preferred habitat. It soon became evident that the wallabies in Kalihi lived in a very restricted section of the valley. They were to be found only on the south-facing cliff and were bounded on the southwest by a ridge dropping down to the grounds of the Kalihi Elementary School, and bounded roughly to the northeast by the second line of *kukui* trees (*Aleurites moluccana*). There are several eroded gulches on this cliff face and I noted that the wallabies lived only in the caves of the southwesterly facing slopes, even though they fed and scampered about on the faces looking toward the Wilson Tunnel. A careful study of these opposing gulch slopes soon showed the reason. In Hawaii the tradewinds blow, more than 80 percent of the time, from the northeast or east; whistling down through Kalihi Valley, they pick up clouds and moisture from the head of the valley and carry these down along the valley edges, where they dissipate as the valley broadens. The effect on the wallaby habitat has been to cause a subtle change in the vegetative pattern of the opposing slopes of the gulches, as well as permeating the east-facing caves with continual moisture.

After reviewing the facts that all the Kalihi wallabies lived on the south-facing, and consequently drier and less heavily vegetated slopes; that they carefully avoided the wetter caves; that they did not penetrate into the forest deeper than the *kukui* trees, which characteristically prefer the 60- to 80-inch rainfall zone, the conclusion was reached that the species was a predominantly dryland one. In 1942 Ripperton and Hosaka proposed a series of vegetation zones for Hawaii, and after comparing over 50 plant species collected in the immediate vicinity of the colony, I tentatively assigned the habitat to one known today as the "guava zone." More specifically, the wallabies' habitat preference appears to be at the transitional point where the guava zone blends into the "*koa* zone."

The next step in the study was to determine the overall distribution. Sighting reports were confusing, spotting animals in such diverse places as Makapuu Point, in the forest above Waimea, "somewhere" in the Waianae Range, and in the mountains north of Kaneohe, where rainfall occasionally reaches over 250 inches annually. Through dozens of interviews it was possible to discount all of the reports; I interviewed scores of pig hunters, who frequented both the Koolau and Waianae mountain ranges with their packs of dogs, and never met one who had seen a wallaby anywhere other than on Fort Shafter Ridge, overlooking Kalihi. Edward Y. Hosaka, who did an intensive ecological and floristic study in Kipapa Gulch from 1931 through 1935, never saw any tracks, runs, or droppings in Kipapa although he was familiar with the Kalihi animals. Kipapa and Waipio gulches are the only two possible avenues of approach to the Waianae Range since they cut down through the Schofield Plateau toward Pearl Harbor and are intersected by stream beds emanating from the Waianaes. In 1957 a male wallaby was captured on the second floor of a barracks building at Tripler Hospital and given to the Honolulu Zoo. Earlier, around 1950, Mr. William Mullahey had seen one on the upper reaches of the Moanalua Golf Course, just north of Tripler. Other than these reports on the areas north of Kalihi, the only verifiable sightings have been of occasional animals seen on the north slopes of Kapalama Stream, just below Kamehameha School, one ridge south of Kalihi.   **1741795**

Beginning at Kipapa Gulch and working south and east as far as Niu Valley, I explored caves in every valley, concentrating on the areas known as the *"koa haole"* and guava zones.

Although I hoped to see wallabies, my primary goal was to search for droppings and skeletal remains, which would have been protected from the elements in caves. The wallaby dropping is somewhat similar in composition to goat droppings but is uniquely shaped and easily discernible from that of any other local animal species. I found many goat droppings, and quite a number of goat skeletons, even in areas where the last goat had been shot out in the early 1930s, but never once did I find an indication that the wallabies had spread toward Honolulu beyond Nuuanu Valley. The density of housing, the golf course intersecting the favored habitat, and the Pali Highway seem to have provided an effective barrier to further population extension in this direction. The Nuuanu population may in fact not be a colony at all, but merely an occasional animal which finds its way over the ridge, around the upper curve of the Oahu Country Club, and then to the sheer cliff about half way up Nuuanu Valley, on the south-facing slope. Only further intensified observations will tell the whole story.

To the north of Kalihi, I found occasional "runs," and an occasional dropping in a cave, but the droppings all appeared to be fairly old. Nowhere north of Moanalua Valley was there any evidence of a colony, past or present. In this area, the portions of the cliffs with the most shelter caves were near the heads of the valleys, and housing developments were under construction on the floors of these areas. Farther up these valleys, before reaching the wetter, less-preferred habitat, there are few caves and most of these are heavily obscured by dense brush. Indications are that the wallaby will not tolerate these areas of poor visibility, being dependent primarily upon his eyesight, rather than hearing or sense of smell, as a protective measure. Therefore, being aware from both visual observations and old newspaper reports that the wallaby did on occasion traverse the flatter lands heading out toward lower Kalihi and the Salt Lake area, the question arose as to why they did not now exist on the lower slopes of these areas, as well as on the sheer cliffs. The population pressures on this small cliff face certainly indicated potential for expansion, if I could give credence to the fact that nearly every female wallaby I observed had a joey in her pouch. The answer became obvious when I examined these slopes; the wallaby had indeed formerly used these lower areas, but today these relatively gentle slopes are the scene of continued passage, not only by humans but, of more definite impact, by dogs. The lower slopes are literally a crisscross of trails and I have often, in the course of one morning, seen old men, young boys with their .22 caliber rifles, romping dogs, and returning pig hunters with their leashed dogs, using the many trails to ascend or descend from Shafter Ridge. Our little kangaroos just could not tolerate, nor survive, the passage of so many transients.

Today we are left with a remnant colony which exists merely because the primary breeding and resting grounds are in excess of 60 degree slopes (in fact they more often vary from 80 to 90 degrees) and cannot be traversed by dogs or any but the most determined humans.

FOOD HABITS

Usually the first question posed by Hawaii's naturalists, after they get over their initial amazement at finding wallabies present, is "What do they eat? Do they cause any damage?" Their concern is based upon the important fact that over 1,700 species and varieties of plants have been described in the Hawaiian Islands that are "endemic," a term meaning that they have evolved their own specific configuration and unique character and are not found in a natural state anywhere else in the world. The naturalists are concerned that the wallaby, a strictly herbivorous animal, might destroy a floristic community that took millions of years to create. Fortunately for the plants, as well as for future generations of wallabies, the studies show little danger; the terrain that they presently inhabit was initially destroyed by the overgrazing of cattle, with subsequent erosive effects, and the plants that have revegetated the area have, for the most part, been "exotics" or those which are also found growing naturally in other areas of the world.

The food habits were studied over a period of 17 months by three methods: direct observation of animals eating portions of a plant, examination of plants consumed along wallaby runs, and evaluation of the contents of 450 fecal droppings. This latter method proved disappointing because the plant material was so thoroughly masticated that it was most often impossible to determine the species, although I could separate out the portions of the plant consumed. One hundred and seventy-four (38 percent) of the droppings contained grass parts, 180 (40 percent) had portions of woody stems or bark, and 396 (87 percent) contined leafy material from various shrubs and trees.

Three hundred and forty-one droppings (76 percent) contained seeds of 'ūlei (*Osteomeles anthyllidifolia*), which was one of only five species of endemic or indigenous plants on the food list I gathered (see Table 1). This woody shrub literally cascades down the major cliff area in dense tangled masses and its pea-sized white berries probably form the primary source of water for the wallaby. The other four native species were taken only occasionally.

There were a great number of other plant species in the wallaby habitat, but I could find no definitive evidence that they were used as foodstuff. It is important to note that *hamakua pāmakani* (*Eupatorium riparium*) was succeeding and crowding out the *ūlei* by 1968; this prolific seeder dominates all understory vegetation in areas it invades and is of no forage value. It has been declared a noxious species under Regulation 2 of the Noxious Weed Law of the state of Hawaii.

HABITS AND BEHAVIOR

Anyone with a consuming desire to study this small animal must be an early riser, because the rock wallaby is primarily a nocturnal or crepuscular animal (crepuscular meaning one which is most active during the dawn and twilight hours) although you can find one or more animals out at any hour of the day. On hot, sunny days the large majority of wallabies retreat to a cave by 9:30 A.M. after briefly sunning and washing themselves after a night foraging on adjoining grassy slopes and ridgetops. On cold, wet days after a night of rain you can find wallabies venturing forth, apparently reluctantly, all day long; the ap-

Table 1. Foods of the brush-tailed rock wallaby
on the island of Oahu, June 1960–November 1961

SCIENTIFIC NAME	COMMON NAME	KNOWN	PROBABLE	OCCURRENCE
Chloris inflata	swollen-finger grass		x	introduced
Paspalum fimbriatum			x	introduced
Paspalum conjugatum	hilo grass	x		introduced
Paspalum orbiculare	rice grass	x		introduced
Paspalum dilatatum	dallis grass	x		introduced
Setaria geniculata	yellow foxtail grass	x		introduced
Setaria verticillata	bristly foxtail grass		x	introduced
Tricholaena rosea	Natal grass		x	introduced
Amaranthus viridis	slender amaranth	x		introduced
Amaranthus spinosus	spiny amaranth		x	introduced
Osteomeles anthyllidifolia	'ūlei	x		indigenous
Acacia koa	koa	x		endemic
Cassia leschenaultiana	Japanese tea	x		introduced
Crotalaria incana	rattlebox	x		introduced
Desmanthus virgatus	slender mimosa	x		introduced
Indigo suffruticosa	indigo	x		introduced
Leucaena glauca	koa haole		x	introduced
Sida fallax	'ilima	x		indigenous
Passiflora foetida	foetid passionflower		x	introduced
Vaccinium dentatum	'ōhelo		x	endemic
Styphelia tameiameiae	pukeawe	x		endemic
Stachytarpheta mutabilis	changeable vervain	x		introduced
Stachytarpheta jamaicensis	Jamaica vervain	x		introduced
Schinus terebinthifolius	Christmasberry	x		introduced
Psidium cattleianum	strawberry guava	x		introduced
Psidium guayava	guava	x		introduced
Casuarina equisetifolia	ironwood		x	introduced

parent conclusion is that they do not feed heavily on nights like this. A look at my field notes in February show a typical morning observation: "Sunrise – 0650; Wind – 5–7mph; Weather – light rain blowing up valley [Kona], overcast and cloudy until 0830 when sun came out; Temperature – about 67–68 degrees. At 0800 saw wallaby under ledge where one was seen twice before; no food available on or in ledge. It remained unmoving until 0830 when the sun came out; then it moved out onto the edge of the ledge into the sunlight. It just sat, looking downward with no particular interest in any one thing—did not move its head—the only movement was shifting of rump to more comfortable position and scratched ear with right hind leg. Wild white pigeons zoomed by it, at which wallaby opened its eyes wide, noted with what appeared to be interest, then took a deep breath and exhaled heavily. It maintained the two common sitting postures; tail behind, leaning forward like a squirrel, or with body positions the same but with tail curved around to front and tip hanging over edge of the ledge. A white-eye (*Zosterops*) started chittering loudly and intensely; the wallaby noted this and looked intensely in that direction. Identified as a male; saw scrotum. He licked the right hind leg at 0841, then yawned, took several deep breaths and resumed posture; shifted rump again at 0844. Ears relaxed and not directed back now. At 0846 eyes shut. Shifted six inches forward at 0848, yawned, eyes half-shut, then looked down into valley steadily at 0850. Dog barked loudly in valley; no response from wallaby. At 0851 he licked his right hind leg again at the same place as before, yawned, licked his leg again, then proceeded to lick all over abdominal region and left foreleg; uses forepaws to separate the fur—very adept at this—separates, then licks between paws at base of fur. At 0900 he turned, hopped back into cave and sat facing the opening. He sat first in normal posture, then, flipping his tail to the left, pushed it under the left hind leg with the left forepaw. The tail then hangs forward between the hind legs with the wallaby actually sitting on the dorsal part of his coccyx. He then leaned back and stretched fore and hind legs as stiff in front of him as he could, then relaxed and remained in this position with his head very low on his chest.

"At 0910 spotted another; female; joey in pouch; pouch opening noticeable due to circular hole expanded about one-half inch with what appears to be line (no guard hairs) running posteriorly about two inches, toward the urogenital opening. She washed herself more or less steadily until 1000, left the rock at 1030, hopped off down the hill and through the Christmas-berry bushes. At one time the joey's lightly haired, blonde-brown tail protruded from the pouch opening about one and one-half inches.

"Male wallaby left when the sun fully entered its ledge. He washed himself about the same time that the female did. The female with young did not appear to be as bothered by itching as was the male."

Two months later, on an overcast wet day in April, I saw a rarely viewed, but common occurrence; a baby wallaby about two-fifths the size of an average adult. Assuming that it takes about one year to attain full size (including about four months in the pouch), I would guess it had not been out of the pouch for more than a month. The baby was alone in an almost inaccessible cave on a sheer rock face. It was washing itself in much the same pattern observed in adults. It washed its out-stretched hind legs first, then moved either up to the belly (most common in females about the region of the marsupium) or to the upper (fore) legs, where it washed from the tip of its claws back to the scapular region on both legs. It then proceeded to wash its face in the manner of a squirrel, with both forelegs at once, stopping occasionally to lick the inside of the wrist region. It then hopped farther out on the ledge where it nibbled at a Jamaica vervain plant.

A pair of wallabies were seen playing or fighting on the ridge just above the baby. At first it appeared they were battling but they then raced up the side of the cliff, stopped, then raced down, with one now obviously following the other with no harm meant. They both ended up going to the cave with the baby, where one wallaby halted about ten feet away from the joey and the other stopping about five feet away. All play between these two ceased from that time on, but no form of antagonism was shown. The baby hopped up to the closest one as soon as it arrived, and nursed for five minutes. To do this it stood next to the female, pulled the marsupial pouch out and down, and inserted its head into the pouch, helping hold it open with at least one paw at all times. These three stayed together for about 15 minutes with the other adult (male?) finally disappearing, the baby moving back into the cave as the heavy rain started, and the female just sitting unconcernedly in the rain.

Another look at some December notes say: ". . . an adult, dark-reddish-colored wallaby darted out from hiding and raced nonstop up the sheer face of the cliff for perhaps 20 yards where it leaped to a small indentation in the cliff face and squirmed headfirst into an almost unnoticeable hole barely large enough to accommodate its body; certainly no more than five inches in diameter. Not five seconds later, a second wallaby of the same size and coloration followed the identical route of the first where it also immediately entered the same hole, which probably opens up inside in a manner common to many lava tubes. They remained in this hole until at least 1:00 P.M. when I left."

After careful examination of dozens of field notes, a broad picture of the wallabies' individual and social habits begins to take form. Although the animals are colonial, they have a very loose social structure; more often than not each animal fends for himself, and during the heat of the day retires alone to any suitable cave that is not already occupied. Throughout the year one can note two adults, or two adults and one young, consorting but I have never noted three or more adults together.

I believe that the two adults are always a male and female, tolerating each other's presence for breeding purposes. This assumption is further borne out by the fact that young have been seen, or are known to have been present in the pouch, in every month of the year. The males are very pugnacious, a trait mentioned by Australian writers (LeSouef and Burrell, 1926) and further evidenced by the instance that occurred in the Honolulu Zoo—the female, which had been captured in May 1954, had been kept separate from the male until March 1960, when it was put in the same pen. The animal keepers noted extensive scraping and hair pulling having taken place on the neck and sides of the female for four days (an obvious attempt at breeding on the part of the male); on the fifth day the female was found dead in the pen. Close examination showed the brain case severely fractured; death was attributed to a powerful kick delivered by the male wallaby.

After spending the hotter hours of the day sleeping, scratching, and occasionally venturing to the mouth of the cave to sun itself, the rocky emerges from his solitude just at sundown. Following well-worn courses, he will browse slowly along, hopping two or three times then stopping for periods of up to five minutes. Suddenly, as though inspired, he will make a scrambling dash across the cliff at speeds estimated at 20 miles per hour. In doing so he will leap unhesitatingly, and apparently heedlessly, off a ten-foot cliff, touch for the merest fraction of a second a projecting rock or tree limb, and careen back to some tiny foothold on the cliff face where he launches himself once more with no perceptible hesitation. During this scramble his forelegs remain neatly positioned at a 30-degree angle from the body, with the forepaws tucked inward, and the long cylindrical tail flickering from side to side horizontally as he uses it as a balancing organ. Just as suddenly he will stop, usually on some bare, projecting rock, or occasionally on a leaning tree trunk, and not moving, will fade into the obscurity of the landscape. About this time the sun has disappeared and we can only follow his movements by conjecture and by observing footprints and droppings on fresh runs in the light of day. Many of the

Kalihi wallabies merely move to the wetter, open grassy slopes to feed, but some of the animals head up to the top of the ridge, where they browse on the grasses and plants alongside the jeep trail that follows the ridge and drink from the rainpools formed from the tire tracks of the army jeeps that patrol this area. Just before dawn the majority of animals head back toward their shelter caves; now is the time of greatest danger to them. The pig hunters with their dogs pass through the area on their way to the upper forest level and many a wallaby has been killed when caught by the pack. Wise pig hunters usually leash their dogs while passing through this area because a number of dogs have been killed by chasing a wallaby too closely; the rocky bounds off a cliff and goes home while the dog plummets down to a broken neck. The wallaby defecates while feeding, and prior to retiring to a cave to wash and sunbathe; it seldom, if ever, defecates in its sleeping cave. Wallabies do not necessarily use the same cave night after night; it seems to be merely a matter of who gets there first.

LeSouef (1926) says that if an intruder comes near a wallaby cave a "thump, thump" sound is made by the wallabies' foot pounding on the ground and that if there is no answering thump it will retreat, but I have found no evidence of this. In fact, it appears that, when in the vicinity of a protective cliff, the wallabies' sense of self-preservation is so amazingly low as to be almost nonexistent. Wakefield (1961) relates that ". . . Dempster came upon the wallaby . . . at the top of the rock chimney. He had been making considerable noise, crawling over rocks and breaking through dead twigs, but the animal had not been alarmed. Coming around the corner of a large rock, he saw it sitting quite relaxed, with the tail underneath and extended forward. Occasionally it looked at him—only six feet away— and then relaxed once more. The wallaby stood up and moved a few feet when Dempster withdrew to get in touch with me, but it was still there about ten minutes later. A colour photograph was taken from about six feet away as the animal stood with ears pricked, intent on the apparition half-emerged from the rocks that almost blocked the top of the chimney. It moved around then and sat on a large platform about 14 feet away and two more photographs were obtained . . ."

Another instance of this generally low sense of self-preservation occurred one day when, belayed by a rope tended by a friend, I worked my way along a crack in a sheer cliff wall. Rounding a small outcropping I came face to face with a rocky reclining on his back in a shallow cave. We looked at each other carefully, but the wallaby seemed not the least disturbed. I stood there for sometime, trying to decide what to do, and then decided to photograph him. Until the moment the shutter clicked the animal gave absolutely no indication of fear, and even then he merely tilted forward, hopped once to the front of the cave, and then hopped down onto my left knee which was wedged into a crack! As I came to my senses and grabbed for him, he quite casually bounced down to my narrow ledge and proceeded slowly around the corner.

Troughton (1944) reconfirms our observations by his statement that, "as with many Marsupials, the lack of an acute sense of self-preservation, which would make them such attractive tourist assets in our national reservations, actually endangers their survival beyond the next few decades of our civilization."

In addition to the supposed thumping sound, LeSouef (1926) also stated that the rock wallaby emits a single coughing note, and Norman Lewellan, a young Kalihi resident who knows the wallabies well, states that "they give a loud scream when chased." I accept this statement since Mr. Lewellan and his relatives captured quite a number of wallabies over the years and kept them in a backyard pen for a long while before releasing them when one of them bit his mother on the leg while she was cleaning the pen. Since it is presently illegal to capture or hunt this species, the relatively simple capturing technique will remain undescribed. Of interest is the observation that, with a wallaby captured with a broken leg in 1961, from nine in the morning, when it was caught, through a two-hour operation involving a hip incision and driving a steel pin in the length of the femur with minimal anesthetic, until its death the next morning, this unfortunate animal did not utter any sound at all, although the pain must have have been intense.

An observation made in June 1961, by Mrs. Hope Lee, while her husband and I scrambled up the cliff face she was watching, seems to be the first observation on the courtship behavior of the rock wallaby. Her notes record that "an adult female and a young wallaby were seen perched on a brushless rocky ledge. A male charged down toward them, then halted about six feet above them and stood erect with front paws 'reaching for the sky' and testicles prominently displayed. This display lasted two or three seconds. The male then rushed between the mother and the young, startling and scattering them. The female hopped up to the left about three feet, while the young hopped down to the right about six feet. The male then followed the female. The female then backed away from the male approximately three feet. After staring at each other a few seconds, the male began to bow to her. He stood up with his hind legs straight, assuming the 'reach-for-the-sky' posture and then bent from the hips toward the female, still keeping his forepaws stretched upwards near his ears. He did this four or five times, then the female acknowledged in the same manner. Then she hopped away a few feet. The male followed until she turned to face him. Both animals rose on their hind legs and bowed simultaneously to each other four or five times. Although they were about one foot apart at the low point in their bow, they continued this action in almost perfect rhythm. The female then hopped down to the young animal; the male did not follow but remained where he was. The mother and the young then began to feed casually, moving toward the cover of the Christmasberry bushes. About five minutes later, the male dropped from his higher position, landing on the female's back. All three animals milled about awhile and then disappeared into the brush."

GESTATION AND BIRTH

There was little study of marsupial reproduction until the mid-1920s but since that time there has been considerable work done on the physiology of reproduction in the larger kangaroos and wallaroos. Unfortunately, there have been no specific studies carried out on the brush-tailed rock wallaby. This is probably because of its relative rarity. By comparing studies done on other species it is possible to assume that certain statements probably hold true for our Hawaiian animal, but only a careful study under penned conditions will give us the ultimate truth.

LeSouef (1926), in describing the kangaroo family, states that "in the birth of the young we find a striking instance of the apparent lack of that maternal care and affection that is so strongly manifest in other animals, as the mother is seemingly unaware of the baby's existence."

Excerpts of David Fleay's observations on a smaller wallaby (1926) are indicative of the relatively premature stage at which most members of this family are born, and probably approximate those of *Petrogale*. Fleay writes, ". . . the young female . . . was sitting on her tail, which projected forward between the outstretched hind legs, and her head was bent forward, hiding the ventral surface. The animal was shivering violently and a muscular contraction of the abdomen was taking place. Then the keeper saw that the little creature was licking the cloaca and also holding her pouch open and cleaning that as well, while between times she cleaned her face with saliva-covered forepaws.

"In this crouching ball-like attitude the cloaca and entrance to the pouch . . . were no more than two inches from each other on a horizontal plane, and a definite furrow or parting in the fur of the abdomen formed a pathway between the two openings. A few minutes later, as the animal lifted its head from the licking process, the watcher noticed, for the first time, moving through the fur near the base of the tail, a minute red embryo (later found to measure one-half inch in length). The mother took little notice of it, but concentrated on licking away a small quantity of blood and embryonic membrane which had also been extruded." Fleay goes on to tell how the mother, getting nervous in the presence of other wallabies, moved, and the embryonic creature fell to the ground, then grasped the hairs of the female's tail, and continued crawling, but toward the tip of the tail instead of toward the pouch. Other writers have indicated that, in the kangaroos, the mother makes no effort to consciously place the newborn in the pouch, and babies have been observed to have crawled upward, missing the pouch opening and continuing up the mother's body until they died from exhaustion or were knocked to the ground by an inadvertent movement on the mother's part. These tiny, embryonic bodies, which are ten to fifteen millimeters long in *Petrogale penicillata* (Chiarugi, 1931), are naked, have only blue pigment spots marking the position of the eyes, and a tiny round hole at the tip of the muzzle which marks their mouth opening. Their forepaws show the most marked development and possess definite grasping powers.

Fleay, after describing how he had to eventually place the embryo in its mother's pouch himself, goes on to record that ". . . teats . . . were well developed, erect, and firmly pointed. From the botton of the moist glandular pouch into which it had rolled the creature instinctively concentrated on the mammae, moving first from one pair and then to the other. Between each of the two members of a pair grew a small tuft of reddish hair, and the embryo lost no time in grasping these in order to support itself. From this vantage point it made definite efforts to fasten its circular mouth opening to the mammae at various points along their respective lengths. . . . at 3:00 P.M. . . . and on opening the pouch it was found the much travelled "Joey" . . . was attached to the lower mammae on the animal's right side. The tiny fore limbs were still moving, as if the embryo was continually working to become more firmly fixed." Fleay continues, ". . . with the embryo aged exactly two months, the mother's pouch was again subjected to examination. Though still blind, and attached to the teat, it had grown considerably, and was now a much darker bluish-pink in color. Its shape was quite definite, and the total length of four inches . . ." He goes on to describe how this smaller species (*Setonix brachyurus*) was, at 16 weeks, "a well developed and very wild miniature edition of its mother."

We do not know just what the exact gestation period of the brush-tailed rock wallaby is, but because of the extremely undeveloped state of the emerging embryo, it is very doubtful if it is much over five weeks, if that much. Although Troughton (1947) has recorded instances of twins and even triplets occurring rarely in the larger kangaroos, it is believed that only one young is born to the wallaby.

The situation is made even more confusing by the fact that, in the marsupials, the female has two separate vaginal canals and uteri, either of which may be functional. Certain marsupials have given birth to young after long periods of isolation from males, and since it is known that some of these animals come into heat the day following birth (known as postpartum oestrus) and will copulate, it has been hypothesized that if fertilization takes place at that time, the resulting embryo remains as an unimplanted blastocyst during the time the pouch is occupied by a suckling fetus; this inactive stage of life will proceed to normal development if the first baby is removed from the pouch. It appears that the suckling of the young is the inhibiting factor to development of the blastocyst. As hormonal changes occur due to less nursing on the joey's part, the blastocyst begins its regular development. Eventually we end up with one baby too large to stay in the pouch, nursing on an elongated nipple from the outside and one still-helpless young yet in the pouch.

PARASITES

Due to the relatively small number of animals present in Hawaii, it was not thought advisable to kill any just for examination of parasites or measurements; therefore all data were derived from only one specimen, or from examination of feces gathered from the cliff face.

The one animal, an adult male, autopsied on October 5, 1961, initially exhibited no parasites in either the intestinal tract, the lungs, or the heart. The kidneys were noted to be slightly nephritic, there was evidence of cystitis of the bladder with no urinary calculi; the prostate gland was slightly gelatinous—comparable to that of a dog; and there was the possibility noted of the animal having biliary coccidiosis. Closer microscopic examination revealed roundworm eggs in the contents removed from the blind cardiac extremity of the stomach; these ova were initially identified as *Strongyloidea sp.,* just as were ova from fresh wallaby droppings. Larval stages were sent to Mrs. Pat Thomas at the University of Adelaide, South Australia, who identified them as really belonging to the genus *Cloacina,* a roundworm found only in the kangaroo family. It was impossible to positively determine the species due to distortion caused by the preservative, but it was believed to be either *C. gallardi* or *C. petrogale.* What is fascinating is how this parasite has, from only two animals, contrived to propagate and survive for more than 50 years; especially since, as Mrs. Thomas notes, none of these, or related forms, has ever been taken from other animals feeding or watering in the kangaroos' locale.

Coccidial oocysts of unknown species were found in four out of five fecal samples examined, but the true incidence of infection, as well as the impact upon the wallaby population is unknown. In a study on the red kangaroo and grey kangaroo, Mykytowycz (1964) indicated that of 658 wild animals examined, not one could be found that showed pathological symptoms attributable to coccidiosis; but he also indicated that mortality due to coccidiosis has been observed in one-year-old joeys in experimental enclosures just after heavy rains and flooding occurred.

Biting lice of the family Boopiidae are known from the Australian wallabies (McKeown, 1944), but it has not been established that any external parasite is present on the Hawaiian colony. In view of the continual scratching behavior of most of the animals observed it is highly likely that they are infested with some type of ectoparasite.

THE FUTURE OF THE WALLABY IN HAWAII

In view of the fact that the brush-tailed rock wallaby has been officially designated as a "rare and vanishing species," and due to the circumscribed range, which is bounded on the east by unfavorable habitat, and on the south, west, and north by the encroaching demands of human expansion, it is incumbent on the proper state authorities to institute a study on the life history of these animals to determine their future status. Evidence to date indicates that they have innocuous feeding habits and pose no threat to either the native flora, or to the economy of Hawaii. At the same time, they are a singularly unique animal and are easily seen; with little effort they could become an interesting tourist attraction, just as they were at Jenolan Caves in Australia a few years ago.

Hawaii has no law protecting "non-game" mammals, so it was necessary to call the wallaby a "game mammal" and then declare a closed season. This rather negative approach to protection serves merely to keep the honest hunter from securing a trophy, but does nothing to reduce the primary mortality factors, which are predation by dogs, illegal shooting, and possibly, mortality caused by strife between members of the "supersaturated" colony, which cannot extend its range.

The future of the Kalihi cliff that is most heavily colonized is also in doubt. At the time of this writing bulldozers are at work scooping out a level area at the base of these cliffs and some sort of a multistoried research center is expected to be built there in the near future. Whether or not the proximity of this building will have any effect on the wallaby colony is unknown, but if this animal is to be considered important enough to be allowed continued residence in Hawaii, steps should be taken soon to transplant some of them to a similar but quieter area.

LITERATURE CITED

Anonymous

1916a Teddy bears will prove excellent attraction. Pacific Commercial Advertiser, Aug. 20: p. 1.

—— 1916b Richard H. Trents' wallabies flee from their cages. Pacific Commercial Advertiser, Aug. 21: p. 1.

—— 1921 Kalihi wallabies increase; big hunt being arranged. Pacific Commercial Advertiser, Mar. 29: p. 1, Sec. 2.

—— 1937 Dogs mangle baby wallaby. Honolulu Advertiser, July 5: p. 5.

—— 1939 Wallabies at home in wilds of Kalihi. Honolulu Advertiser, Feb. 5: p. 1.

—— 1951 "30 years ago—1921." Honolulu Advertiser, March 30.

Chiarugi, G.

1931 Note sulla embriologia dei Marsupiali. II Osservazioni di embrioni de *Petrogale (Macropus) penicillata.* Monit. zool. ital. Firenze. 42: 177–179.

Fleay, D.

1926 Observations on the birth of a wallaby. Proc. Roy. Soc. N.S.W.: 25–27.

Harper, F.
1945 Extinct and vanishing mammals of the old world. Am. Comm. for Int. Wildl. Prot.; Spec. Publ. No. 12, N.Y. Zool. Park, N.Y., 60, N.Y., Lord Baltimore Press, Baltimore, Md.: 850pp.

Hosaka, E.Y.
1937 Ecological and floristic studies in Kipapa Gulch, Oahu. Bernice P. Bishop Mus. Occ. Pap., Vol. XIII, no. 17: 175–232.

LeSouef, A. S.
1926 Notes on the habits of certain families of the order Marsupialia. Proc. Zool. Soc. London: 935–937.

——
1930 Alteration in character of wallabies acclimatized on Kawau Island, New Zealand. Aus. Zool. 6(2): 111.

LeSouef, A. S., and H. Burrell
1926 The wild animals of Australasia. Geo. G. Harrap and Co., Ltd., London: 388pp.

Lydekker, R.
1894 A handbook to the Marsupialia and Monotremata. London: 302pp.

McKeown, K. C.
1944 Australian insects. Roy. Zool. Soc. N.S.W., Sidney, 2nd Edit.: 303pp.

Mykytowycz, R.
1964 Coccidia in wild populations of the red kangaroo, *Megaleia rufa* (Desmarest), and the grey kangaroo, *Macropus cangaru* (Muller). Parasitology 54(1): 105–115.

Ripperton, J. C., and E. Y. Hosaka
1942 Vegetation zones of Hawaii. Hawaii Agri. Exp. Sta. Bull. 89: 61pp.

Tinker, S. W.
1938 Animals of Hawaii. Nippu Jiji Co., Ltd., Honolulu: 188pp.

Troughton, E.
1944 The kangaroo family—rock wallabies. Aus. Mus. Mag. 8(9): 295–299.

1947 Kangaroo twins—and triplets. Aus. Mus. Mag. 9(5): 160–164.

Wakefield, N.
1954 The re-discovery of the rock-wallaby in Victoria. The Victorian Naturalist 70(11): 202–206.

1961 Victoria's rock wallabies. The Victorian Naturalist 77(3): 322–332.

The Hawaiian Bat

Lasiurus cinereus semotus

Many tens of thousands of years ago, one of the most remarkable mammalian flights of all time occurred. From somewhere along the coast of North America a hoary bat—perhaps a single pregnant female—somehow became disoriented and was blown far out to sea. Pushed along by powerful winds the bat (or, doubtfully, the group of bats) somehow survived an energy-draining flight of at least 2200 miles, to land at last on one of the Hawaiian Islands.

Here its progeny remained and, over the course of thousands of years of isolation, changed slightly in appearance and perhaps in habits, from its mainland ancestors. It is quite possibly the rarest bat in the world, not because it is threatened with extinction, but because the population has never been large. Because it is so rare, with only locally common populations, it is still almost as unknown to the majority of Hawaiian residents today as it was to the original Hawaiians.

The Hawaiian bat was seen by some of the earliest visitors to Hawaii, primarily because Kealakekua Bay was a major port of call, and this bay happens to be one of the more common locations of bats, but the true relationship of this animal to other bat species was a somewhat muddled affair until 1939. Peale, who was on the 1838–1842 United States Exploring Expedition to Hawaii, rightfully identified the bat as belonging to the family Vespertilionidae and noted that "it has the same aspect and color of *Vespertilio noveboracensis,* but is larger" (Cassin, 1858).*

In 1862 Dr. J. E. Gray of the British Museum received a specimen of the Hawaiian bat from a Mr. W. H. Pease of Honolulu. He identified it as belonging to the genus *Lasiurus,* and noted that he could not find any distinction between it and a specimen then called *L. grayii* from Chile. (Tomes had written, five years earlier, that *L. grayii* was "a little larger than *Vespertilio noveboracensis*"); Gray was perhaps the first person to hint at the origin of the Hawaiian bat by writing that "this Bat . . . is curious, as showing the similarity of the fauna in some particulars with that of the Western Coast of America."

It was not until 1890 that the Hawaiian bat was finally scientifically described and given a name of its own. It was called *Atalapha semota* (for some obscure reason, taxonomists were then using the name *Atalapha* instead of *Lasiurus,* but this decision was later reversed), but Dr. H. Allen, who described the new species (Allen, 1890), made a serious error in the measurement of the forearm bone—40 mm. instead of the correct 50 mm.—which made the bat appear related to the red bat group (*L. borealis*) instead of being relegated to its proper ancestor, the hoary bat (*L. cinereus*). This error went unnoticed

* At that time, the red bat of the Americas (*Lasiurus borealis*) was considered to be in the genus *Vespertilio,* and it is interesting to note that, in a study of the genus *Lasiurus,* Tomes (1857) writes that *V. noveboracensis* undergoes fur coloration changes in the southern populations: "In tropical parts of America, a bright ferruginous color completely supercedes the original hoary-brown." Tomes goes on to record that while North American forms of *Lasiurus* show pelage colors that are mixtures of brown and rufous, thickly sprinkled with white, tropical American forms almost uniformly showed a ferruginous hue without any mixture of white. Variations of color in specimens he examined appeared to depend on the tint of the brown color near the tip of the hairs.

for 49 years, until Dr. Miller of the U.S. National Museum re-examined the original specimens (Miller, 1939). Today, it is generally agreed that the Hawaiian bat is merely a subspecies of the hoary bat, and properly known as *Lasiurus cinereus semota*.

DESCRIPTION

Bats are the only mammals capable of true (flapping) flight. The forearm (radius) has become elongated, and, along with the long finger bones of the hand, has been modified into a wing. The thumb is not included in this wing but is used instead for climbing and clinging, and is armed with a tiny claw for this purpose. A thin, double layer of skin stretches from the shoulders, over the arms to the fingertips, and down to the ankles; from there it continues down to the tail. This latter portion of skin is known as the interfemoral membrane and, in *Lasiurus* at least, extends to, and includes, the last bone of the tail.

The hind limbs are rotated so the knees are bent backward instead of forward as they do in other mammals; the short toes on these hind legs bear recurved claws that are the primary means of support when the bat rests in its typical upside-down position. A slender bone known as the calcar extends from this hind foot and supports the edge of the tail membrane, but it is not a sixth "toe." The muscles and bones of the shoulders, rib cage, and collarbone, as might be imagined, are much more developed than those of the pelvic girdle. The sternum (breastbone) has a keel to accommodate the large flight muscles, but this is not as large as the keel of birds of similar size.

Bats are true mammals and appear to be most closely related to such insectivores as the shrews and the moles; contrary to common opinion they are not even closely related to the rodents. Their mammae are pectorally located and they suckle their young in the same manner as other mammals. The teeth of *Lasiurus* are relatively primitive, but can be differentiated into the four common sorts (see Appendix C.).

The Hawaiian bat is a member of the family known as the Vespertilionidae; members of this family are characteristically known as "simple-nosed bats," meaning that they do not have any of the weird facial excrescences or "nose-leafs" common to many other families. But as Dalquest and Werner (1954) point out, this family, histologically speaking, has a most complex facial area with "enormous nests of sebaceous glandular cells swirling and coiling around in amongst the connective tissue."

The body fur of the Hawaiian bat covers the same body portions as it does in other species of the hoary bat, but, as in the red bat *(L. borealis)*, there are two, well-defined color phases. According to Miller *(op.cit.)*, the gray phase of the Hawaiian bat differs only slightly from its progenitor, but in its red phase Miller notes that it "is unlike any specimen of *L. cinereus* that I have seen. The red is probably never as bright as in the brightest skins of *L. borealis;* but between some individuals of the two species . . . there is no essential difference."

The Hawaiian bat is slightly smaller than the hoary bat of the mainland, with tip-to-tip wing expanses of about 10.5 to 13.5 inches, and a total body length of 3.2 to 3.8 inches, of which the tail makes up 1.5 to 1.7 inches. Like the hoary bat, the Hawaiian bats' ears are relatively small (in comparison with many other species), and lie close to the sides of the head. They are not joined at the anterior basal edge nor do they exhibit any of the intricate foldings of the ear that are common to many other species.

Tomich (1965) said that Hawaiian bats usually weigh about 14 grams ($\frac{1}{2}$ ounce), but noted that when body fat accumulated in the fall they may weigh as much as 22 grams.

DISTRIBUTION

Information about the distribution and abundance of the Hawaiian bat is sketchy and very meager. Since most of Hawaii's residents are not aware of the apparently peculiar distribution of the native bat(if in fact they are even aware that it exists), they do not bother to record or report the sighting of one of these animals to any specific agency. Worse, the agencies which do receive reports have no particular place to channel their information, and these data eventually get buried among other files. Readers who see a bat or a group of bats are requested to call any Division of Fish and Game office—there is one on every island—and report the date and exact location of each sighting, and remind the biologist that this information should be recorded in his monthly report.

To date, it appears that the Hawaiian bat occurs primarily on the island of Hawaii, and appears only irregularly on the islands of Maui, Oahu, and Kauai. I have interviewed many long-time residents of Lanai and Molokai and have never talked with a person who could recall either having seen or heard of bats on these latter two islands. Gay (1965) said that bats were found all over the island of Lanai, but in view of the fact that he said they made their homes in the cliffs, and included this information under the categories of either birds seen or rodents seen, I do not put much faith in the comments.

I have collected records indicating that the bat is present year round on the island of Hawaii, but observations for Maui, Oahu, and Kauai are interesting since the bats seem to appear only during the months from August to December. The type specimen of the Hawaiian bat, along with several other specimens of the period, was collected from Kauai, but the labels unfortunately do not have the dates of collection on them.

The northern island records are interesting in that they indicate that some Hawaiian bats are migratory. The hoary bat of the western states is also migratory, but flies northward in the spring months, and returns to the south in the autumn! If the Hawaiian bat is indeed of a migratory nature it provides animal behaviorists with a puzzling turnabout in behavior. If bats migrate to Oahu from Hawaii they would have to fly past Molokai and Lanai; hence it is a puzzle as to why they have never been recorded from those islands. Obviously, it is only by compiling many sight records that we shall someday be able to interpret the actions of these unique creatures.

Baldwin (1950) reports that bats have been seen from sea level to 13,200 feet on the island of Hawaii but he felt that they were most common from sea level up to 4,000 feet. Vaughan and Krutzsch (1954), in their studies of the hoary bat in southern California, found indications that there is a segregating of the sexes during the late spring, with males keeping to the foothills and mountains, and females staying in the lowlands and in the coastal valleys. Vaughan (1953), in the earlier part of his work, collected 22 bats of this species over a water hole in the month of May, and discovered that all were males. Sexual segregation of at least three other species of bats on their summer range is known to occur (Winsatt, 1945), so it appears that someone will have to capture or kill a number of Hawaiian bats from different altitudes, and during different times of the year, before we can make further statements about this facet of the life history of *Lasiurus cinereus semotus*.

Baldwin *(op.cit.)* noted that bats were seen in both wet and dry areas with yearly rainfall averages of from 20 to 90 inches, but he did not preclude the possibility of them being found in wetter areas. He also noted that they apparently prefer habitats of either open or mixed character and that he had never seen them in dense, closed, wet forests. The existence of open bodies of water is not essential, but those animals along the sea coast venture consistently out over the open ocean; three of the best viewing spots that I know of are over Hilo Bay, Kailua Bay, and just offshore (300–400 yards) from the mouth of the Waipio River.

HABITS

The Hawaiian bat, like other members of the genus *Lasiurus*, is considered a solitary-roosting, nonhibernating species. Roosting does not apparently require any particular species of tree or plant; I observed one for three days (on Oahu) returning to an overhanging porch beam on a Pacific Heights house. Ernest Akana (personal communication) has seen one hanging from a window screen, and Gerry Swedberg recalls seeing one roosting next to the entrance to the Kawaihae Beach Park Public Restroom, about four feet off the ground in a bush. Some years ago David Woodside flushed one from a *pukeawe (Styphelia tameiameiae)* bush at the 6,000-foot level of Kipuka Kekekaniho on Hawaii. Baldwin *(op. cit.)* records a bat being flushed from the exposed tree roots of an 'ōhia tree *(Metrosideros collina)* and notes two instances of them being taken from *hala,* or screwpines *(Pandanus odoratissimus).*

For two years I lived in Waipio Valley, Hawaii, and I often observed one or two bats leave a large grove of this latter species of tree and begin their very purposeful flight to the lower reaches of Waipio Valley. They roosted at about the 500-foot level and shortly after the sun had set behind the cliffs the first bat would appear. Normally it moved along at an altitude of 200 to 300 feet and almost directly over the Waipio River, but on occasion it would begin a low course and drop down to a search pattern of perhaps 20 to 50 feet. Often, within one minute or less of the first sighting, a second or even third bat would appear. In my observations, they almost invariably followed the same course, and hunted at the same altitudes. Since they roost separately, I suggest that the first bat's echo location sounds first stimulated nearby bats into action and perhaps secondly (or by a different series of hunting signals) made known the hunting course that the first animal was taking. Despite the fact that the animals continually veered several feet in all directions, it was obvious that they were progressing to a predetermined feeding ground. In this valley the feeding area is along the lower Waipio River bed or along the beach. I once counted 14 bats darting and weaving about at altitudes of perhaps 500 feet. A few individuals were over the beach area, but the majority were several hundred yards out to sea. This unusually large gathering remained in sight for over a half hour, when it became too dark to observe them.

Another indication of purposeful flight was recorded by David Woodside (pers. comm.) at Pohakuloa at the 6,600-foot level. He used to "fairly commonly" see a lone bat in the early afternoon that was always flying toward Pohakuloa Gulch from the direction of Hualalai. This type of purposeful flight has been described for many other species of bats and has been labeled by Cockrum (1956) as a "diurnal movement." Baldwin *(op. cit.)* estimated the duration of these daily flights to be about two hours or more; most people mistakenly assume that, because a bat is nocturnal, it flies about all night. If a bat can collect sufficient flying insects to satisfy itself in two or three hours it returns to its roost. No one knows for sure how much energy it takes for a bat to sustain itself during flight but Griffin (1958) has suggested that a bat on the wing may consume as much as 200 calories per gram body weight per hour, and that as much as 78 percent of the annual metabolism of the animal is required for two hours of active flight during the warmer months of the year. To understand this fantastic energy transfer better, Griffin performed an interesting experiment with a bat of the genus *Myotis* and a room full of mosquitoes. He found that the mosquitoes weighed 0.002 grams each and that the bat weighed 3.5 grams. The food consumption was determined by weighing the bat after feeding and he found that, in 15 minutes, the bat's weight had increased by 10 percent. This indicated that it had caught 175 mosquitoes in 15 minutes (about 1 every 5 seconds).

In this time of rockets and moonships it is easy to forget that until World War II radar and sonar techniques were only poorly known, and that it was not possible to prove the techniques by which bats fed and maneuvered through the dark until after certain highly sophisticated instruments were invented. As early as 1793, Lazar Spallanzani (the same man whose experiments disproved spontaneous generation) became interested in the fact that bats were not inconvenienced by the dark, and he found that, while blinding bats did not interfere with their ability to avoid objects in flight, plugging their ears caused complete disorientation. He concluded that "the ear of the bat serves more efficiently for seeing, or at least for measuring distances, than do their eyes" (Griffin, *ibid.*). Much of his work went unnoticed, and it was not until 1920 that Hartridge theorized that bats made use of high frequency and short-wave lengths to avoid objects in the dark. It was not until after the invention of radar, some 20 years later, that the works of Griffin finally defined "echolocation."

Griffin (1955) simplifies the intricacies of echolocation by saying that "echolocation . . . [is] hearing echoes of the intense pulses of high frequency sound which they emit at the rate of 10 to 200 per second. The frequency of the sound making up these pulses ranges from 20 to 120 kilocycles per second, and it usually drops by about an octave between the beginning and ending of each pulse, even though the pulse duration is only one to five milliseconds. But under some circumstances these bats emit somewhat longer pulses with a nearly constant frequency, and during the pursuit of flying insects marked changes occur, both in the frequency pattern and the pulse repetition rate." Griffin, in his 1958 book, describes a cruising bat as emitting a lazy "putt – putt," but this sound increases to a "buzz" as it locates and closes in on an insect. These sounds are detectable only with special instruments.

Each species of bat creates its own sound variation, and transmits and receives it in a different manner; these latter functions are believed to be responsible for the great variations in the facial structures of the different species. For example, the "leaf-nosed" bats transmit their pulses through their nostrils (with their mouth closed) and it is believed that the fleshy "leaf" on the nose is involved in directing or focusing the sound. On the other hand, the vespertilionid bats, which include the Hawaiian bat, transmit their sound beams from the mouth. The structure of these bats' facial muscles is such that, at the moment they emit a pulse, they are deaf; if this did not occur the bat would be unable to separate an outgoing signal from an incoming one. Although I do not know of any studies to prove the point, the fact that vespertilionid bats all have relatively simple ears, but at the same time have such a complex of glandular cells on the face, may indicate that these glands serve to help pick up rebounding signals.

REPRODUCTION

Virtually nothing is known about reproduction or reproductive behavior of the Hawaiian bat; the only reference I have been able to find concerning these subjects is that of Baldwin (*op. cit.*), who recorded finding two fetuses in a female's reproductive tract in May, and no sign of fetuses in another female examined in November. This scanty information would indicate that birth occurs at the same time of year as it does in its close relatives, the hoary bat and the red bat. In the United States mainland, most hoary bat young are born in the months of May or June; two young are usually produced, but this number may vary from one to four. Bourliére (1964) notes that parturition may take place in one of two ways: in some species it occurs with the female in the normal, head down resting position, while in others, the female suspends herself by all four feet, back downward, in such a way that the newborn baby is received in an "apron" formed by the interfemoral membrane. Unfortunately, we do not know which method the Hawaiian bat chooses, but we do know that, like other members of the genus *Lasiurus*, the baby attaches itself to its mother's belly fur, and remains there, even in flight, until it is nearly full grown. Stegeman (1956) records finding a female hoary bat that had two well-developed young attached to her nipples and it is believed that she was flying with them; the amazing thing is that their combined weight was 24.1 grams or 90.6 percent of the weight of the mother. In another instance, Sanborn (1954) tells of finding a hoary bat lying on the ground with two young weighing 25 percent more than she weighed.

OTHER BATS INTRODUCED TO HAWAII

In 1897, Mr. Albert Koebele, an entomologist employed by the sugar planters of Hawaii, sent a report to the *Planters' Monthly* (Koebele, 1897) that stated: ". . . it was found advisable to introduce bats. . . . so far the results of the introduced California bats, of which over 600 reached the Islands living, has not been very encouraging, since little is seen of them in Honolulu. Several trials with Japanese bats resulted in a failure." Fifty-nine years later (May 31, 1956) the *Honolulu Advertiser* quoted a report from the May 30 edition of the *Pacific Commercial Advertiser* that said: "Two hundred and twenty-five bats are received per the SS *Australia,* addressed to Prof. Koebele. They are set free at dusk, after being fed a meal of beetles. They enjoyed the repast."

Unfortunately, we do not have any indication as to which species were introduced, or when. Evidently there were two or more species released, but so far as we know, they all failed to survive (although Perkins [1925] indicated that individuals were seen alive for a year after one of the introductions). There is, in the Bishop Museum, a specimen of the silver-haired bat (*Lasionycteris noctivagans*) with a label attached that says "Hawaiian Islands?" and it is conceivable that this was one of the bats introduced from California, but it is doubtful that anyone will ever know for sure.

There was some agitation in 1904 to introduce and release bats in Hawaii for insect-control purposes (Blackman, 1904 and Lowrie, 1904), but Perkins, who would like to have seen this method of biological control used, noted the past failures, and wrote: "It is probable that for some reasons most bats cannot flourish here. The so-called 'native' bat, a very widely-ranging immigrant species, has been here no doubt for centuries, yet it exists with difficulty. . . . the fact that a species so long acclimated . . . cannot flourish, makes it doubtful whether the Islands are suited to these useful creatures . . ." (Perkins, 1904). The same suggestion arose again in 1914 and in 1919, but Perkins (anon., 1919) once again reiterated his stand, and the question of further introductions was finally dropped.

The only other "almost introduction" of a bat species to Hawaii involved the discovery of a fruit bat (family Pteropodidae) found asleep in the rigging of a ship that had just arrived from the Philippine Islands (anon., 1946). This animal was captured and killed.

LITERATURE CITED

Allen, H.
1890 Description of a new species of bat. *Atalapha semota.* U.S. Nat. Mus., Proc. 13: 173–175.

Anonymous
1919 Bats as leafhopper enemies. In: Director's Report for October-November. H.S.P.A., Honolulu.

——
1946 Unwelcome visitor to Hawaii. Honolulu Advertiser, April 10, p. 1.

——
1956 "60 Years Ago." Honolulu Advertiser, May 31.

Baldwin, P. H.
1950 Occurence and behavior of the Hawaiian Bat. J. Mammal. 31(4): 455–456.

Blackman, L. G.
1904 Introduction of bats. Hawaiian Forester and Agriculturist 1: 115–117.

Bourlière, F.
1964 The Natural History of Mammals. 3rd Edit. A. A. Knopf, Inc., New York: 387pp.

Cassin, J.
    1858   United States exploring expedition. Vol. VIII, Mam-
            malia and ornithology. C. Sherman and Son, Philadel-
            phia: 466pp.

Cockrum, E. L.
    1956   Homing, movements, and longevity of bats. J. Mammal.
            37(1): 48–57.

Dalquest, W. W., and H. J. Werner
    1954   Histological aspects of the faces of North American bats.
            J. Mammal. 35(2): 147–160.

Gay, L. K.
    1965   True stories of the island of Lanai. Mission Press,
            Honolulu: 85pp.

Gray, J. E.
    1862   Notice of a species of *Lasiurus* sent from the Sandwich
            Islands by Mr. W. H. Pease. Zool. Soc. London Proc.,
            Part XXX: p. 143.

Griffin, D. R., and A. Novick
    1955   Acoustic orientation of Neotropical bats. J. Exp. Zool.
            130(2): 251–299.

Griffin, D. R.
    1958   Listening in the dark. Yale U. Press. New Haven: 413pp.

Koebele, A.
    1897   Report of the entomologist. Planters' Monthly 16: 65–
            85.

Lowrie, W. J.
    1904   Notes on bats. Planters' Monthly 23: 354–355.

Miller, G. S.
    1939   Note on the lectotype of *Lasiurus semotus* (H. Allen).
            J. Mammal. 20: p. 369.

Perkins, R. C. L.
    1904   Introduction of bats. Haw'n. Forester and Agriculturist
            1: 138–139.

    ———

    1925   The early work of Albert Koebele in Hawaii. Haw'n.
            Planters' Record 29: 359–364.

Sanborn, C. C.
1954 Bats of the United States. Publ. Health Report, Wash. 69(1): 17–28.

Stegeman, L. C.
1956 Record of a female hoary bat, *Lasiurus cinerius*, and young in Syracuse, New York. J. Mammal. 36: p. 455.

Tomes, R. F.
1857 A monograph of the Genus *Lasiurus*. Zool. Soc. London, Proc., Part XXV: 34–36.

Tomich, P. Q.
1965 The hoary bat in Hawaii. Elepaio 25: 85–86.

Vaughan, T. A.
1953 Unusual concentration of hoary bats. J. Mammal. 34: p. 256.

Vaughan, T. A., and P. H. Krutzsch
1954 Seasonal distribution of the hoary bat in Southern California. J. Mammal. 35: 431–432.

Winsatt, W. A.
1945 Notes on breeding behavior, pregnancy, and parturition in some vespertilionid bats of the eastern U.S. J. Mammal. 26: 23–33.

The Rabbit

Oryctolagus cuniculus

HISTORY

No one knows precisely when the first rabbits were introduced
to Hawaii, but Andrew Bloxam recorded visiting "Rabbit Island"—now known as Ford Island—in Pearl Harbor, for the
purpose of shooting some in 1825. He mentioned that they were
offspring of an earlier release and "are now wild and numerous;
they are of a black and white color . . ." (B. P. Bishop Mus.,
1925). Chung (1931) makes reference to an article appearing in
The Polynesian on October 22, 1853, which reported that
"Mr. Tanner has recently introduced from Australia . . . a pair of
white rabbits," and Vollrath (1952) records that in 1873
a government permit was issued to allow rabbits to be raised on
Coconut Island in Hilo Bay. At least three more introductions
were made to islands of the Hawaiian chain but unfortunately
they were not recorded.

The known history of the European rabbit is interesting because this animal was "a disappearing species before man
reversed its fortunes so dramatically" (Corbet, 1966). Apparently this one-species genus was originally found only in the
Iberian district of Spain, but eventually was domesticated by
the conquering Romans, who kept them for a living food supply

in walled enclosures and on islands. These animals were distributed throughout western Europe during the Middle Ages, and reached England in the 12th century (Corbet, *ibid.*). The Dutch peasants were responsible for breeding the European rabbit into several distinctive forms and into larger configuration. Today's "Dutch rabbit" is typically white and either gray, blue, black, or buff; the English, by selective breeding, produced the well-known "white rabbit"—which is merely a large albino—from the Dutch rabbit (Wender, 1946).

In the middle 1800s some sailing ships carried a stock of rabbits on board for a supply of fresh meat and it may be assumed that they occasionally liberated surplus animals upon islands and islets as a potential food source in case of shipwreck. In many cases the rabbits simply failed to establish themselves and disappeared; in other notable cases they flourished. The reasons for success or failure are unknown; while some island rabbit populations have been intensively studied, ordinarily the data derived are applicable only to that particular island and are consequently of little help for comparison with other island ecosystems.

Certainly the most destructive introduction of rabbits to an island of the Hawaiian chain occurred on the tiny coralline island of Laysan in 1903. This important sea bird nesting area is 790 nautical miles west-northwest of Honolulu and is the home of several truly unique bird species. Between 1903, when the manager of a guano mining firm, Max Schlemmer, introduced several breeds of rabbits to the island with the intent of starting a commercial meat venture, and 1923, three species of birds were wiped from the face of the earth.

In 1911, two years after President Theodore Roosevelt had declared the "leeward islands" (excluding Midway) to be protected and henceforth known as the "Hawaiian Islands Bird Reservation," an expedition to Laysan was formed under the joint auspices of the U.S. Department of Agriculture and the University of Iowa. The observations made by members of the party were lamentable. Bryan (Dill and Bryan, 1912) wrote, "Rabbits now literally swarm over the island by thousands. The amount of damage done by them can better be imagined than told. They are exterminating first one species of plant then another. Several species that were common eight years ago have entirely gone, others are already doomed. Unless some drastic measures are resorted to within a very short time, not a bush or spear of grass will be alive."

Dill (Dill and Bryan, 1912) went on to say, "In the latter part of the afternoon they may be seen feeding. They are very fond of the green juncus that grows near the lagoon, and, while they are eating, their bodies are concealed among the thick growth and only their ears show. At times there are so many ears protruding that they resemble a vegetable garden."

A year later an unsuccessful attempt was made to eliminate the rabbits by a United States Biological Survey team, but, for some unknown reason, no further attempts were made until April 1923. Alexander Wetmore, who was a member of this "Tanager Expedition," reviewed the destruction. He wrote, "On every hand extended a barren waste of sand. Two coconut palms, a stunted hau tree and an ironwood or two, planted by the former habitants" were the only survivors except for three patches of *Sesuvium* on the lake flat. He wrote of the rabbits: "Of the vast army of destroyers, only a few hundred remained. . . . The destruction of the majority was simple, but the survivors became wary and it was necessary to hunt them out one at a time. . . . Pursuit, therefore, was relentless and effective. A party sent to Laysan a year after our visit reported no sign of a single survivor" (Wetmore, 1925).

In the intervening years, the beautiful red Laysan honey creeper (*Himatione sanguinea freethii*), the Laysan Miller bird (*Acrocephalus f. familiaris*), and the flightless Laysan Island rail (*Porzanula palmeri*) all disappeared from Laysan forever. The rail had been transplanted to Midway sometime before 1923 and managed to survive there until 1944, but eventually it fell prey to a newly established population of rats (Baldwin, 1947). The extinction of these birds was undoubtedly caused primarily by the rabbits' destruction of the vegetation, which provided shelter, nesting material, and food in the form of nectar or insects.

Shortly after introducing rabbits to Laysan, Schlemmer also released a number of animals on Lisianski Island, which is about 140 miles northwest of Laysan and is slightly less than half the size of the latter (.7 square miles of dry land compared with 1.56 for Laysan). By 1914 the rabbits had almost completely destroyed the vegetation of this smaller island, and themselves as well (Elschner, 1915), and by 1923 the last of the rabbits had perished naturally (Ball, 1923 *from* Warner, 1963:7). The destruction of the vegetation on Lisianski not only immediately affected certain sea birds nesting there but forced biotic changes which have assuredly caused a variation in the present-day species' composition from that of the prerabbit days.

DISTRIBUTION AND ABUNDANCE

The distribution of wild rabbit populations in Hawaii today is well known, but the population numbers fluctuate seasonally, and from year to year, and have not been studied.

Rabbits are presently found on Manana, or Rabbit Island (not the same island as mentioned by Bloxam), which is a secondary tuff cone lying just off Makapuu Point on Oahu; on Lehua, a tuff cone just north of Niihau; and on Molokini, which is a tiny semicircular tuff cone part way between Kahoolawe and southwest Maui. It is not likely that the average tourist or resident will ever see any wild rabbits because all three islets are protected bird sanctuaries where landing except for scientific purposes is forbidden.

The status of the Molokini population is the most uncertain of the three. In 1913, Mr. C. N. Forbes explored Molokini and recorded 15 plant species and some birds but did not mention seeing rabbits (Forbes, 1913), and in 1930 Caum recorded 21 plant species and certain birds, but no rabbits (Caum, 1930). Joseph Medeiros, on the other hand, made a quick visit to Molokini in 1954 and recorded seeing a small number of rabbits (Medeiros, 1954). They were all believed to be of a black-and-white color pattern.

Rabbits have been on Lehua since at least 1930 (Caum, 1936), and Swedberg (pers. comm.) says they are of every conceivable color pattern, including the wild "agouti" pelage. On a comparative basis, Lehua probably has the largest population of all three islands.

Manana, or Rabbit Island, as it is more popularly called, is better known to local scientists than are the other two because of its ease of access by small boat. There are no written records of the first sightings of rabbits on this island, but local legends in the area have it that an unnamed Waimanalo resident released a number of animals there about the turn of the century in the hope of starting a business. It would be interesting to get the complete story because the present-day animals all have the wild-type agouti pelage with very little indication of having received color characters of the domesticized breeds. Although earlier observers had tentatively thought this animal was an American cottontail (*Sylvilagus sp.*), a New Zealand scientist who is a leading expert on the European rabbit passed through Hawaii in 1961 and unhesitatingly pronounced the four specimens he saw to be typical European rabbits.

So, here we are with a puzzle! On two of the Hawaiian Islands the rabbits have reproduced and destroyed the vegetation to the extent that in one case they eliminated themselves, and in the other would have eliminated themselves if man had not stepped in to help them. On three other islands rabbits still exist, and have done so successfully for at least as long a period of time, even if the chronology does not quite match. We know that certain plant species were similar on all five islands, but that on two of the islands certain of the species disappeared along with the rabbits, while on the other three islands they continue to persist. The solution may very simply be that on Laysan and Lisianski the soft sand made it possible for the starving rabbits to dig to the base of the root system in their search for food, but they could not do this on the compressed soils of the other three islands. However, because no study has been made, we have not the slightest idea of the real reasons.

I have also been told that a small colony of rabbits lived, in ever dwindling numbers, on the island of Kauai, near Hanalei, for several years until they finally disappeared (Richard Fuller, pers. comm.), and it is well known that pet rabbits continually get loose on all of the main islands but never seem to prosper. It is for this reason that the author does not intend to go further into the *possible* life history of this species; there are literally thousands of papers and scores of books written about *Oryctolagus cuniculus* in all parts of the world, and doubtless much of the material applies to the Hawaiian situation, but until local biologists and ecologists undertake some semblance of a study further writings in this chapter would be mere conjecture.

LITERATURE CITED

Baldwin, P. H.
1947   The life history of the Laysan rail. Condor 49: 14–21.
Bernice P. Bishop Museum
1925   Diary of Andrew Bloxam, naturalist of the "Blonde", on her trip from England to the Hawaiian Islands, 1824–25. B. P. Bishop Mus. Spec. Publ. 10: 96pp.
Caum, E. L.
1930   Notes on the flora of Molokini. B. P. Bishop Mus. Occas. Papers 9(1): 15–18.

——
1936   Notes on the flora and fauna of Lehua and Kaula Islands. B. P. Bishop Mus. Occas. Papers 11(21): 1–17.
Chung, H. L.

1931   Rabbit raising in Hawaii. U. of Hawaii Agri. Exten.
        Ser. Bull. 12: 34pp.
Corbet, G. B.
1966   The terrestrial mammals of western Europe. London,
        G. T. Foulis & Co. Ltd.: 264pp.
Dill, H. R., and W. A. Bryan
1912   Report of an expedition to Laysan Island in 1911. U.S.
        Dept. Agri., Biol. Surv. Bull. 42: 30pp.
Elschner, C.
1915   The leeward islands of the Hawaiian group. Honolulu:
        68pp.
Forbes, C. N.
1913   Notes on the flora of Kahoolawe and Molokini. B. P.
        Bishop Mus. Occas. Papers 5(3): 3-15.
Medeiros, J.
1954   "Outdoor Life." Maui News, Oct. 23.
Vollrath, H.
·   1952   Rabbit Production in Hawaii. U. of Hawaii Agri. Exten.
        Ser. Bull. 52: 32pp.
Warner, R. E.
1963   Recent history and ecology of the Laysan duck. Condor
        65: 3-23.
Wender, L.
1946   Animal encyclopedia: Mammals. London, Geo. Allen
        and Unwin Ltd.: 266pp.
Wetmore, A.
1925   Bird life among lava rock and coral sand. Nat. Geog.
        Mag. 48(7): 73-108.

The Rats *and* The Mouse

The three species of rats and one species of mouse that inhabit Hawaii all belong to the family Muridae, which is the largest grouping of animals within the order Rodentia. The very fact that the rodents make up about one-third of all known genera and species of the mammals in the world is indicative of their amazing ability to undergo adaptive physiological change in order to respond to varying environmental conditions. Some form of rodent is presently found in almost every habitat in the world except in Antarctica, or on a few remote and uninhabited tropical islands. The four species of murids in Hawaii are the black rat *(Rattus rattus)*, the brown rat *(Rattus norvegicus)*, the Polynesian rat *(Rattus exulans hawaiiensis)*, and the house mouse *(Mus musculus)*;* these four animals are perhaps the most widespread of all mammals. *Rattus rattus, R. norvegicus,* and *Mus musculus* have followed (or accompanied) man to almost every corner of the earth and can be described as being truly cosmopolitan. *Rattus exulans* has its own form of rat in Hawaii, but its close cousins (often known as *Rattus concolor*) can be found all the way from Tahiti through the rest of Polynesia, Melanesia, the Malay Archipelago, and on up through parts of Burma.

As exhibited by their ability to successfully inhabit so many

* The guinea pig is a rodent, but is in a different suborder.

House Mouse

areas of the earth, almost every facet of their life process appears susceptible to change; the result is that probably more studies have been carried out on these animals than on all the mammals of Africa, and yet, when we try to examine such things as methods of control of cane field or urban populations we find such a staggering array of conflicting information from other geographical areas as to render any sort of previously gathered qualitative or quantitative data almost without applicability in the Hawaiian situation. An example of this need to do individual studies for individual problems can be seen by the apparent fact that, although *Rattus exulans* (or *R. concolor*) is considered a household pest throughout much of its range, and has obviously achieved its wide distribution through its close association with man, the Hawaiian subspecies is extremely uncommon in human habitations, and seems to prefer more wild and un-inhabited regions.* Similarly, studies of such things as food habits, reproduction, population densities, and even parasitic infections, tend to show great variation from area to area. Agencies in Hawaii, such as the Hawaiian Sugar Planters' Association, the Plague Research Unit of the State Department of Health, and recently the U.S. Fish and Wildlife Service, are spending, or have spent, hundreds of thousands of dollars in attempting to understand more about the varied life histories of these animals. They have yet to arrive at many definitive conclusions that might be applicable on a state-wide basis, and it will probably be many years before they do so, but certainly no one else could try harder.

Because of this great diversity, it would be impossible to cover here the Hawaiian murids in depth; in fact, this subject is so complicated as to call for the writing of a separate book devoted solely to rats and mice. Therefore, I merely give a short

---

* The reason for this is unclear but may be related to interspecific competition with the brown rat; this latter animal prefers to live around human habitation and is clearly the superior, in size and aggressiveness, of both the Polynesian rat and the black rat.

Hawaiian Rat

Black Rat

Brown Rat

description of the form and habitat of each species, leaving the intricacies of their life histories to someone more qualified.

THE BLACK RAT *(Rattus rattus)*

The black rat (also commonly called roof, house, or ship rat) originated in southern Asia but has spread throughout most of the world. In the northern areas of Europe it has been replaced by the more aggressive and cold-tolerant brown rat and is now absent from the British Isles, Denmark, Scandinavia, and Finland except in the form of isolated urban populations, especially in seaports (Corbet, 1966). Hawaiian populations were apparently derived from these European-type stocks because our animals show a variety of color patterns similar to those of Europe. For many years scientists separated this species into three subspecies on the basis of coloration. The black rat, *Rattus rattus rattus,* was typified by having its upper surface black, and its underparts (or "venter") a slate gray. The Alexandrine rat, *Rattus rattus alexandrinus* had a gray-brown dorsal surface and a slate gray venter. The fruit rat, *Rattus rattus frugivorous,* also had a slate gray back but was noted for its white belly. As Tomich and Kami (1966) have pointed out, actual ecological separation has never been demonstrated among these various-colored animals, and they, like Caslick (1956), Johnson (1946), and Nicholson and Warner (1953), feel that all these various-named animals are merely the result of genetically inherited pelage colors and that all animals of this type should be solely referred to as *Rattus rattus rattus.*

The full-grown black rat is about seven inches long, from the tip of the snout to the base of the tail, and the tail is usually over eight inches long. The average weight of a full-grown animal is five to seven ounces. The tail is sparsely covered with coarse hairs that grow from areas between the rings of small epidermal scales. The ears and feet are naked, and while the tail and parts of the ears are sometimes darkly pigmented, the bottoms of the feet are usually flesh colored. The teeth of all the murids are very highly specialized; the incisors grow throughout life and neither they nor the molars are replaced. There are no canine teeth. The anterior (labial) surface of each incisor is covered with enamel which is formed by a special enamel-producing organ (Figure 1.); this enamel is pigmented a bright orange from the fifth week after birth (Rowett, 1960). The posterior (lingual) and the lateral surfaces are covered only with a thin layer of cement. Since the enamel is harder than either the cement or the underlying dentine, there is a differential wear which produces the chisel-like edges so characteristic of all rodents. Ordinarily, wear of the incisors occurs at the same rate as does growth, but if one tooth is damaged, the opposite one will overgrow and may eventually perforate the lip and palate, and cause death by starvation.

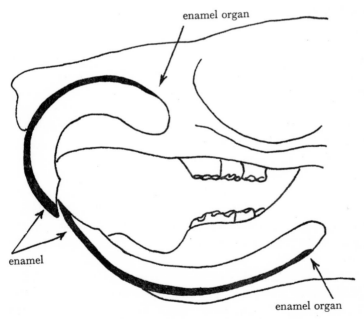

Fig. 1. Rodent incisors (Adapted from Rowett, 1960, p. 27)

A great majority of the rats inhabiting Hawaii are nocturnal, and it is interesting to note that rats' eyes have no cones, only rods (Rowett, *ibid.*). Since only cones can discriminate light of different wave lengths, rats are colorblind; cones also have a high threshold of stimulation and can function only in relatively bright light. It is an interesting question as to whether this lack of cones evolved as a result of their nocturnal habits, or whether their nocturnal habits came about because of a lack of cones. Further adaptations to their nocturnal existence are indicated not only by their long, sensitive whiskers (vibrissae) but by their apparent ability to send and receive ultrasonic sounds in much the same manner as do bats (Anderson, 1954, and Bourlière, 1964).

The black rat is an agile climber and not only often builds its nests in trees (a loose structure that is somewhat larger than English sparrow [*Passer domesticus*] nests) but often preys on the eggs and young of tree-nesting birds. Because of its propensity for climbing, it is said that when frightened it tends to climb upward to hide (Rowett, *op.cit.*), and is most often found in the upper stories of the buildings it inhabits (Corbet, *op.cit.*). Rowett *(op.cit.)* also notes that it is an unwilling swimmer and is therefore seldom found in sewers.

As far as is known, the black rat inhabits the islands of Hawaii, Maui, Lanai, Molokai, Oahu, Kauai, and Midway Atoll. Black rats escaped onto islands of this latter group from ships in 1943, and were probably primarily responsible for the extirpation of the Laysan finch *(Psittirostra cantans cantans)* from that atoll, and for the total extinction of the flightless Laysan rail *(Porzanula palmeri)*; the last rail ever seen was observed in November of that same year (Fisher and Baldwin, 1946).

Rats of unknown species are present on Lehua Island (Richardson, 1963) and were at least present in 1938 on barren Kaula Island (Bryan, 1938). Since both these islands are so close to Niihau we might presume that some species of rat inhabits that island as well, but there is no published information to confirm this.

In Hawaii breeding takes place throughout the year; some studies indicate that, like the other species of rats, there may be seasonal peaks of intensified breeding but there is not yet sufficient evidence available to delineate these times. The gestation period in the black rat is normally 21 days with four to eight young commonly being produced; Jackson's study (1965) showed *R. rattus* averaging a litter size of 6.5 young in Hawaii. The young may attain sexual maturity in about three months.

Kami (1966) studied the food habits of rodents in the Hamakua district of Hawaii; in the process of investigation he collected animals from three general types of habitat (cane fields, gulches adjacent to cane fields, and areas of human habitation), and found that "under present conditions . . . the most versatile of the three species of rats appears to be *R. rattus*, which utilizes a wide variety of domestic and wild food sources and adapts itself readily to field habitats as well as to domestic environments." In cane fields the black rat fed primarily on the internodes of sugar cane, but in nearby gulches they fed heavily on grass stalks and fruits, and near areas of human habitation they ate mostly garbage, other waste materials, and mixed livestock rations (Kami, *ibid.*).

Spencer and Davis (1950) found that in fairly open fields on Oahu, the black rat had a home range of about 200 feet in diameter; this appears to be almost twice the home range diameters of the other two rat species.

THE BROWN RAT *(Rattus norvegicus)*

The brown rat (also commonly known as the Norway, sewer, or wharf rat) is believed to have originated in western China. Its specific name *norvegicus* is definitely a misnomer since it is not necessarily any more common in Norway than elsewhere in Europe. The brown rat is the largest of our local rats, averaging about 16 inches in total length, but, in opposition to the black rat's similar total length, the brown rat is much heavier (averaging 14 to 17 ounces) and has a tail that is shorter than its body length. Although *Rattus norvegicus* is generally brown on its dorsal surface, color alone is not sufficient to separate this animal from the black rat; many brown rats are of a gray color.

Titian Peale, a naturalist with the United States Exploring Expedition of 1838–1842, was perhaps the first person to write about the presence of the brown rat in Hawaii. He wrote: "The common brown or Norway rat was observed at the Hawaiian, and some other islands in the Pacific Ocean, where it has been introduced by commercial intercourse with Europe and America. It was observed to retain its partiality for the habitations of mankind, with all its burrowing and destructive habits, but does not seem to multiply so rapidly as it does in those countries where the cereal grains are grown, or dealt with as a matter of commerce. We did not find it on islands uninhabited by mankind" (Tinker, 1941).

The brown rat is presently known to inhabit the islands of Hawaii, Maui, Molokai, Lanai, Oahu, and Kauai, but it appears that they are not nearly as adapted for a life away from mans' habitations as are the black and the Hawaiian rats, and are consequently found in greatest abundance in cities and villages. Eskey (1934), in his studies of plague in the Hawaiian Islands, found that the different species of rats varied considerably in abundance according to the distance from buildings.

Of all rats captured inside or within 50 feet of buildings, the brown rat contributed 36 percent, the black rat 56 percent, and the Hawaiian rat 8 percent. Fifty-one to 500 feet from buildings the brown rat proportion dropped to 16 percent, the black rat group rose to 64 percent, and the Hawaiian rats occurred at the 20 percent level. Further than 500 feet away black rats were caught 72 percent of the time, the Hawaiian rat catch remained almost constant at 19 percent, but brown rats contributed to only 9 percent of the captures. Kami *(op.cit.)* found much the same pattern in his aforementioned food habit study: of 394 rats examined from Hamakua cane-field habitat only 1 was a brown rat, and of 272 studied from nearby gulch lands only 3 were of this species.

Of further interest are two reports made in 1961 stating that while the brown rat made up 7 percent of rats caught in Hamakua cane fields on the island of Hawaii (Tomich, 1961), brown rats had not been found on the plantations of central Maui, and were normally scarce on Oahu and the drier cane areas of the other islands (Bianchi, 1961). On the other hand, Doty (1945) states that on Kauai, the most destructive cane-field rat "has always been the Norway."

No one is sure just what the highest elevation record is for rats on any of these islands, but Tomich (1965) captured all four murid species at the 4,000-foot level in Hawaii Volcanoes National Park, and Woodside (pers. comm.) said that an unknown species of rat was common around the 6,000-foot high Pohakuloa Military Base garbage dump.

Although the brown rat is capable of climbing it is much more terrestrial in preference and is not known to nest in trees. Both the Hawaiian rat and the brown rat dig burrows, but those of the Hawaiian rat are considerably smaller and less complicated than those of the brown rat. Most burrows are located at depths of less than two feet, but the galleries they build may be 10 to 15 feet long and may contain from one to four or five nests (Tinker, *op. cit.*). Inhabited burrows almost always have some fresh soil showing in front of the main openings, but there are often blind galleries that can serve as "emergency exits." Doty (*op. cit.*) points out that a favorite place for a brown rat's nest is directly under a clump of cane or a rock; in the loose soil of an irrigated field the rat then receives the advantage of overhead support from the roots or rock. The nest, which is usually roughly spherical, six or seven inches in diameter, and lined with dry cane leaves or grass, is generally placed so that it cannot be submerged by irrigation or excessive rain.

The gestation period of the brown rat is variously quoted as being from 21 to 24 days, but this period may be extended up to a week longer if the rat is carrying a large number of young and is nursing a previous litter at the same time (Rowett, *op. cit.*). Females commonly bear 4 to 12 young; although Doty (*op. cit.*) notes that one-and-a-half year old females are said to have larger litters than younger animals. Rowett (*op. cit.*) states that females undergo the menopause at about 15 to 18 months of age. Although the babies are born blind, naked, and helpless, they are well developed in about three weeks and are usually weaned about that time. The young are sexually mature at three to six months of age (Rowett, *ibid.*).

The famous "white rat," so commonly used in laboratories, is an albinistic breed of the brown rat known as *R. norvegicus* var. *albinus;* it will interbreed with the brown rat, but not with other species. It has been selected for its tameness and is smaller in size than its wild relative. Pigment is usually totally lacking in this animal and the fur is pure white with the ears, feet, tail, and eyes being pink. It has a gestation period of from 21 to 22 days.

THE HAWAIIAN RAT *(Rattus exulans hawaiiensis)*
According to Sir Peter Buck, the Hawaiian rat arrived with the ancestors of the present-day Hawaiians about 1,500 years ago (Hiroa, 1964). The first mention of it in writing was made by Captain Cook, who, on first visiting Kauai in 1778, noted that there were "rats, resembling those seen at every island at which we had, as yet, touched" (Donaldson, 1940). Little mention was made of this animal in the next 130 years although the naturalist Titian Peale noted, for Polynesia in general, that "nearly all of the coral islands visited . . . were found to be inhabited by rats, so like the common Brown or Norway Rat . . . that they might be pronounced a diminutive variety, had we not found them inhabiting islands many thousands of miles apart, but still retaining their peculiar habits, with but very little variation in size. . . ." A quick glimpse into pre-European times shows that the Hawaiians were very much aware of the presence of rats,

and in fact apparently invented a tiny bow and arrow for the specific purpose of shooting at them. According to David Malo (1951), "*Pana 'iole*," the shooting of rodents with a bow and arrow, "was the only use the Hawaiians made of the bow and arrow." This comment was also confirmed by Bryan (1915), and Stokes (1917). According to the latter author, the small (extinct) flightless rail (*Pennula sandwichensis millsi* Dole) was sometimes substituted for the rat as a target. Stokes also notes that no contrivance that could be deemed a rattrap has been described from Hawaiian artifacts in any museum collection although such items occurred on some of the other Pacific islands.

In the 19th century it is apparent that very little attention was paid to speciation and "a rat was a rat!" For some reason the Hawaiian rat was believed to have become extinct; Bryan. (*op. cit.*) attributed its extinction to the introduction of the brown rat, but this same year (1915) Stone formally described, for the first time in scientific annals, several specimens caught on Popoia Island, which is several hundred yards offshore from Lanikai, Oahu. Miller (1924) visited that island again in 1920 and captured a number of animals, and lists, in his later publication, the measurements of ten specimens, including two from Kahoolawe and one from Maui. He concluded that it was similar in form to rats of the *R. concolor* group and that it had come, through the agency of man, to Hawaii in relatively recent times. Despite the fact that in 1923 members of the Tanager Expedition found "thousands" of Pacific island rats on tiny Kure Island (Gregory, 1924), many people continued to consider the Hawaiian rat as being almost extinct on the main islands until at least 1930 (Barnum, 1930).

Illingworth (1931) was perhaps the first person to point out that the species was abundant, at least on Oahu, and later reports have shown that it is indeed common on all of the larger islands. In 1957 Gross noted that this species made up over 60 percent of rats captured in the Hamakua district of Hawaii, and

four years later Tomich (1961) reported that, in terms of biomass, the Hawaiian rat accounted for 48.2 percent of nearly
3,000 animals weighed. This same year Bianchi stated that the
Hawaiian rat "is ubiquitous on all the plantations. It maintains
populations independent of sugar cane from sea level to the
highest elevations at which cane is grown and from the driest to
the wettest regions. These populations expand gradually but
steadily into the cane fields and leave evidence of their presence
in characteristic feeding injuries known as 'canoe damage'. "

Today we know that this species is found on the islands of
Hawaii, Maui, Molokai, Lanai, Kahoolawe, Oahu, Kauai, and
on Popoia islet. It is also present, although perhaps in a slightly
different form, on Kure Island, and may very well be the species
reported as inhabiting Kaula, Lehua, and Mokolii (Chinaman's
Hat).

The Hawaiian rat is considerably smaller than either the
brown or black rats. Its total body length averages about five
inches and its tail is approximately the same length, or slightly
longer. Adult males average 65 grams (just over 2 ounces), and
females weigh slightly less at 60 grams (Smythe, 1965). Their
color has been described by Stone (*op. cit.*) as being a cinnamon
brown or russet shading on the dorsal surface, shading into
cinnamon buff on the sides, and light buff or buffy white on the
venter; the back and sides have many black hairs mixed among
the brown. The feet are nearly white above, but the whole
undersides of the hind feet are dark. The tail is covered with
fine, rather than coarse hair (as exhibited by the other two
species), and the ears are small and ovoid.

Of some interest is the fact that recently (1963) Quay and
Tomich discovered a specialized "midventral sebaceous glan-
dular area" in this species which is unknown in other forms of
Rattus. The significance of this gland is not known.

The gestation period is 23 days (Smythe, *op. cit.*), and Jackson
(*op. cit.*) has shown that they average a litter size of just over
4 young each (from a sample of over 50 females). Smythe felt

that under natural conditions this rat probably produced four to six litters a year. He noted that, while some animals reproduce throughout the year, breeding was at a low level from December through February; during this time less than 5 percent of the females he examined were pregnant, while from June through August 20 percent were pregnant.

The Hawaiian rat digs burrows in well-drained soil, but builds nests slightly off the ground in the wetter areas. Burrows are three to eight feet long, are not interconnected, and generally have only one entrance. A succession of rats may use one burrow over a period of time; when doing this they often enlarge or extend the burrow (Smythe, *ibid.*). Inside sugar-cane fields nests made from a mass of cane leaves worked into a hollow ball are the most common home.

Smythe's studies also indicate that this species has a home range of approximately 100 feet in diameter although he states that some animals, such as male rats under a breeding stimulus, young rats just out of the nest who are searching for new territory, and a few chronic wanderers, will exceed this distance. In Spencer and Davis's study on Oahu (*op. cit.*), 82 Hawaiian rats (of an initial sample of 102) were recaptured within 200 feet of the place they were banded, and 53 of these were caught at "zero feet"—apparently meaning that they were found in the same trap from which they were first captured and released.

THE HOUSE MOUSE *(Mus musculus)*

The house mouse is the smallest of our island mammals, but at the same time is probably the most successful and most abundant. Like the other murids the exact date of introduction is unknown, but some animals may very well have come ashore in one of Captain Cook's longboats. We know that it was well established in villages and towns at least by 1825 (Perkins *in* Pemberton, 1925), and that it is indigenous today on the islands of Hawaii, Maui, Molokai, Lanai, Oahu, Kauai, and much of Midway Atoll. A unique population also exists on Manana, or

Rabbit Island, just off the coast of Oahu, and there is the possibility that a population exists on Kaula Island south of Kauai, since E. H. Bryan, Jr., reported one occurring there in 1938. Whether or not mice are present on Kahoolawe or Niihau is uncertain, but there most probably are some on both islands.

Although this mouse is usually thought of as inhabiting areas close to man, the fact that there are no other species of mice in Hawaii has allowed them to expand their population into ecological niches which would, on less-isolated land masses, be inhabited by various species of field mice. Consequently this species can be found inhabiting almost every biotic community that occurs from sea level up to at least 6,500 feet.

The house mouse is easily distinguishable from the rats because of its diminutive size; its total body length, including the tail, is generally six and one-half to seven inches, and it weighs just about one ounce. Graf (1963) did a limited survey of mice from eight different island locations, and found a definite trend toward individual population uniformity; coat colors were different in different areas as were foot measurements and tail lengths. Therefore a description of pelage color in this chapter would hold true only for one of these genetically isolated strains. It is interesting to note that the mice from Rabbit Island were the largest in the collection and showed a pale, sandy color that is often characteristic of wild mice inhabiting arid, light-colored, sandy soils—an apt description of Rabbit Island.

Tomich (1961) trapped nearly 3,000 rodents, during all months of the year, on the Hamakua coast of Hawaii, and found that *Mus* made up 56.2 percent of the catch, although in terms of total biomass it contributed only 18.9 percent of total rodent body weights. The overall sex ratio was 125 males to 100 females, but adult mice showed a ratio of 140 males to 100 females. The females weighed 13.5 percent more than the males. Litter size of 127 females averaged 4.8 young, and it was discovered that few females were pregnant in midsummer or midwinter, indicating a bimodal breeding peak in summer and fall.

The gestation period is from 18 to 21 days; the young are weaned at about 18 days, and they may be sexually mature at 6 weeks.

Around human habitation the house mouse might be termed omnivorous, but it is believed that when living in a totally wild state its primary foods are insects and grasses. Kami's food habit study (*op. cit.*), wherein he examined 345 mice, showed that insects (primarily egg masses), and three species of grass made up over 70 percent of the diet of those animals living in sugarcane fields; sugar cane, on the other hand, was eaten by only 7.2 percent of the mice and formed less than 10 percent of the volume. Other items such as fruits, berries, nuts, and lower invertebrates amounted to 5.5 percent, and 10.9 percent was unidentified. Forty-eight percent of the mice living in nearby gulches consumed insects at a volume level of 20 percent of their total diet, and also ate *kukui* nuts (*Aleurites moluccana*) in about the same amount. Grass seeds (14.6 percent volume) and unidentifiable material (41 percent) made up the rest of the animal's diet.

PARASITES AND DISEASE CONNECTED WITH RODENTS

As might be expected, rodents in Hawaii carry a large number of parasites, and are at the same time responsible in large part for carrying and spreading several human diseases. The three rodents and one mouse are known to carry a total of 36 parasites, including two blood flagellates, 11 nematodes, three tapeworms, four flukes, and 16 external arthropods. For a description of these species, see Alicata's 1964 book *Parasitic Infections of Man and Animals in Hawaii*, pp. 78–86, 108, and 112–114.

They also serve as at least intermediate hosts for an as yet untotaled number of diseases. Some of those transmissible to man include endemic typhus, salmonellosis (gastero-enteritis), leptospirosis, and plague. Plague first occurred in the Hawaiian

Islands in Honolulu in December 1899. At that time no one was really sure what caused this disease but local doctors believed that rats, in combination with unsanitary conditions, might be to blame. The Hawaiian Board of Health surrounded China-town with a "sanitary cordon" and began a house-to-house search for further cases. No communication was permitted be-tween Chinatown and the rest of the city, the residents were evacuated to detention camps, the furnaces of the Honolulu Iron Works were turned into a crematorium for victims (Bergin, 1945), and buildings where plague cases occurred were con-demned and burned. All ships venturing between islands were detained, away from wharves, for seven days before leaving, and steamships were kept breasted off from docks and were required to "tar all mooring lines and to provide them with ratproof funnels" (Link, 1954). By January 20, there had been 44 plague cases and 36 of the victims were dead; on this day about 5,000 persons were made homeless when a plague victim's house was being burned and nearby Kamakapili church caught fire. The blaze then quickly spread and all of Chinatown, from River Street to Nuuanu Avenue, and from Queen Street to Kukui Street, was destroyed.

Dr. V. B. Link has done an excellent job of documenting the history of plague in Hawaii (*ibid.*), and the reader is referred to his article for further information, but it might be noted that from the time plague was first discovered here until 1949, at least 410 persons have contracted this disease, and 374 (91 per-cent) of them died. Although plague disappeared from the island of Oahu after 1910 and never reappeared (it disappeared from Kauai after 1902, and from Maui in 1938), plague-infected rats have been found in the Hamakua district of Hawaii every year from 1933 and are still being reported; human cases were reported up until 1949, and all cases but one were fatal (Link, *ibid.*). Consequently the State Department of Health formed a "Plague Research Unit," based at Honokaa, in the Hamakua area; members of this unit not only catch large numbers of rodents every month and test them for plague bacilli to have advance warning of an impending epidemic but do considerable study on the habits and life histories of these animals in the hope of eventually finding a "weak link" that will allow the rats to be kept under better control and in reduced numbers.

LITERATURE CITED

Anderson, J. W.
1954 The production of ultrasonic sounds by laboratory rats and other mammals. Science 119 (3101): 808–809.

Barnum, C. C.
1930 Rat control in Hawaii. Haw'n. Planters' Record 34: 421–443.

Bergin, W. C.
1945 Bubonic plague in Hawaii—1899–1900. Paradise of the Pacific 57(3): 28–29.

Bianchi, F. A.
1961 The rat population of the Hawaiian sugar cane fields. 10th Pacific Science Congress, Abstr. Sympos. Paps., Star Bull. Printing Co., Honolulu: p. 209.

Bourlière, F.
1964 The natural history of mammals. 3rd Ed., Alfred A. Knopf, Inc., New York: 387pp.

Bryan, E. H.
1938 Kaula—an island of Hawaii. Paradise of the Pacific 50(4): 27, 38–39.

Bryan, W. A.
1915 Natural history of Hawaii. Hawaiian Gazette Co., Ltd., Honolulu: 596pp.

Caslick, J. W.
1956 Color phases of the roof rat, Rattus rattus. J. Mammal. 37(2): 255–257.

Corbet, G. B.
1966 The terrestrial mammals of Western Europe. G. T. Foulis and Co., Ltd., London: 264pp.

Donaldson, R.
      1940   Let's be rough on rats. Paradise of the Pacific 52(6): 17.
Doty, R. E.
      1945   Rat control on Hawaiian sugar cane plantations. Haw'n.
             Planters' Record 49(2): 71–239.
Eskey, C. R.
      1934   Epidemiological study of the plague in the Hawaiian
             Islands. Publ. Health Bull. 213: 70pp.
Fisher, H., and P. H. Baldwin
      1946   War and the birds of Midway Atoll. Condor 48(1):
             3–15.
Graf, W.
      1963   The effects of isolation on house mice *(Mus musculus)*
             and the feral goat *(Capra sp.)* on the Hawaiian Islands.
             Amer. Philos. Soc., Yearbook: 326–329.
Gregory, H. E.
      1924   Report of the Director for 1923. B. P. Bishop Mus. Bull.
             10: 38pp.
Gross, B.
      1957   Observations on rodent plague in Hawaii. 9th Pacific
             Science Congress, Abstr. Sympos. Paps., Pacific Science
             Assn., Bangkok, Thailand: p. 241.
Hiroa, Te Rangi (Sir Peter Buck)
      1964   Arts and crafts of Hawaii. B. P. Bishop Mus. Spec. Publ.
             45: 606pp.
Illingworth, J. F.
      1931   Entomology. Report of the Director for 1931. B. P.
             Bishop Mus. Bull. 82: 18–20.
Jackson, W. B.
      1965   Litter size in relation to latitude in two murid rodents.
             Amer. Midl. Nat. 73: 245–247.
Johnson, D. H.
      1946   The rat population of a newly established military base
             in the Solomon Islands. U.S. Naval Med. Bull. 46:
             1628–1632.
Kami, H.
      1966   Foods of rodents in the Hamakua District, Hawaii.
             Pacific Science 20(3): 367–373.

Link, V. B.
1954 A history of plague in the United States. U.S. Pub. Health Service, Publ. Health Monogr. 26: 120pp.

Malo, D.
1951 Hawaiian Antiquities. B. P. Bishop Mus. Spec. Publ. 2, 2nd Edit., Honolulu: 278pp.

Miller, G. S., Jr.
1924 The characters and probable history of the Hawaiian rat. B. P. Bishop Mus. Bull. 14: 2–6.

Nicholson, A. J., and D. W. Warner
1953 The rodents of New Caledonia. J. Mammal. 34: 168–179.

Pemberton, C. E.
1925 The field rat in Hawaii and its control. Haw'n. Sugar Planters' Assn., Expt. Sta. Entomological Series Bull. 17: 46pp.

Quay, W. B., and P. Q. Tomich
1963 A specialized midventral sebaceous glandular area in *Rattus exulans*. J. Mammal. 44: 537–542.

Richardson, F.
1963 Birds of Lehua Island off Niihau, Hawaii. Elepaio 23: 43–45.

Rowett, H. G. Q.
1960 The rat as a small mammal. John Murray, Ltd., London: 94pp.

Smythe, W. R.
1965 Notes on the natural history, behavior and control of the Polynesian rat, *Rattus exulans*. Haw'n. Sugar Technologists, 24th Ann. Conf.: 167–171.

Spencer, H. J., and D. E. Davis
1950 Movements and survival of rats in Hawaii. J. Mammal. 31: 154–157.

Stokes, J. F. G.
1917 Notes on the Hawaiian rat. B. P. Bishop Mus., Occas. Paps. 3(4): 261–271.

Stone, W.
1917 The Hawaiian rat. B. P. Bishop Mus., Occas. Paps. 3(4): 253–260.

Tinker, S. W.
    1938   Animals of Hawaii. Nippu Jiji Co., Ltd., Honolulu:
            188pp.
Tomich, P. Q.
    1961   Reservoirs and vectors of plague in Hawaii: rodent
            populations of the Hamakua District. 10th Pacific Sci-
            ence Congress, Abstr. Sympos. Paps. Star Bull. Printing
            Co., Honolulu: p. 210.

    ——

    1965   A survey of rodents in Hawaii Volcanoes National Park.
            Dept. of Health Field Rept., State of Hawaii, Honokaa:
            4pp.
Tomich, P. Q., and H. T. Kami
    1965   Coat color inheritance of the roof rat in Hawaii. J. Mam-
            mal. 47(3) : 423–431.

The Guinea Pig

Cavia cobaya

The guinea pig is generally considered to be a purely domesticized rodent of the family Caviidae, but it has made an impact
on the biota of one island of the Hawaiian chain and therefore
deserves a passing mention.

This tiny animal is apparently a domestic form of the brown-
ish Peruvian cavy (*Cavia tschudii*), and was being bred by the
Incas of Peru at the time of the discovery of America. It was
taken from there to Europe in the 16th century (Wender, 1946)
and has since become a standard subject for biological experi-
mentation.

For some unknown reason, the manager of a guano mining
company introduced a number of these animals to the island of
Laysan shortly after 1903. Whether they were initially kept in
pens is not known, but when the Nutting Expedition of 1911
visited that island, Dill (Dill and Bryan, 1912) noted that
"guinea pigs were found on the south end of the island in the
thick juncus. They were rather abundant in this one place,
seven being seen at one time, but they have done no harm."

In view of the fact that rabbits were drastically destroying the
vegetation at that time (see rabbit chapter), and that guinea
pigs are not only strictly herbivorous, but fairly rapid breeders

(a gestation period of from 63 to 66 days with six to eight young usually born), I suggest that the guinea pig was in fact doing harm with every mouthful of food it ate.

In 1923, when members of the "Tanager Expedition" visited the island, only the rabbits were left and they were on the verge of eating themselves out of house and home; the guinea pigs were not able to compete with these more prolific breeders and became extinct from that island sometime during the intervening 12 years.

LITERATURE CITED

Dill, H. R., and W. A. Bryan
    1912   Report of an expedition to Laysan Island in 1911. U.S. Dept. Agri., Biol. Surv. Bull. 42: 30pp.

Wender, L.
    1946   Animal Encyclopedia: Mammals. London, Geo. Allen and Unwin Ltd.: 266pp.

The Dog

Canis familiaris

An adequate discussion of the dog in Hawaii would require far more space than can be devoted to it in this book. The Polynesian dogs that were originally brought to these islands by the early Hawaiians still remain enigmatic animals although the many legends associated with them are well documented. When European breeds were introduced to the islands, the Hawaiian dog quickly lost its identity through crossbreeding. Dogs of later eras have played diverse roles that have ranged from the usual role of domesticated pet or hunters' companion, to the unusual (in the United States) circumstances of being considered the *pièce de résistance* at a *lūʻau*, or being used to sniff out sea bird burrows. Feral dogs have, in the past, served a positive value as the sole predators on the vast herds of feral sheep, goats, and cattle that were denuding the uplands of Hawaii. They also have, in recent years, been of economic significance through their depredations on domestic livestock and introduced game animals. This chapter can therefore provide little more than an overview of some of the activities and uses of the dog in Hawaii; it is hoped that someday soon, some enterprising dog enthusiast will take upon himself the vast but interesting task of compiling a book on the history and status of the dog in Hawaii.

THE HAWAIIAN DOG

Anyone reading this chapter for the specific purpose of obtaining a validated description of an original Hawaiian dog is, I am afraid, going to be disappointed. Katherine Luomala (1960a) in attempting to understand more about the Polynesian dog has done a masterful job of accumulating nearly all the writings and etchings about the dog during the era of Cook's discovery, not only for Hawaii but elsewhere in the Pacific, and after intensively reviewing these materials she remarks that "latter-day concepts, like that of genetic drift, have not been considered in connection with the possible emergence of local varieties as the result of line breeding from perhaps a single pair isolated on an island.

"Progress toward . . . learning more about *Canis familiaris* Linneaus of pre-European Polynesia must depend on studying museum skeletal remains and artifacts made of dog bones, teeth, and hair, and recent archeological finds of remains of dogs that are datable by radio-carbon analysis as pre-European in age."

There are two schools of thought concerning the appearance of the Hawaiian dog. There are those who, following Captain Cook's account, feel that one description suffices for Hawaiian dogs on all of the islands, and there are others who claim that there were at least two distinct breeds. Certainly, if the latter claim is correct, there must have been an intergrading of the bloodlines of the two (or more) which would have led to considerable variation in morphological, and perhaps temperamental, characteristics. For those readers who might prefer only one breed of dog, I offer two similar descriptions. Captain Cook wrote: "The dogs are of the same species with those of Otaheiti [Tahiti] having short, crooked legs, long backs, and pricked ears. I did not observe any variety in them, except in their skins; some having long and rough hair, and others being quite smooth. They are about the size of a common turnspit. . . ." Wood-Jones (1931) offers a similar description (although he cites no references): "We know that it was a long-bodied, short-legged dog of the short-haired terrier type. In general build it has been likened to the dachshund but, unlike this breed, its large ears were held erect. The tail was carried with an upward curve and the coat color appears to have been varied; but white and pale yellow are said to have been predominant. The fore limbs are described as being bandy, and it is said that very commonly one leg was markedly more bent than the other."

Charles Kenn (1947a), on the other hand, stated that the Hawaiian dog was white with black spots; at least one dog shown in an etching in Luomala's first article is spotted. In a second, even more extensive report on the Polynesian dog, Luomala (1960b) mentions black, brown, yellow, and hairless dogs as playing various roles in the mythology, taboos, or even daily culture of the Hawaiians. Kenn also notes (1947b) that, while all dogs were generally known as *'ilio,* the dog kept for general purposes was called *i'i,* while a brindle-colored animal "which enjoyed the fellowship of man and was never eaten at any time" was known as *mo'o.* This latter animal was sacred to the reptilian deity, Kihawahine, and figures prominently in Hawaiian mythology.

It is thus obvious that no simple description will suffice to please everyone. We must wait until more skeletal material of a datable period is available, at which point a competent vertebrate physiologist will be able to reconstruct, with a skeleton and modeling clay, the overlying musculature of the specimen and give us an accurate picture of at least one original Hawaiian dog.

Despite the importance of the dog in the legends of the Polynesians, it was kept primarily as a source of food; in some other island groups such a delicacy was reserved for the ruling class, but among the Hawaiians people of all ranks could eat dog. They were bred and reared in much the same manner as were pigs, and were kept on a vegetarian diet. Captain Cook noted that they were "exceedingly sluggish, though perhaps this may be more owing to the manner in which they are treated than to any natural disposition. They are in general fed and left to herd with the pigs; for I do not recollect any instances in which a dog was made a companion in the manner we do in Europe. Indeed, however, the custom of eating them is an insuperable bar to their admission into society . . ." (Tinker, 1941). Ellis, in 1823, also implied that the animals did not appear too alert by recording that "they have few of the characteristics of the English dog. . . . This probably arises from their different food" (Ellis, 1917). Wood-Jones (*op. cit.*) studied the skulls of two dogs unearthed on Kauai, and found that there were very definite cranial modifications brought about by the imposition of soft vegetable food on these animals of primarily carnivorous background; the skull had changed, but the animals retained the large teeth of their ancestors. A later study (Svihla, 1957) showed that dental caries were common in pre-European dogs and were probably due to the sugar-rich diet on which they were kept.

Ellis (*op. cit.*) wrote: "Numbers of dogs, of rather small size, and something like a terrier, are raised every year as an article of food. They are mostly fed on vegetables; and we have sometimes seen them kept in yards, with small houses to sleep in. A part of the rent of every tenant who occupies the land is paid in dogs for his landlord's table.

"In their feasts the flesh of the dog constitutes their principal meat. I have seen 200 dogs cooked at one time; during the last visit which Taümuarii, late king of Tauai, and Kaahumanu his queen, paid Kuakini, the governor of this island [Hawaii], a feast was prepared for them by the latter, at which Auna was present, and counted 400 baked dogs, with fish and hogs, and vegetables in proportion."

The practice of dog-eating at *lūʻaus* continued until at least the early 1840s, according to McClellan (1940). In an article describing a number of *lūʻaus* held in the past, McClellan documents some of the various comments made by guests; Capt.

Amasa Delano wrote, sometime around 1805: "The conversation turned upon having a dog cooked and served. I made reply that I did not desire to have one cooked for our table. . . . I was answered that I should not know the difference between a dog and a pig when it was cooked. The next day at dinner two pigs, as they called them, were brought on to the table; one was without a head, which was placed opposite to where I sat. I was very politely asked what I would be helped to? My answer was, a piece of pig. The gentlemen who sat near the one which had no head asked if he should help me to a piece of it, which was baked in that country style; and said he would recommend it far before the other, which was roasted. Yes, was my answer. I was helped, and ate very heartily of it. . . . I never tasted anything better, and was again helped, and finished my dinner of what I thought to be the baked pig. Later there were jokes passed on the subject of eating dogs, and I learned that what I had made so hearty a meal of was a dog." Lucy G. Thurston (McClellan, *ibid.*) wrote in 1820 that "once they mischievously attached a pig's head to a dog's body, and thus inveigled a foreigner to partake of it to his great acceptance." McClellan cites another diner who said: "Near my place was a fine young dog luaued, the flesh of which was declared to be excellent by all who partook of it. To my palate, its taste was what I can imagine would result from mingling the flavor of pig and lamb, and I did not hesitate to make my dinner of it, in spite of some qualms at the first mouthful."

Despite the fact that Cook did not see dogs being kept in the "usual European manner," it is obvious that this animal played a role in Hawaiian society beyond that of being a mere foodstuff. Ellis (*op. cit.*) wrote that "we have often had occasion to notice the fondness of the natives for their dogs. . . . the pets are usually of small size; and though the females generally evince the greatest regard for them, frequently carrying them in their arms or on their backs, yet the men are occasionally seen attended by their favorite dog." It is probable that these pets were

the animals that were buried or hidden away in caves or at
shrines; if such is the case, and if Kenn (1947b) is correct in his
assumption of two distinct breeds being present, then it is
entirely possible that when the known skeletons are finally un-
wrapped from their tapa covering and reconstructed by a
scientist, we shall see *mo'o,* the pet dog, and not *i'i,* the "poi
dog."

Dogs served not only as food and as pets but as raw material
for dancers' ornaments. The Bishop Museum anthropologists
counted 9,381 canine teeth used in the construction of 11 dog-
tooth leg ornaments. Since only canine teeth were used, and
because each dog only possesses four of these, it was an easy
matter to determine that it took 2,346 dogs to provide this
material (Hiroa, 1964).

Kenn (1947b) also found, in *Fornander's Collection of Hawaiian
Antiquities and Folklore,* a reference to the use of "a number of
ferocious trained dogs used in warfare" by Kaeo of Kauai in
1791,* and Bryan (1908) notes that Hawaiians of his time used
"'ua'u dogs" to locate burrows of the dark-rumped petrel
(*Petrodroma phaeopygia*) on Molokai; the Hawaiian dog was, of
course, long gone by this late date but it is entirely possible
that this form of training was a carryover from earlier times.

Jack Throp, director of the Honolulu Zoo, has done careful
research into the history of the Polynesian dog and hopes that
someday, through careful selection of local "poi dogs," he can
put on display an animal resembling, in shape and mannerism,
a characteristic dog of pre-European times.

THE FERAL DOG
As with other domesticated animals, the dog may revert to a

* Luomala (1960b) notes that Hawaiians used the term "wardog"
metaphorically for vassals who fought for their masters and were mythol-
ogized as supernatural dog-men. Thus, it appears probable that men, and
not dogs, were the primary participants of this battle.

feral existence from time to time. Like the cat, some dogs may step back and forth from the hearth to the wild; these animals cannot be called feral, but they are treated as such when caught preying on wildlife or domestic stock. There are a few truly feral dogs in Hawaii that are born, raised, live and die far from the proximity of man, but certainly the majority of economic damage presently attributable to dogs is caused by bands of straying animals who, after several days or even months of creating havoc, slowly disband and once again take up the company of either former or new "owners." Some dogs may stray only once in their lifetime, while others break loose from domesticity one or more times a year and run loose on an ofttimes dangerous rampage. It is these animals that create many headaches for stockmen, game managers, and Humane Society trappers; when a wild pack of dogs is reported, these people spend vast amounts of time, effort, and money to set out traps or poison stations, but more often than not the marauding pack merely disappears, or shows up later many miles from the trapping grounds.

No one knows when the first damage attributable to dog packs occurred, but it seems likely that such problems came about sometime after the settling of Europeans in Hawaii; there are no reports or comments on this subject in any of the old Hawaiian legends or folklore. Many new breeds of dogs were brought by the first European settlers (these were given names by the Hawaiians, such as the "apuwai," "makue," "ohune," "olohe," [Kenn, 1947c], and such names are still in use today in more isolated Hawaiian communities) and we must imagine that many were abandoned and left to forage for themselves. As early as 1840 wild dogs were numerous in the interior of Hawaii (Wilkes, 1845), and by 1848 citizens of that island had set up a poisoning program to eliminate some of the many wild dogs that were living off the sheep and goats (and presumably wild cattle) of the Waimea region of that island (Ana, 1848). During this period, and for about 90 years thereafter, we owe a certain debt of gratitude to the dog. Although they certainly caused considerable economic loss to owners of domestic stock, they were, at the same time, the only significant predator on the feral sheep and goats, who were increasing in unbelievable numbers and causing irreparable damage to the native vegetation. Although untold numbers of dogs were poisoned, shot, or trapped, feral dogs still range the high mountains of Hawaii; early-rising campers and hunters who stay at the Pohakuloa cabins can often look up on the slopes of Mauna Kea and see swirling clouds of dust, which indicate that a normally slow-moving herd of sheep is probably being chased by a pack of dogs.

Generally, when persons concerned with domestic stock or wildlife management come across a single dog, they whistle and call to it, to see if it is perhaps a lost and confused pet, but if these same persons run into a pack of three or more animals, they usually do one of two things: if armed, they start shooting, and if unarmed, they seek cover. When I first saw a pack of seven feral dogs, in a Game Management Area on Molokai, I recalled the stories of several other biologists who had been attacked by dogs on the slopes on Mauna Loa; both men had been charged the moment that the dogs became aware of them. There was no growling or snarling or uncertain movement on the dogs' part, they just raced in a straight line at the men. Both men had escaped unhurt by either shooting the dogs or jumping into their nearby vehicles; they later said they believed the animals had probably never seen a human before and that they (the men) were probably considered by the dogs as no more dangerous than the sheep and goats on which they normally preyed. I shot three animals of this pack and threw them into the back of my pickup truck so that I might study them later. On leaving the area I ran into a foreman from a pineapple company; on seeing the animals he told me that I should take the two black ones up to the little town of Mauna Loa, which is situated on the western end of Molokai, and "trade them for beer." This was when I first became aware that dog was still eaten in the islands.

I did not take the animals up to the town that day, but at a later date made inquiries and found that a large, well-fed black dog (preferably alive or only freshly killed) could bring a case of beer in trade—in the right quarters. A few months after this discovery, Edward Norbeck's sociological treatise *Pineapple Town Hawaii* (1959) was released, and described the prevalence of this custom in Mauna Loa. Norbeck writes: "A practice which is restricted to Filipinos and principally to single men among them is the holding of parties at which dogs are cooked and eaten. . . . Participants estimate that from half a dozen to a dozen such parties may be held throughout the year. . . . Dogs are sometimes purchased and—it is said—often stolen. They should be fat, . . . short-haired, and darkly pigmented, preferably black. It seems that white dogs are never used because they taste bad or because of vaguely remembered taboos against eating them. After the hair has been singed and scraped off, the animal is eviscerated and the viscera cleaned for future consumption. Various recipes, differing according to the organ being prepared and the preference and state of drunkenness of the cook, involve boiling, frying, simmering, broiling, or only partial cooking. All the soft parts of the animal including the brains are eaten, and the blood is also consumed, sometimes while raw and warm. . . . The prevailing attitude among Filipinos is that this practice is revolting if not immoral. Dog-eaters are well aware of this sentiment and seem in a curious way to share it, speaking of the dog feast in a defensively laughing tone as if it were a form of delinquency. . . ." I later found that some Filipinos in plantation towns on other islands also occasionally have a dog feast; it would appear that the custom had almost died out in the first half of this century but, when large numbers of Filipinos moved to Hawaii to work just after World War II, they brought a revival of this custom.

Feral or "loose" dog packs run free from time to time on all islands, but determination of abundance or habit patterns is difficult because their presence is so seldom made public until sometime after they have done their damage. The dogs are looked upon, not as a subject for biological study, but strictly as pests. About the only effort put into a study of feral dogs is the study of methods of extermination, and this is haphazard at best. The island-wide economic loss attributable to these animals has never been calculated but must be considerable if we can rely on the sporadic newspaper articles that appear from time to time. It would seem that after one person protests to a newspaper about dog damage, there is a rash of sightings and damage reports; when the subject becomes "old news," such articles disappear from the paper for a time despite the apparent fact that damage continues to occur. The Humane Society wages a continuing battle to keep the numbers of loose or wild dogs in control.

In 1954, the manager of this organization, Arthur McCormick, reported that over 1,000 dogs, half of which were "wild," were trapped on Oahu during the seven preceding years (Maneki, 1954). Two years later Mr. McCormick estimated that there were still about 500 dogs running free in packs ranging from three to nine or ten (anon., 1956). The situation was still so bad on Oahu in 1959 and 1960 that the Honolulu City Council appropriated $4,800 for a feral dog extermination program that, in five months, netted about 100 dogs. At this time McCormick estimated that losses (on Oahu) due to dog predation averaged between $10,000 and $12,000 a year. He also noted that in the preceding six months dogs had killed nine calves, seven pigs, two goats, and sixty-two chickens (anon., 1960). Losses on other islands were certainly equally if not more severe, but there was no standardized method of reporting this information. A 1946 report of "packs of 30 and 40" dogs making nightly raids on a ranch at Pupukea, Oahu—and killing three or four pigs nightly—immediately brought forth reports of simultaneous stock damage occurring at Koko Head, Kaneohe, and near St. Louis College (anon., 1946); this same report prompted George Munro to write and tell how, a few years earlier, two dogs on Lanai had killed twelve sheep, two goats, and one wild pig in just one night (Munro, 1946). An unusual economic loss occurred in 1954 when a pack of dogs splashing around in a watercress field ruined a $300 crop (anon., 1954).

There are too many damage reports to list; some of the more significant depredations—such as one small rancher losing 16 calves in one year at Waikane, Oahu (anon., 1955); two dogs killing 13 calves in Kau, Hawaii (the cowboys who killed the dogs were given a $100 reward) (anon., 1959); and 65 lambs being killed in one night at Parker Ranch's Humuula sheep station (McMurray, 1961)—point out the magnitude of the problem. Worse, the packs will sometimes attack humans. Maneki (*op. cit.*) tells how "four huge dogs once attacked Territorial surveyors at Koko Head who picked up some puppies they found. The men would have been in serious danger if they had not thrown their equipment at the animals." A woman patient at the Kaneohe Hospital was bitten on the leg by one of a pack of ten or more dogs that invaded the hospital grounds in 1957, but was not seriously injured (anon., 1957). Therefore it is urgent that any citizen who sees or even suspects the presence of dogs wandering loose about their homes should immediately call the Humane Society and request that immediate action be taken; those of us who have found it necessary to confront these animals are aware of their unpredictable behavior and potential savagery.

LITERATURE CITED

Ana, K.
    1848   Letter dated November 16 for William Beckley, Waimea, Hawaii. Int. Dept. Translations, Book 2. Hawaii State Archives, Honolulu.

Anonymous

    1946   Wild dog packs roam hill, kill hogs, cattle. Hono. Advertiser, Feb. 1.

    1954   Wild dog menace back again. Hono. Advertiser, Sept. 30: A4–1.

    1955   Calves killed in dog attacks. Hono. Star Bull., Sept. 27.

    1956   Wild dog packs on rampage again. Hono. Advertiser, May 25: B1–6.

    1957   Wild dog pack attacks Kaneohe woman patient. Hono. Advertiser, April 21: A10–7.

    1959   Cowboys shoot 2 calf-killing dogs, get bounty. Hono. Star Bull., Jan. 9.

    1960   100 'killer' dogs shot or trapped. Hono. Advertiser, Feb. 9: A1–1.

Bryan, W. A.
    1908   Some birds of Molokai. B. P. Bishop Mus., Occas. Papers No. 4: 133–176.

Ellis, W.
    1917   A narrative of a tour through Hawaii, or Owyhee; with remarks on the history, traditions, manners, customs, and language of the inhabitants of the Sandwich Islands. Hawaiian Gazette Co., Honolulu: 367pp. (Reprint of the 1827 London edition).

Hiroa, Te Rangi (Sir Peter Buck)
    1964   Arts and crafts of Hawaii. B. P. Bishop Mus., Spec. Publ. No. 45. Honolulu: 606pp.

Kenn, C.
    1947a The dog. Hono. Star Bull., Sept. 8.

    1947b The dog. Hono. Star Bull., Sept. 10.

    1947c The dog. Hono. Star Bull., Sept. 11.

Luomala, K.
1960a A history of the binomial classification of the Polynesian native dog. Pacific Science 14: 193–223.

———

1960b The native dog in the Polynesian system of values. In: S. Diamond, Culture in History. Columbia U. Press, New York: 190–240.

Maneki, R.
1954 Wild dog packs increasing, Humane Society man warns. Hono. Star Bull. Oct. 22: p. 2.

McClellan, E. N.
1940 Ahaaina or Luau in old Hawaii. Paradise of the Pacific 52(1): 9–12, 25.

McMurray, T.
1961 Bloodthirsty wild dogs slay Big Island lambs. Hono. Advertiser, June 7.

Munro, G. C.
1946 Wild dogs a real menace, says Kamaaina; tells of depredations. Hono. Star Bull., March 9.

Norbeck, E.
1959 Pineapple Town/Hawaii. Univ. Calif. Press, Berkeley and Los Angeles, California: 159pp.

Svihla, A.
1957 Dental caries in the Hawaiian dog. B. P. Bishop Mus., Occas. Papers 22(2): 7–13.

Tinker, S. W.
1941 Animals of Hawaii. Tongg Pub. Co., Honolulu: 190pp.

Wilkes, C.
1845 Narrative of the United States Exploring Expedition. Vol. IV, Lea and Blanchard, Phila.: 539pp.

Wood-Jones, F.
1931 The cranial characters of the Hawaiian dog. J. Mammal. 21: 39–41.

The Small Indian Mongoose

Herpestes auropunctatus auropunctatus

DESCRIPTION

The mongooses are small to medium-sized carnivores belonging to the family Viverridae which encompasses such other animals as the civet cats, genets, and merrkats. Most people are surprised to find this family most closely related to the Felidae, or cat family. In the classification of animal life they fall into the superfamily known as Feloidea along with the cats, and are thus considered to be more evolutionarily advanced than the dog family. Though most viverrids superficially resemble animals of the family Mustelidae, such as the weasel, mink, or ferret, the viverrids actually replace these animals in much of the Indo-Malayan and African regions of the Old World. Our concern is for one of twelve species (Corbet, 1966) of the genus *Herpestes,* which has been introduced to Hawaii, the West Indies, the northern portion of South America, and parts of southern Europe.

The name of the Hawaiian species of mongoose, *Herpestes,* from the Greek word *herpein* (to creep), and *auropunctatus* (gold spotted) is an apt summarization of this long-bodied, short-legged predator. In the local literature the Hawaiian animal is given other scientific names, such as *Herpestes mungo, H. griseus, H. edwardsi,* and *H. javannicus auropunctatus,* but as Baldwin *et al.* (1952)* reported, the latter name is now reserved only for that species in Java, and the preceding names were technical misnomers.

Undoubtedly the mongoose is the most commonly observed wild animal in Hawaii, with only a few sequestered residents of Kauai, Lanai, and Niihau not having seen any. Certainly any tourist who has left the environs of Waikiki has observed a mongoose scurrying across a road, but many think they have seen a large rat and dwell no further on the subject. Indeed, with a total body and tail measurement ranging from 20.3 to 26 inches in males, and from 18.7 to 23 inches in females (Baldwin *et al., ibid.*), and with the erectile hairs of the tail in a normal relaxed position, it is difficult for the casual visitor to differentiate a mongoose from a rat at any considerable distance.

Not only is the male mongoose usually larger than the female, it may weigh half again as much as the female; in the Baldwin and Schwartzes' study, females were found to range in weight anywhere from .7 to 1.35 pounds with adult males weighing from 1 to 2.8 pounds.

The grayish brown hair has a definite yellow cast and the broad, alternating rings of dark brown and yellow pigment in the individual outer or guard hairs give the mongoose the appearance of having had a faulty permanent wave; hence the appearance of clusters of yellow areas or "golden-spots." There are color variations (not reported by Baldwin *et al.*) ranging

---

* The author wishes to acknowledge the fine publication *Life History and Economic Status of the Mongoose in Hawaii,* by Paul Baldwin, Charles and Elizabeth Schwartz, from which much of the information in this chapter is gleaned. Statistical information given is quoted accurately from this or other referred sources, but the author takes full responsibility for conclusions presented.

from a rich red-brown to dark yellow-brown, to a dirty gray-blonde tone. The latter color seems most prevalent in the extremely dry coastal areas, with the darker colorations occurring in the wet areas.

The mongoose's tail, averaging eight to ten inches in length, serves several useful functions. When traveling, the tail hairs are most often relaxed, with the subsequent appearance of being a not-too-thick nontapering tail; when the mongoose is excited, frightened, or in a fighting stance, the hairs become erected to an almost 90 degree angle to the tail, increasing the apparent diameter of the tail almost to that of the circumference of the body. One obvious advantage is the appearance of being a larger animal than it really is, and another is in the distraction to its foe, who sees half the body waving in the air and upon striking at this focal point finds little but a wisp of hair, while the mongoose, in turn, pivots and strikes a telling blow to his fully extended foe. Another useful function of this furry tail is in the maintenance of warmth while the animal is sleeping; almost invariably the captive animals I have observed sleeping have done so much in the manner of the American squirrel, with their bodies curled into the fetal position and the tail curling up between the forelegs and over the crown of the head. The individual hairs of the tail, like those of the dorsal body hairs, have alternating bands of dark and light pigment (known as agouti pelage) and are somewhat longer than those of the body, which average four-fifths inch in length.

The head of the mongoose is long, relatively narrow, and quite pointed. This weasel-like appearance is further enhanced by the low cranial structure and the fact that the ears are short, rounded, with the external opening almost obscured by rear-directed hair. There are skin folds inside the ear which, when the ears are laid back, also help close the aperture to the inner ear; Baldwin *et al.* felt that the ear shape was more indicative of an adaptation to a life of living in burrows than it was to suggest poor hearing ability. The eyes are positioned so that they can look up and to the sides, as well as forward, without moving the head. Normally they are of a pale yellowish-green color with a horizontally slotted pupil, but when the animal becomes excited, the eyes develop a distinctly reddish color, which is due to suffusion of the blood vessels in the eye. The nose and the genital region are the only areas of the body that are normally pigmented, but I have seen a number of mongooses with pigment only on the upper half of the nostrils, as well as several with unpigmented noses, leaving them a conspicuous flesh pink.

The soles of the feet are of the normal pink color and the foot is of a structure common to bears, members of the weasel family, and man, known as "plantigrade"; defined as walking on the sole of the foot with the heel touching the ground. Five claws are present on each foot; in contrast to reports on certain other species of mongoose, these claws are not the least bit retractile. The claws grow continually, but normal walking wears them down and keeps them sharp.

Like most members of the family Viverridae, both sexes of mongoose have a pair of anal glands about the size of a large pea which opens into the anal pouch. Certain other species of *Herpestes* are said to be capable of ejecting or producing a foul-smelling fluid, similar to the ejection of musk by skunks, and Baldwin *et al.* found a cream-colored, cheesy substance in the glands, but stated that this secretion did not seem notably odorous. During the 1967 rabies scare on Oahu, when more than 7,000 mongooses were trapped, Swedberg (pers. comm.) said that, in the autopsy room, a definitely acrid and pungent odor was noticeable, but that this smell was not distinguishable on individual animals.

The shape of the teeth indicate the mongoose has adapted to a partly omnivorous but primarily carnivorous diet. Baldwin *et al.* noted that in animals presumed to be four or five years old the majority of teeth were excessively worn down, occasionally to the rims of the bony socket. See Appendix C for the dental formula.

The female mongoose possesses three pairs of mammary glands, all of which are fully functional.

HISTORY

Assuredly, anyone who is even aware of the mongooses' presence in Hawaii is also roughly conversant with the fact that they were brought here to combat rat depredation in the sugar-cane fields. If only the plantation owners had waited another 15 years, it is certain that they would have concentrated on other means of control, but knowledge of the impact of these small carnivores on an island community which formerly had only a few feral cats and dogs as predators was sadly lacking at that time.

In February 1872, four male and five female mongooses arrived in Jamaica from Calcutta (Espeut, 1882) for exactly the same purpose—rat control—that descendants of theirs were later brought to Hawaii. Espeut doubted that any further introductions were made, but an anonymous writer in Hawaii (anon., 1883) mentioned that other animals from a source in England at least arrived in Jamaica. On first sight, and from the limited viewpoint of the Jamaican planters, the mongoose was an instant success and this word soon spread to sugar planters elsewhere in the Caribbean and in Hawaii. Paying little attention to the life history of the animal, and little heed to depredations among native birds and reptiles, only favorable reports initially came forth; after all, it must have taken several years for the population to have built itself up sufficiently to have become noticeably efficient in its primarily delineated task.

In 1883, after hearing of the "good job" being done on cane-field rats in Jamaica, and ignoring vague reports of damage done to at least the native reptiles (after all, Hawaii had no snakes!), the Hilo Planters' Association raised the sum of $1,100 and commissioned a Mr. J. Tucker to go to Jamaica and bring back as many mongooses as possible. He returned on September 30, 1883, on the *City of New York,* with 11 cases containing 72 live mongooses. They were delivered to Hilo and divided among the planters along the Hamakua coast who had shared the expenses (Tinker, 1938). Then, two years later in 1885, another "large number of mongooses" were brought back to the Hamakua planters by Mr. Joseph Marsden, who acquired them in Jamaica on a trip to the New Orleans Exposition (anon., 1885).

The plantation managers obviously were more optimistically than mathematically inclined because in 1884, only one year after the original introduction of 36 pairs of animals, a representative of the Planters' Association, Jonathan Austin, stated that at least one plantation could find no evidence of rat damage and concluded that the mongoose had saved them at least $50,000 (Walker, 1945). Using the absolute maximum breeding season and reproductive data formulated by Baldwin *et al.*, and allowing for no mortality, I find it impossible to raise the 1884 mongoose population higher than 850 members; in fact I would place it closer to 200 animals.

In 1888, an editorial comment on the mongoose appeared in the *Planters' Monthly* stating that, in former years on the Hamakua coast, one-quarter to one-half of the cane crop was destroyed by rats, but "now a field is harvested clean and not a stalk of cane is damaged" (anon., 1888).

The rush was on, and planters on Maui, Molokai, Oahu, and Kauai asked for stock. Animals were shipped to these islands, but a fortunate event took place at the Kauai dock and the mongoose was never established there. There are several accounts of the story, one being that a gentleman from that island could not stand the idea of so vicious an animal being liberated on his beloved island and forthwith threw the crate off the dock, and the other has it that an unidentified gentleman attempted to pet the new arrivals by putting his hand in the crate, receiving in return a fierce nip, and in wrath, threw the animals into the sea where they drowned before they could be rescued by onlookers (Tinker, *op. cit.*). The island of Lanai was at that time being used strictly for ranching purposes, as were Kahoolawe and Niihau, and no requests were made for introduction; consequently, these four large islands are without mongooses today, as are all the small islets.

DISTRIBUTION AND HABITAT

Mongooses live from sea level to the summits of the highest peaks on Oahu and Molokai, and from sea level to approximately 10,000 feet on Maui and Hawaii. The upper limit of contiguous vegetation ceases at about this altitude; the immediate decline in suitable foodstuffs is the apparent reason for not finding the animal at even higher altitudes during the summer. Although a majority of mongooses living at these upper levels probably range downward in the winter months, I once saw tracks made in a light snow at about the 7,500-foot level on Mauna Kea. Baldwin *et al.* found that mongooses living at higher elevations developed much finer coats in summer than animals living at lower elevations; it was assumed that since the outer guard hairs are relatively coarsely scattered and since the underhair is also relatively sparse, the animal could not withstand long periods of cold.

Baldwin *et al.* found that the best habitat seemed to be the warm humid areas below 2,000 feet elevation where there was a natural mixed vegetative pattern with an abundance of cover and shelter such as rock walls, cracks and crannies in the lava, and heavy grass or brushy litter. In comparison to these lower areas, the forest regions are not densely occupied, but there is no forest trail which, on close investigation, will not reveal mongoose sign. Seaman (1952) noted that in the Caribbean the preferred habitat was in dry brush country, with humid forest areas being generally avoided, but in Hawaii I have found that, though certainly abundant in the dry leeward areas of the islands, sightings are much more common in the 30- to 60-inch rainfall zone of the windward sides; Baldwin *et al.*'s trapping results agreed.

I once watched for two days a mongoose living in a crack in a rock less than two feet from the ocean edge at the extreme outer ledge of the City of Refuge at Honaunau. When the tide was high this animal was completely isolated from land and its home was less than six inches from the calm water of the cove. It appeared to subsist entirely on crabs which ventured up onto this narrow ledge, since there was absolutely no other animal or vegetable life for a hundred yards; there were sufficient crab remains in and about the crack to indicate that it had been there well over a week. I have also seen mongoose foraging on the bare tidal flats of Molokai at dawn, and LaRivers (1948) records seeing them on a peninsula in Pearl Harbor where they exist on crustacea and other littoral animals.

FOOD HABITS AND PREDATION

If one were to believe an anonymous writer of 1897, who wrote of the depredations of the mongoose in Jamaica, islands inhabited by the mongoose today would probably be barren deserts. He noted that after having "abated the pest of rats which infested the sugar canes," the mongoose "increased and multiplied to such an extent that not only the rats and mice but most of the living species of the island were threatened with extinction. Poultry suffered first, but the depredations extended to young pigs, kids, lambs, newly dropped calves, puppies and kittens. Game of all kinds was attacked, both living and in the egg. The marauder even ate fish, and made such a specialty of snakes, ground-lizards, frogs, turtles, and land crabs, that many of these entirely disappeared. Finally the mongoose developed a ravenous desire for bananas, pineapples, young corn, avocado pears, cocoas, yams, and the sugar-canes, which it had been called in to protect, winding up its tastes with an appetite for salt meat."

At the end of this article, after further erroneous explanation about the eventual decline of the mongoose and subsequent reestablishment of these "vanished species," the writer stated that "the renewed depredations of the rats are hailed as an advent of salvation, and, odd as it may sound, the increase in numbers of the crocodile is taken as a happy omen."

In reality, the mongoose is an omnivorous eater with the typical characteristics of most small predators; that is, it will eat that food which is most commonly available with the least amount of effort.

With regard to control of rodents, Kami (1964) found rodent hair and bones in 72 percent of cane-field droppings, and in 24 percent of those examined from pasture lands on the windward side of Hawaii. Baldwin *et al.* analyzed 86 droppings from rocky, open grass pastures at 2,000 to 4,500 feet elevation on the opposite, leeward side of Hawaii and found them to contain 39.6 percent volume of rat and mouse remains. Pemberton (1925) examined some 365 droppings from Honokaa cane fields and reported that "52.2 percent . . . contained nothing but rodent parts . . . 36.2 percent containing a mixture of insect and rodent parts . . . and 11.5 percent contained nothing but parts of insects." Obviously, the mongoose does perform at least a portion of the job for which it was originally imported. Doty (1945) felt that from the viewpoint of the sugar-cane agriculturists, the mongoose does much more good than harm and his paper quoted Barnum (1930) as believing that the uniformly higher rat damage on Kauai in 1927 and 1928, in comparison to that of other islands, was due to the absence of mongooses.

Kami (*op. cit.*) found that 80 percent of the scats collected in pasture areas contained various insect species' remains and considered them the most important food under those conditions, while Baldwin *et al.* found various plant species, at 29.3 percent volume, slightly more important than insects, of which 27.0 percent volume was found. However, this latter study was conducted in a very dry area and it is perhaps significant that five-sixths of the plant remains were those of the succulent cactus; in wetter areas, or where constant water is available, we might expect to see a commensurate decrease of vegetable material in the diet. Insect remains, as might be expected, prove to be largely those of cockroaches, dung beetles, and grasshoppers.

The author has on several occasions observed mongooses catch and eat lizards, and has also watched them ferret out gecko eggs from rocky crevices on Molokai, but most other Hawaiian studies make only passing mention of lizards as a food source. It was thought for a long time that the common large toad (*Bufo marinus*) would not be susceptible to the hunger of the mongoose due to the poison glands on its back, which violently irritate and occasionally kill dogs or cats that bite into them, but the late Charles S. Judd once kept five captive animals and fed them some 20 toads, which they ate with apparent relish and no sign of ill effect (Baldwin *et al.*, *op. cit.*).

In most areas the mongoose feeds on birds only to a limited extent, due to the difficulty of capturing them. Baldwin *et al.* shows that only 4.1 percent of the volume of 86 scats contained bird remains, but this is undoubtedly because of the terrain from which the sample was collected. On the leeward west end of Molokai, where bird census figures occasionally show up to 10,000 barred dove (*Geopelia s. striata*) per square mile, this bird provides one of the common foods, if one is to judge by the large number of feather remains found daily. It is interesting to observe the "distance factor" allowed by the different species of birds when they are aware of a mongooses' presence; the Kentucky cardinal (*Richmondena cardinalis*) is certainly the most skittish, never allowing an approach of closer than four or five yards before flitting off to another location. The California quail (*Lophortyx californica*) is next in wariness, allowing an approach of eight to ten feet before running rapidly away for five or so feet before resuming feeding; the lace-necked dove (*Streptopelia c. chinensis*) will allow approach to about six feet before taking wing, and the bold mynah (*Acridotheres tristis*) will stroll, always with a sideways movement, as close as three feet from a semihidden mongoose, but never takes its eye off the animal and will from time to time, bounce into the air and away for two or three feet before approaching again. The barred dove, on the other hand, with its eyes seemingly glued to the ground, will quite commonly walk within two feet of the mongoose before turning its back and starting to feed off in the opposite direction. It is no doubt this lack of wariness that accounts for the 43 separate kills I observed one day over a six-mile stretch of trail.

Although Charles and Elizabeth Schwartz (1950) admit to some mongoose predation on the quail, they did not consider it to be a critical limiting factor; on the other hand, studies by biologists of the Division of Fish & Game (Smith and Woodworth, 1951; Woodworth and Woodside, 1953) indicated that pheasant brood success increased in areas where heavy mongoose poisoning was carried on, even though no differences in brood size were noticeable. The latter report also noted that ranchers in the study area agreed that there was an increase in the feral turkey population in the poisoned areas. The obvious differential in size between a mongoose and a turkey weighing five to ten times as much certainly does not bother an aggressive, hungry mongoose. It is known that certain mongooses unhesitatingly attack and kill such large birds as the black-crowned night heron (*Nycticorax nycticorax*) (Bryan, 1908) and the nestling red-footed booby (*Sula sula*) (Ord, 1964) even though it took some 10 to 15 minutes to kill this latter bird.

Seaman and Randall (1962) describe how one or two mongooses were seen on three occasions to have attacked young white-tailed deer (*Odocoileus virginianus*) in the Virgin Islands with apparent success, and Lewis (1940) records an instance in India where a large mongoose (undoubtedly of a different species) seized a grazing donkey by the snout and held on, much to the consternation of the donkey, who fell over on its back with "feet kicking in the air." Seaman (*op. cit.*), in discussing *H. auropunctatus* in the Caribbean, said, perhaps overdramatically: "Were this animal the size of a fox terrier, no man would dare enter the woods unless properly armed. As it is, females with young will attack humans on occasion."

Baldwin *et al.* list numerous bird species where it was definitely known that a mongoose had eaten eggs, chicks, or poults; on two occasions I have caught mongooses in my chick brooder. On both occasions the animal, in a manner exactly reminiscent of the "killing lust" of weasels, stoats, and ferrets, had killed every chick by identical means—by a single bite at the base of the skull—but had fed on only one or two birds. On the second occasion all 26 birds were known to have been killed in less than three minutes! Several authors have mentioned the manner that the mongoose uses to crack open an egg that is too big or thick shelled for it to bite through. Walker (1948) perhaps describes the technique best: "After straddling the egg like a football center, he suddenly passes it between his hind legs. On the green grass it rolls and bounces, with the animal in close pursuit. This is repeated time after time, and the animal works into a frenzy of excitement. Sometimes a second mongoose intercepts the rolling object and a battle ensues, with the game being carried on by the winner. Finally success rewards the labor, as the egg on its careening journey strikes a rock and cracks. Within a few moments only an empty shell is left."

Certainly the mongoose must be charged with an immense amount of destruction to certain species of ground-nesting native birds. The nonnative, ground-nesting "game birds" are all exotic and evolved in areas of the world where small predators were common; in consequence, during the eons of time when it was necessary to cohabit any given area, these birds took to concealing their nests in one manner or another, thus allowing at least a few members of the species to escape detection, to survive, and to reproduce. The sea birds, on the other hand, nest in colonies with no regard for concealment and innocently tolerate almost any intrusion. Many of the smaller ones actually dig burrows in the earth, thus tempting even more the exploration of the inquisitive mongoose. Bryan (*op. cit.*)

noted at the turn of this century examples of the mongoose occupying the burrows of the dark-rumped petrel *(Petrodroma phaeopygia)* on the 2,000 to 3,000-foot high Molokai cliffs, and Munro (1947) states that by 1936 the mongoose had succeeded in eliminating not only this species but also the Newell's shearwater *(Puffinus puffinus newelli)* from that island. Today the dark-rumped petrel is found only on the islands of Maui and Hawaii, nesting at altitudes of 7,000 to 9,000 feet, which, as mentioned, is just at the upper altitudinal range of the mongoose. The Newell's shearwater, which is known to have also nested in low areas of Maui is found today only on Kauai. It may also be significant that, only on Kauai, of all the larger islands, are wedge-tailed shearwaters *(Puffinus pacificus)* found nesting. This bird, and many other smaller sea birds, are found on many offshore islets of the chain.

While there is no definite proof that the mongoose is capable of killing an adult nene *(Branta sandvicensis)*, Walker (1966) records the destruction of clutches of nene eggs and hearsay evidence has it that they can kill young goslings.

Cannibalism has been mentioned by some writers (Baldwin *et al.* and Doty [*op.cit.*]); carrion in the form of any dead animal in the field is taken, and Pemberton (1933) reports that mongooses in captivity eat everything from bread and ripe bananas to centipedes and any insect fed them.

REPRODUCTION

Powell (1914), who kept five pet mongooses of this species in Ghazipur, India, was the first person to record some good reproductive data. He said that the first female he captured was bred at the age of one year by a wild mongoose and bore three young just seven weeks later. Pearson and Baldwin (1953) agree that the gestation period in Hawaii is seven weeks, and their studies show a number of fetuses ranging from two to four, with an average of 2.7 fetuses per female. There is however, the possibility that a female may occasionally bear up to five young. Bryan *(op. cit.)* records finding a litter of five in a Molokai petrel burrow, and Baldwin *et al.* have counted up to five uterine scars (which indicate that perhaps five young had been born) in several females examined. Walker (1948), who observed "several score of family groups" on Oahu, says that there were normally only two pups to a litter, with only one female being seen with triplets.

In India the breeding season seems to extend from at least late February into July, while Baldwin *et al.* indicate that the breeding season in Hawaii extends from February into September, with two peaks, one between February and April and the other between May and July. Since Walker *(op.cit.)* indicated that young were absent only during the months of October, November, and December, and also since Pearson and Baldwins' work did not seem to include a standardized sample each month, the author questions the double peak and suggests that more work be done in this area. There is no doubt that a well-nourished, healthy female can bear two litters a year; in fact, Pearson and Baldwin conclude that each adult female does bear two litters per year, which would lend credence to the double-breeding peak. Powell *(op.cit.)* relates how one of his females gave birth to two young on April 14 and then, 12 weeks and 2 days later, gave birth to a second litter. He goes on to say that when they are born they are "practically hairless and of a dark mouse colour." Their eyes open on the sixteenth to seventeenth day. In the meantime, his female carried them as a cat would carry its kittens and constantly moved them from place to place.

Pearson and Baldwin *(op.cit.)* examined some 221 skulls and, using skull characters and tooth wear as an indication, found that the mean age of captured males was 25 months, while females were somewhat younger, at 22 months. Dover (1932) stated that in zoos in Calcutta and London these animals averaged a captive life of seven years.

HABITS AND BEHAVIOR

The mongoose is a terrestrial animal that is active by day and quiescent at night, hence the Hawaiian saying that the mongoose and the rat often share the same burrow, with "one working the day shift and the other the night shift." Unfortunately, no information is available about the extent of its home range, hunting range, or territory, excepting that of pet animals, who seldom range far from their adopted home.

It is a common sight to see five or six mongooses all feeding at one garbage dump, or over one carcass with little intraspecific competition noted, provided of course, that one animal does not try to steal a specific morsel that another has in possession. LaRivers *(op. cit.)* described how two animals seemingly worked together, with one turning over stones while the other pounced on any crab flushed. The two animals then consumed each crab before resuming the hunt. Paired mongooses can quite often be seen hunting together in an apparently coordinated manner, and my own observations indicate that, nearly always, the male leads the way; this habit may in fact lead to the unusually high catch of males which has been noted by trappers and has sometimes been accredited to a highly unbalanced sex ratio within the species. Though information is sparse, I do not believe that the male remains with the female once the young are born as one most often sees only one adult, usually leading the way, as a family group traverses the scrub. If this theory is true, it is also important to learn when the female re-pairs with a male and whether this male is the former mate or a new one. Information of this sort can only be acquired by capturing, marking, and releasing paired adults.

Walker *(op. cit.),* who started out running a bird-feeding station, and ended up running a mongoose-feeding station, says that "until about one-fourth grown, the young are kept well hidden deep in some underground burrow. They are not brought

to the station until they are well able to walk, run, and fight—
and in spite of their small size they do plenty of the latter with
strangely victorious results. These babies can rush and snarl at
an adult two or three times their size, and even steal a tasty
morsel of food with impunity. If a full-grown mongoose were to
try the same tactics, a ferocious battle would surely ensue."
These young pups can utter several types of weak, high-pitched
sounds and several owners say that the young mongoose purrs
like a cat when it suckles; the adults make a variety of sounds,
ranging from the threatening "spitting" sound that seems to
serve as a warning, through soft growls and snarls, to a short,
sharp "tchak" as the mongoose lunges. The rattling "rikk-tikk-
tikki-tchk" cry of the famous Rikki–Tikki–Tavi of *The Jungle
Books* fame has not been heard, leading us to believe that this
mighty warrior was, unfortunately, of a different species!

When walking, the tail is held straight to the rear and off the
ground. In high grass, or even on open ground, the animal will
stop from time to time and sit up straight on its haunches, peering at a questionable object for up to two or three minutes in
this position. At this time it is reminiscent of the pose of the
prairie-dog *(Cynomys sp.)*.

When attacking its prey, or doing battle with one of its kind,
it becomes quite oblivious to its surroundings and can be closely
approached. As mentioned before the hairs, not only of the tail
but also of the back, are erected, and the animal will strike out
with the coiling manner of its occasional Asian adversary, the
snake. As Baldwin *et al.* pointed out, in retreat, those seen never
backed up but "turned tail and dashed," even if cover was but
a short step away.

The mongoose can swim when necessary, but usually seeks
other means to cross a stream before finally taking to the water;
emerging on the other side they stop, and with a violent quiver,
shake the water from their fur. Curious, they seem to take a
different route everytime from point to point rather than use
any self-created trail; even on taro-patch walls surrounded by

water one is just as liable to find them moving along the waters' edge as up on the well-trodden foot path.

The first comment heard from many tourists, upon first learning of the presence of mongooses in Hawaii, is, "How can there be? You don't have any snakes here!" This common association undoubtedly stems from the many legends of the mongoose feeding primarily on snakes. In fact, there is one tiny burrowing snake *(Typhlops brahminus)* that has been established on Oahu for more than 30 years, but since these tiny creatures have much the same appearance and habits of an earthworm, on which they feed, it is doubtful that there has ever been much of a confrontation. In 1966 and 1967 some seven or eight larger snakes of various species were caught on Oahu, and early in 1968 a boa constrictor about four feet long was captured on Maui. Although it is believed that all of these snakes were escaped pets and that no large snake is established yet, the mongoose may in the future prove to be a blessing in disguise. It is a fact that a hungry mongoose will unhesitatingly attack a large snake and, quite often, win the battle. Occasionally they will lose, as evinced not only by the fact that snake/mongoose fights are staged in India for betting purposes but by Olivers' comments (1955) that several kinds of boa constrictors in Trinidad rather commonly kill and eat mongooses. Contrary to common belief, the mongoose is not immune to snake venom, and must rely on his speed, stamina, erected hairs and thick skin to protect him from a fatal bite. The belief in many parts of the Far East is that the mongoose, when bitten by a snake, seeks an antidote, a herb or root known in India as *manguswail;* this is, of course, only folklore (Blanford, 1891).

PARASITES AND DISEASE

The discussion of parasites and disease in this species, their effect on the individual animal, and possible danger to man, is too complicated for the scope of this book. The interested reader is directed to Joseph Alicata's *Parasitic Infections of Man and Animals in Hawaii* (1964) for an in-depth review. The parasites listed below are from page 108 of that publication.

Common Name	Scientific Name	Location in Host
NEMATODES:		
Trichinosis	*Trichinella spiralis*	Adult in small intestine, larvae in muscles
ARTHROPODS:		
cat flea	*Ctenocephalides felis*	external
stick-tight flea	*Echidnophaga gallinacea*	external
mouse flea	*Leptopsylla segnis*	external
northern rat flea	*Nosopsyllus fasciatus*	external
mange mite	*Notoedres cati*	external
Oriental rat flea	*Xenopsylla cheopis*	external
Hawaiian field rat flea	*Xenopsylla vesabilis hawaiiensis*	external

Baldwin *et al.* *(op.cit.)* also mentions that one example of an animal with *Pulex irritans,* the human flea, was found.

Alicata and Breaks (1943) recorded the spirochete *Leptospira* in the kidneys of 4 of 12 mongooses examined from Oahu, 12 of 60 from Kohala, Hawaii, and 6 of 26 from Olaa, Hawaii. In addition, in 1965, five medical technologists training for Peace Corps duty examined 52 mongooses from Waipio Valley, Hawaii, and found 5 of these animals showing positive pool antigens, with one specifically identified as being *L. ichtero-hemorrhagica.* This is the organism responsible for the disease known variously as Weil's disease, infectious jaundice, or Leptospirosis. Almost every member of the permanent Waipio staff, the author included, at one time or another exhibited symptoms and illness resembling that of Weil's disease. The rat, and in particular the Norway rat *(Rattus norvegicus),* is the prime carrier of this disease and it is quite likely that the mongoose has acquired the infection because of its predation on the rat.

The presence of trichinosis in the mongoose has concerned state wildlife biologists because of the possibility of wild pigs eating infected carcasses, becoming infected themselves, and eventually passing this disease on to humans. Also, it is reported that Chinese herb doctors occasionally use parts of the mongoose in their medicines; unless this meat is properly cooked, the danger of consumer infection is present, though remote.

THE FUTURE

It is apparent that the mongoose is a conspicuous resident of Hawaii and will probably remain so in the future. Only hunters, bird watchers, and a few poultry farmers raise their voices from time to time, demanding some means of extermination. The remainder of the public does not care and the sugar-cane growers feel that the mongoose helps rather than hinders their efforts to control rat damage. The present laws prohibiting the possession of mongooses except for scientific study should be carefully enforced; granted that young mongooses make delightful pets, it is still imperative that none of these pets be innocently introduced to either Kauai, Lanai, Niihau, or to the United States mainland (where such introduction is in violation of federal law), where the potential damage to endemic wildlife would far outshadow any economic gains.

LITERATURE CITED

Alicata, J. E. and V. Breaks
    1943   A survey of leptospirosis in Honolulu. Hawaii Medical Jour. 2(3): 137–142.
Alicata, J. E.
    1964   Parasitic infections of man and animals in Hawaii. Hawaii Agri. Exp. Sta. Tech. Bull. 61: 138pp., illus.
Anonymous

1883 The mungoose. Planters' Monthly. 1: 307–308.

Anonymous
1885 Planters' Monthly. 4: 65.

Anonymous
1888 Editorial on the mongoose. Planters' Monthly. 7: 196.

Anonymous
1897 The mongoose in Jamaica. Planters' Monthly. 16: 437–438.

Baldwin, P. H., C. W. Schwartz, and E. R. Schwartz
1952 Life history and economic status of the mongoose in Hawaii. Jour. of Mammal. 33: 335–356.

Barnum, C. C.
1930 Rat control in Hawaii. Hawaiian Planters' Record. 34: 421–443.

Blanford, W. T.
1891 The fauna of British India. Mammalia., London: Taylor & Francis: 617pp., illus.

Bryan, W. A.
1908 Some birds of Molokai. Bernice P. Bishop Mus., Occas. Papers. 4: 133–176.

Corbet, G. B.
1966 The terrestrial mammals of western Europe. London: G. T. Foulis & Co., Ltd.: 264pp.

Doty, R. E.
1945 Rat control on Hawaiian sugar cane plantations. Hawaiian Planters' Record. 49(2): 241pp., illus.

Dover, C.
1932 The duration of life of some Indian mammals. Bombay Nat. Hist. Soc., Jour. 36: 244–250.

Espeut, W. B.
1882 On the acclimatization of the Indian mungoos in Jamaica. Zool. Soc. Proc., London: 712–714.

Kami, H. T.
1964 Foods of the mongoose in the Hamakua District, Hawaii. Zoonoses Research 3(3): 165–170.

La Rivers, I.
1948 Some Hawaiian ecological notes. The Wasmann Collector. 7: 85–110.

Lewis, E. S.
 1940 Mongoose attacking a donkey. Bombay Nat. His. Soc.,
       Jour. 41: 893.

Munro, G. C.
 1947 Notes on Molokai birds. Elepaio 7: 63.

Oliver, J. A.
 1955 Is the mongoose a snake-killer? Nat. Hist. 64(8): 426–
       429, illus.

Ord, W. M.
 1964 Mongoose attacks young red-foot booby at nest. Elepaio
       25: 3.

Pearson, O. P., and P. H. Baldwin
 1953 Reproduction and age structure of a mongoose popula-
       tion in Hawaii. Jour. of Mammal. 34: 436–447.

Pemberton, C. E.
 1925 The field rat in Hawaii and its control. H.S.P.A. Exp.
       Sta., Ent. Series Bull. 17: 46pp.

 ———

 1933 Some food habits of the mongoose. Hawaiian Planters'
       Record 37: 12–13.

Powell, J. E.
 1914 Notes on the habits of the small Indian mungoose. Bom-
       bay Nat. Hist. Soc., Jour. 22: 620.

Schwartz, C. W., and E. R. Schwartz
 1950 The California quail in Hawaii. Auk 67: 1–38.

Seaman, G. A.
 1952 The mongoose and Caribbean wildlife. Trans. 17th
       N. Am. Wildl. Conf. : 188–197.

Seaman, G. A., and J. E. Randall
 1962 The mongoose as a predator in the Virgin Islands, Jour.
       of Mammal. 43: 544–545.

Smith, J. D., and J. R. Woodworth
 1951 A study of the pheasant, California quail, and lace-
       necked dove in Hawaii. Div. Fish & Game, Terr. Ha-
       waii, Spec. Bull. no. 3, Bd. of Agri. & Forestry, Hono-
       lulu. mimeo.

Tinker, S. W.
   1938   Animals of Hawaii. Nippu Jiji Co., Ltd., Honolulu,
          Hawaii: 188pp.
Walker, L. W.
   1945   The Hawaiian mongoose—friend or foe? Nat. Hist.
          54(11): 396–400. photos.

   1948   Citizen mongoose. Audubon Mag., March–April: 80–
          85. photos.
Walker, R. L.
   1966   Nene restoration project report. Elepaio 26: 96–100.
Woodworth, J. R., and D. H. Woodside
   1953   Mongoose poison experiment. Div. Fish & Game, Terr.
          Hawaii, P.R. Proj. 5-R-4. 19pp., mimeo.

The Feral Cat

Felis catus

". . . I saw cats—Tom-cats, Mary Ann cats, long-tailed cats, bob-tail cats, blind cats, one-eyed cats, wall-eyed cats, cross-eyed cats, gray cats, black cats, white cats, yellow cats, striped cats, spotted cats, tame cats, wild cats, singed cats, individual cats, groups of cats, platoons of cats, companies of cats, regiments of cats, armies of cats, multitudes of cats, millions of cats, and all of them sleek, fat, lazy and sound asleep. . . ."

In March 1866, Mark Twain wrote the above comments in his fourth letter to the *Sacramento Union;* he was writing, as well as anyone could, of the description and abundance of the cat population of Honolulu. The situation has changed little in the intervening century and applies just as succinctly to cats living in the forests and mountains of Hawaii as it did to the "townies."

This barely domesticated animal belongs to the family felidae in the order carnivora, and the cat is probably the most carnivorous of all members of this predatory group. In a wild state the cat feeds almost entirely on vertebrate prey; this habit is reflected by the structure of its skull and feet, which show a most extreme specialization. The face is short, caused evolutionarily by a reduction in the size of the nasal cavity (implying

that the sense of smell is less important than in other carnivores, with senses of sight and hearing being consequently more acute), and by reduction in the length of the jaw. These short jaws are likewise associated with a shortening of the tooth rows, and a reduction in number of molariform teeth. (See Appendix C for dental formulae.) The shortened jaw, operated by extremely well-developed masseter muscles, allows a powerful bite to be taken by the anterior teeth, particularly the long and heavy canines. The feet are also adapted as weapons of attack, with the claws compressed and curved; they are kept sharp by being retracted into sheaths when not in use. There are five toes on the front feet and four on the hind; the palms and soles are hairy with naked pads under each toe and the ball of the foot. They walk on these toe pads and are thus described as being "digitigrade."

Although some biologists feel that if a feral cat population were isolated long enough their coloration would eventually resemble that of the striped European wild cat *(Felis silvestris)*, the fact remains that feral cats in Hawaii show little tendency in this direction and can be found in all common sizes, shapes, and colors. This is true for several reasons; for one, it is almost impossible to determine whether or not any particular cat has not, in recent generations, been infused with the genetic characters of a temporarily straying pet cat, and second, because so many "humane" people take unwanted kittens up lonely roads and quietly "release" them. If the kittens are old enough, and happen to be dropped in an area of good food supply, they will often survive, and take a new stock of "domestic breed" genes into the wild.

Cats who have lived in the wild for some time, or who are the result of several generations of feral animals, usually grow to a larger size than their domesticized counterparts. McKnight (1964) noted many reports of feral cats weighing more than 12 pounds, with a few going twice that weight.

HISTORY

Little is known of the history of the domestic cat in Hawaii, but it must be assumed that they were one of the earliest exotic animals to become established. Undoubtedly some of the earliest sailing vessels, nearly all of which had a complement of rat-catchers aboard, lost some of their number to either the curious, pet-loving natives or to the proprietors of food shops who found themselves increasingly besieged by rats or mice from these same ships. Bloxam (B. P. Bishop Mus., 1925) visited Honolulu and Lahaina in 1825 and mentioned seeing dogs, rats, mice, and donkeys, but makes no mention of cats; in view of his type of narration it is probable that there were not many, if any, cats in Hawaii at that time. One of the few references specifically relating to cats in Hawaiian history was found by Spaulding (1930) and recorded that a ship (presumably bound for a pirating expedition to the southern seas) paid a local shopkeeper for some supplies with "a poignard, a pair of pistols, and a male and female Manx cat," about the year 1850.

The domestic cat is believed to have originally been derived from the wild Caffer cat (*Felis ocreata*) of Egypt and Syria. This small animal was apparently first tamed as a wildfowl retriever, then later taught to protect granaries from mice and rats. Several races still occur in Africa and they are generally described as being a buffy-yellow to buffy-gray with indistinct marks on the neck and back, whitish below; the legs have black cross stripes and the latter half of the tail is ringed and with a black tip (Wender, 1946). Corbet (1966) believes that this ancestral stock received further genetic contributions from the European wild cat and is in fact still interfertile with this larger animal. The variations seen in domestic or feral cats are thus only of color and fur, with an occasional lethal gene causing such phenomena as taillessness in the Manx cat (Todd, 1964) or deafness in white, blue-eyed Persian cats (Wender, *op. cit.*).

DISTRIBUTION AND HABITAT

Feral cats are presently found on all of the eight larger islands of the chain, including Kahoolawe. An occasional cat or two have probably been present from time to time on some of the smaller islands, but with the exception of a cat that ran free on French Frigate Shoal for more than five months (anon., 1964), any that were present should probably have to be considered as pets; at least no feral population is known to have existed.

Cats, unlike our other small predator, the mongoose, have a sufficiently thick coat to allow continual habitation of the higher mountains of Hawaii; consequently they can be found at every elevation and in any vegetative type that allows the existence of mice or rats.

Unfortunately, a population of feral cats does not capture the imagination of the average naturalist; he therefore puts forth less effort, even in the recording of field observations, except when making a specific study of some more "exciting" species. Consequently we have no idea of relative abundance or preferred habitat. At the same time the "preferred habitat" of a truly feral population is difficult to determine because it is obscured, at least in coastal areas where the majority of towns and villages are located, by the wanderings afield of "pet" cats, and there is little to differentiate them in the field. While McKnight (op. cit.) has noted that in the U.S. mainland feral or stray cats are only rarely found far from human habitation, I have found wild kittens being raised six miles away from the nearest village on Molokai, and adult cats more than fourteen trail miles away from the nearest village, in Waimanu Valley, Hawaii. Other biologists report fairly regular sightings of feral cats on the slopes of Mauna Loa near Hualalai, which is truly wilderness country.

Kahoolawe, being totally uninhabited, but with a thriving population of feral cats, would make an ideal area for a complete life history study. In view of the fair number of cats on this island, and the fact that there are only two usually available sources of water on all the 28,700 acres, we must presently assume that some of the animals can exist for many days on metabolic water derived from the rats, mice, and occasional Gambels' quail (*Lophortyx gambeli*) that they catch.

FOOD HABITS AND PREDATION

Three basic theories prevail about the food habits of feral cats; almost every naturalist, biologist, bird watcher, or hunter ardently subscribes to just one of the three. Some people firmly believe that the cat is one of the greatest destroyers of birdlife and small mammals that there is, and should be shot on sight. Other persons are just as convinced that the cat is not a predator of significance and need not be given much consideration. Still others (and this may include the majority of Hawaii's wildlife managers) feel that cat depredations are not important until the hunting population begins to complain or until a particularly unique colony or population of birds show signs of being fed upon. All three ideas probably hold true at one time or another in various locales, but the food habits of the cat in Hawaii have never really been described in either quantitative or qualitative terms. Some general idea of feral cat food habits may be obtained by examining a stomach content table taken from McKnight's publication (*ibid.*) which refers to cat predation in various places throughout the mainland states (see Table 2, on following page).

As noted with the mongoose, it is highly likely that the cats merely react, as do most predators, to the biotic community in which they find themselves by taking that food which is most abundant with the least amount of effort. Jackson (1951) examined some 500 scats from a slum area cat population in Baltimore and found that they contained less than seven percent rat remains (certainly these animals were primarily scavenging

Table 2. Summary of cat-stomach content studies
(Adapted from McKnight 1964)

STUDY	NUMBER ANALYZED	PERCENTAGE OF STOMACH CONTENTS				
		Rodents	**Lago-morphs*	*Game birds*	*Nongame birds*	*Other*
McMurry & Sperry	107	—55—		0	4	41
Nilsson	86	—62—		—19—		19
Hubbs	184	49	13	18	8	12
Llewellyn & Uhler	40	75	small	v.small	v.small	small
Korschgen	110	60	23	1	1	15

* Hawaii does not have lagomorphs (rabbits, hares, pikas) living in a wild state on any of the cat-inhabited islands.

for garbage), while Bradt (1950) studied his pet cat's farmland and pasture catch over an 18-month period and counted 1,600 mice, 4 rabbits, 66 nongame birds, and a few miscellaneous mammals taken.

The innate hunting instinct of even pet cats is evinced by Toner's study (1956). He recorded that, while his pet cat ate six ounces of cat food every 24 hours during the snowy winter months, it took only one and one-half ounces each 24 hours during the rest of the year, but at this time brought in two or three meadow mice (*Microtus*) each day.

House mice (*Mus musculus*) are abundant in Hawaii in even the most remote grassland areas and cats can often be seen, usually at dawn or dusk, pouncing about the peripheries of these pasturelands. They may also be taking lizards or even large cockroaches or grasshoppers in lieu of rodents. Cats quickly learn to ignore the large toads (*Bufo marinus*) because of the unpleasant and poisonous effect that even the slightest bite into the toad imparts.

The author's own observations indicate that cats take a fair toll of barred dove (*Geopelia s. striata*) on certain areas of Molokai, but this is probably because of the immense number of this species available in a relatively constricted area; actually the ground-feeding birds probably serve as a buffer species, cutting down on the number of individuals taken of other bird species.

Richardson and Woodside (1954) considered the cat to be the most serious predator on the dark-rumped petrel (*Pterodroma phaeopygia*) in the Mauna Kea nesting region, but felt that the cat did not do as much damage in the petrel-nesting region on Haleakala, Maui. Other sea birds, such as the wedge-tailed shearwater (*Puffinus pacificus*), and the Newell's shearwater (*Puffinus puffinus newelli*), both of whom nest colonially on the ground on Kauai, are susceptible to reduction by cats, but seem to be able to maintain a fairly stable population nonetheless. Most of the small native birds nest at some height off the ground and seem to be considerably more "flighty" and wary than many of the introduced species; the author feels that, while a fair number of introduced birds may be killed, any effect on the native species of passerine birds is negligible.

The cat undoubtedly takes the native duck (*Anas platyrhynchos wyvilliana*) from time to time, but dogs and man are much more serious decimators, and pose the primary threat to survival of this species. Young nene goslings (*Branta sandvicencis*) are presumed susceptible to cat predation, but because of the rarity of confrontation, and also because of the aggressive attack of the adult goose, it is doubtful whether the feral cat presently exerts much effect on the native goose population. On the other hand, the cat was almost certainly of serious impact on the nene in the 1940s and 50s when this rarest of geese numbered less than 50 wild specimens.

There is no evidence to indicate that a cat would attempt to do battle with a mongoose; even if this happened it is doubtful that the cat is much of a match for its ancestral relative.

GESTATION AND REPRODUCTION

The cat, like many of its small wild relatives, is a solitary animal. Males and females come together only for breeding purposes, then the male goes his own way, leaving the female, some 55 to

63 days later, to seek a birthplace for her helpless young who vary in number from two to as many as nine, with four to six being the commonest litter. As McKnight (*op. cit.*) points out, there is considerable disagreement among observers concerning the frequency of breeding in the wild by cats. Many authorities are convinced that this is a rare occurrence and feel that the major population of feral cats is caused primarily by a "drift" from domesticity into the wild. McKnight cites considerable evidence to support this theory in the mainland states, but he does mention Hubbs's work (1951) which suggests that there may be a direct relation between increase in wild breeding and mildness of climate. Because our Hawaiian cats are, for the most part, blessed with the most perfect of climates, we might therefore expect a commensurate increase, not only in breeding activity but in litter survival and longevity.

I once found a litter of two kittens in one of the more rugged dry gulches on Molokai, some six miles from the nearest village and was amazed at their wildness and ferocity. The kittens heard me before they saw me and instead of peering curiously about as do most domestic youngsters, flattened themselves out on the ground at the base of a large boulder and remained perfectly still as I, pretending not to see them, walked by. I waited a minute, then walked back directly toward them. When they realized they were about to be discovered they scampered clumsily around behind the boulder and a game of "hide and seek" began. I finally dragged each one out of a crack in which they had wedged themselves and where they had hissed, spit, and struck out at me with their tiny claws every time my hand was within range. I attempted to soothe them for some five minutes but they would have none of it and so soon as I put them down they ducked back around the far side of the boulder and crawled into a deeper crack, where I left them. I looked to see whether the mother was about, apprehensively awaiting my departure but there was no sign of her, which was just as well since McKnight (*op. cit.*) mentions a half dozen instances reported of feral cats unhesitatingly attacking humans who bothered them.

The age that a feral cat attains is not known but undoubtedly varies with environment, food supply, and incidence of disease. The maximum authenticated age under household conditions is 27 years for a male cat, but claims of up to 31 years have been made for both sexes (Comfort, 1956). This would make the cat the longest-lived of any of the small domestic animals. It would probably be rare for a feral cat to attain even one-third this age.

PARASITES

The cats, both feral and domestic, are infested with a fairly large number of parasites, some of which are transmittable to man; it is much more likely, however, that anything which might be contracted by humans would be from domestic pets rather than feral animals. The reader is directed to Joseph Alicata's *Parasitic Infections of Man and Animals in Hawaii* (1964); the parasites listed below are on pages 95-96 of that book.

Common Name	Scientific Name	Location in Host
NEMATODES:		
lungworm	*Aelurostrongylus abstrusus*	lungs
lungworm	*Anafilaroides rostratus*	lungs
hookworm	*Ancylostoma tubaeforme*	small intestine
heartworm	*Dirofilaria immitis*	heart & pulmonary artery
stomachworm	*Physaloptera praeputialis*	stomach
dog and cat roundworm	*Toxocara canis*	small intestine
CESTODES:		
dog tapeworm	*Diplidium caninum*	small intestine
cat tapeworm	*Hydatigera taeniaeformis*	small intestine
TREMATODES:		
heterophyid fluke	*Phagicola longis*	small intestine

(cont.)

| liver fluke | *Platynosomum fastosum* | liver |
| heterophyid fluke | *Stellantchasmus falcatus* | small intestine |

ARTHROPODS:

cat flea	*Ctenocephalides felis*	external
stick-tight flea	*Echnidnophaga gallinacea*	external
biting louse	*Felicola subrostrata*	external
mange mite	*Notoedres cati*	external

THE FUTURE

The cat will certainly continue to persist at its present feral population level, and may very possibly increase in number as both urban and rural housing developments continue to spring up in heretofore uninhabited areas. With more people come more pets, and in the case of the cat, with its schizophrenic ability to step from civilization to the wilds and back again, we shall almost certainly record more sightings along our mountain trails.

LITERATURE CITED

Alicata, J. E.
    1964 Parasitic infections of man and animals in Hawaii. Hawaii Agri. Exp. Sta. Tech. Bull. 61: 138pp., illus.
Anonymous
    1964 Coast Guard Searchers: here kitty, kitty. Honolulu Advertiser, Dec. 10, p. A-2.
Bernice P. Bishop Museum
    1925 Diary of Andrew Bloxam, naturalist of the "Blonde", on her trip from England to the Hawaiian Islands, 1824–25. B. P. Bishop Mus. Spec. Publ. 10: 96pp.
Bradt, G. W.
    1950 Farm cat as predator. Michigan Conservation Mag., July-Aug.: p. 25.

Comfort, A.
1956 Maximum ages reached by domestic cats. Jour. of Mammal. 37(1): 118–119.
Corbet, G. B.
1966 The terrestrial mammals of Western Europe. London, G. T. Foulis & Co., Ltd.: 264pp.
Hubbs, E. L.
1951 Food habits of feral house cats in the Sacramento Valley. Calif. Fish & Game Bull. 37: 177–189.
Jackson, W. B.
1951 Food habits of Baltimore, Maryland, cats in relation to rat populations. Jour. of Mammal. 32: 458–461.
McKnight, T.
1964 Feral Livestock in Anglo-America. U. Calif. Publ. Geog. Vol. 16: 78pp., illus.
Richardson, F., and D. H. Woodside
1954 Rediscovery of the nesting of the dark-rumped petrel in the Hawaiian Islands. Condor 56: 323–327.
Spaulding, T. M.
1930 The Hawaiian cat. Paradise of the Pacific 43(11): 8.
Todd, N. B.
1964 The Manx factor in domestic cats. Jour. Heredity 55: 225–230.
Toner, G. C.
1956 House cat predation on small animals. Jour. of Mammal. 37(1): 119.
Wender, L.
1946 Animal encyclopedia: Mammals. Geo. Allen and Unwin Ltd., London.: 266pp.

The Hawaiian Monk Seal

Monachus schauinslandi

From man's first occupancy of the Hawaiian Islands, the monk seal has remained one of the rarest and least known of Hawaiian mammals. It was known to some Hawaiian people (who called it *ilio-holo-i-kauaua,* the dog that runs in the tough elements) before the coming of Captain Cook, and it was well known to sailors who ventured to the leeward islands of Hawaii, but it was not scientifically described until 1905, when it was near extinction. Although occasionally seen swimming about, and rarely landing on the larger inhabited islands, the monk seals prefer the low, mostly uninhabited islands of the northwestern part of the Hawaiian chain.

The genus *Monachus* is limited to three species: the Mediterranean monk seal, *M. monachus,* the West Indian or Caribbean monk seal, *M. tropicalis,* and our Hawaiian animal. They are the only truly tropical seals. The differences between these species are slight and if their populations were not so completely isolated they would probably all be regarded as subspecies. Scheffer (1958) thought that during the evolution of the genus *Monachus* the ancestral seals moved about from one sea to another, in increasing numbers and for longer distances as they developed the attributes of pelagic creatures, and Kellogg

150

(1922) felt that this animal had a very extensive distribution throughout tropical seas "as early as or even before the Lower Miocene" (some 25,000,000 years ago). During this period there was a waterway across Central America, connecting the Caribbean and the Pacific.

Although our Hawaiian seal is little known to residents of these islands, and the Caribbean seal is almost equally unknown, their cousin, the Mediterranean monk seal, was very probably the most familiar of all seals to the people of the European world in ancient times. Jardine (1839) mentions some of the superstitions attached to this animal and wrote that "by the undaunted Romans the skins of these seals were considered as an efficacious preservative against lightning; and hence tents were constructed of them, under which they sheltered themselves during thunderstorms. It is also mentioned by Suetonius, that such was the Emperor Augustus' [27 B.C.–A.D. 14] dread of lightning that . . . when on a journey, he never traveled without carrying along with him one of these skins."

HISTORY

The first mention of the Hawaiian monk seal in the literature appears to be the very short record of the brig *Aiona* setting sail in 1824 for the express purpose of taking seals from the leeward islands. Although Tinker (1941) felt that the Russians hunted this species earlier, he cited no reference. There is no information about the success of the *Aiona*'s expedition except that later writers stated that this ship's crew took the last of the monk seals. The true history of this period will probably never be known, but the seal was obviously not totally exterminated.

Fourteen years later, in 1838, an anonymous writer described Ocean (Kure) Island and noted that ". . . at times, there is a considerable number of hair seals." When the schooner *Manuokawai* visited Nihoa in April 1857, Paty (1857) wrote: ". . . on the sand beach ten or twelve hair seals were found; they didn't take much notice of us until His Majesty [King Kamehameha IV] had shot several, when they became more scared." The next record is that of the voyage of the bark *Gambia*, which left Honolulu on April 26, 1859, and returned 103 days later after making the rounds of all the known leeward islands and, in addition, discovering Midway Atoll. According to newspaper reports (*The Polynesian*, August 13, 1859) the ship had on board "240 bbls., seal oil, 1,500 skins. . . ." Kenyon and Rice (1959) give some very convincing reasons (time and distance factors) for questioning this report, and I would suggest that, since the article does not specifically state that the skins were those of seals, they may very possibly have included large numbers of bird skins (for which there was considerable market for ornamentation purposes).

The next mention in the literature of a monk seal sighting is one by Lyons (1890) who saw and photographed one on Laysan Island. Atkinson and Bryan (1914) reported that a Mr. Williams, who visited Laysan in 1893, had heard reports of 60 or 70 seals being killed on that island on an earlier (undated) expedition. In 1894, Captain King landed on Necker Island and annexed it to the Hawaiian monarchy and it was noted that "one hair seal was captured" (anon., 1894).

In 1896, Schauinsland spent three months on Laysan observing the flora and fauna and noted that "seals came singly, indeed very seldom by this island." Max Schlemmer, manager of a guano mining firm on the island, gave a skull to Schauinsland, and it was upon this skull that Matschie (1905) based the description of the species.

Seals, according to other observations in the next several decades, were not especially common on any of the islands, but since no one specifically went looking for seals through all of the islands in a single trip, sightings on individual islands did not give a true picture of the total population or its growth. Svihla (1959) gives a detailed record of animals seen from 1914 to 1956, and Kenyon and Rice (*op. cit.*), by doing careful aerial and ground censuses in 1956 and 1957, arrived at a minimum population figure of 1,013 animals in the summer of 1957. Rice (1960) counted 1,037 animals in 1958 and estimated the total population to be about 1,350. He did not feel that the animals had reached a maximum density, but predicted that increased pup mortality would become the most obvious natural population control. Counts have been made in later years by U.S. Fish and Wildlife Service personnel but the data have not been recently interpreted.

DESCRIPTION

Karl Kenyon and Dale Rice have done an excellent job in describing the life history of the Hawaiian monk seal in the July 1959 issue of *Pacific Science,* a journal published by the University of Hawaii Press. For this reason I shall give only an abstracted view of this species and its life requirements and refer the reader with more interest to the aforementioned article.

At birth, the pup is covered with short, coal-black hair. When dry the hair appears to have the texture of velvet, but the direction of growth can be felt by rubbing with the hand. When the young seal has moved about on the sand for a short while, the mucous about the eye gathers some of the pure white coralline sand and superficially gives the youngster the appearance of having white eye-rings, but the sand is washed away as soon as the pup goes into the water (the pup can swim at birth, but seldom does for the first three or four days). At an age of 20 to 30 days the pups begin to change body color in a process known as "postnatal molt." As Kenyon and Rice (*ibid.*) point out, the rate of molt varies with individual pups; the size of the mother at the time the pup is born influences the growth of the pup, and thus indirectly the rate of molt. The natal hairs fall out separately and are not attached to large pieces of the cuticle, as happens in older animals. Between 30 and 40 days of age the black coat "begins to appear moth-eaten and has faded from jet black to a dark chocolate brown. . . . by the time the black pup coat is entirely lost, the first postnatal pelage has completely grown in" (Kenyon and Rice, *ibid.*).

After the postnatal molt, the ventral body areas are silvery white, darkening to light silvery gray on the sides and dorsally to dark slate gray faintly tinged with a silvery sheen. When wet, the back appears sooty brown. After about a month the light belly may take on a yellow tinge and before the end of the first year the pup becomes quite yellowish.

The pup is just over three feet (95–100 cm.) long at birth and weighs from 35 to 38 pounds. At about 17 days the pups have doubled in weight; after 28 days they weigh three times as much, and at 37 or 38 days, several days after weaning, the birth weight has nearly quadrupled. Immediately after weaning the pups start to lose weight; they grow very little in length during the nursing period and are very fat when weaned, but for a time afterward they show no interest in food. Most weigh from 130 to 150 pounds at weaning, but the yearlings, while showing a length gain of about 10 to 12 inches, average only about 100 pounds weight. The yearlings must then be living off their store of blubber while they undergo the difficult adjustment period of learning to find and catch their own food. After they do learn to feed they grow quite rapidly; it is believed they attain adult size in their third year (Kenyon and Rice, *ibid.*).

Adult seals in fresh pelage are silver white or silver gray ventrally and dark silvery brown or slate gray dorsally. As the hair ages, the silver color is lost and, while the dorsal hairs become dull brown, the ventral surface takes on a yellowish color. Adult males are usually darker than the females.

The molting process of the monk seal is apparently unique among mammals except for the elephant seal (*Mirounga sp.*) and has been called "reptilelike." When the old faded hair sloughs off (between May and November) it takes with it the outer layer of the epidermis; little or no new hair shows on the rough skin beneath. The molt progresses from front to back, and bottom to top, and comes off in sheets and patches and is quite dissimilar from the hair displacement pattern of the first molt.

It seems that when molting the seal almost or completely ceases feeding; because of this characteristic, denser bands of cementum form in the teeth and, like the annular rings in a tree, can be used as an indicator of age (Kenyon and Fiscus, 1963). Adult female seals appear to be somewhat larger than males, particularly when they are pregnant or have just given birth; the females apparently fast while nursing and, as the pup gains about 100 pounds during this period the female may lose up to 200 pounds. An adult male weighed by Kenyon and Rice scaled 380 pounds and was just over seven feet long while a female seven and three-quarter feet long was estimated to weigh 600 pounds. Another female estimated at 575 pounds immediately after birth of a pup weighed only about 380 pounds some 37 days later.

Despite the fact that the monk seals are of a purely subtropic to tropic distribution, they show few obvious adaptations. Like members of their family from cooler regions they are covered with a thick layer of blubber. On the other hand, they show a body temperature (35.5 degrees) that is lower than that of seals of cooler climates, and the black skin and pelage of the pup may be significant in protecting the animals from insolation.

Most seals, and particularly those which have just emerged from long periods in the water, exhibit a greenish tinge on many parts of their fur; this is a tiny green algae, *Pringsheimiella scutata*. After several days on land this harmless species dries out and the color disappears.

DISTRIBUTION

The breeding range of the monk seal is presently confined to the islands and atolls of "The Leeward Chain." Beginning at Nihoa Island, some 240 miles northwest of Kauai, are the volcanic extrusions of Necker Island, La Perouse Pinnacle (surrounded by the atoll of French Frigates Shoal) and Gardner Pinnacles. Monk seals have been seen basking on the one small beach on Nihoa and occasionally haul out on the rocks of Necker Island, but La Perouse Pinnacle is too steeply faced to allow a seal's presence. There is a small breeding colony on the atoll of French Frigates Shoal. No seals have been reported from Gardner Pinnacles. Beyond this latter island is Maro Reef which, when awash at low tide, temporarily provides shelter for a few resting seals. Farther north are the coral atolls of Laysan, Lisianski, Pearl and Hermes Reef, Midway Atoll, and Kure Atoll. It is on these latter named islands, or groups of islands, that the majority of seals breed and rest.

Every few years, there are reports of a seal visiting the larger islands of the archipelago. Since the old Hawaiians had a name for the animal, we might have expected that it would have played a prominent role in their legends, but it was apparently so rarely seen even then that the natives placed little importance on sightings.

Henshaw was apparently the first to record a seal in the main chain by writing that "in 1900 a sick or helpless seal was caught by the natives in Hilo Bay, Hawaii, towed ashore, killed and eaten. . . . The natives assured me that solitary seals occurred on the coast about once in 10 years or so. They were very curious and asked many questions as to the habitat of the animal, its nature, food, and habits, about which they knew nothing" (Dill and Bryan, 1912).

Kenyon and Rice (*op. cit.*) created a table showing sightings of monk seals from the main islands and I have taken this opportunity to revise and update it as shown in Table 3, on the following page.

There have undoubtedly been many more seals swim past or even land on isolated beaches of the main islands; as the population in the leeward archipelago reaches a saturation point we might even suspect a rash of sightings as younger seals explore new resting grounds. For this reason it is important that people sighting seals record the date and location and report this information to biologists of the State Division of Fish and Game.

Table 3. Monk seals recorded from the main islands

DATE	PLACE	OBSERVER	REMARKS
Nov. 11, 1928	Oahu, N.E., windward shore	T. M. Blackman	". . . in the vicinity for several days."
Oct. 26, 1931	Oahu, north side	J. P. Kaleo	"seal frequently seen three years ago."
May 12, 1948	Kauai, east side	P. Palama	"Seal climbed out of water onto rocks."
Dec. 1950	Hilo Bay, Hawaii	D. Krebs	Notes "last seal seen" off Kauai in 1936.
Oct. 1951	Oahu, Kewalo basin entrance	R. Dodge	Seal bit at fish line about 25 feet from shore.
Dec. 1951	Kaneohe Bay, Oahu	?	Captive animal from zoo, released in bay after 6 mo. captivity;not seen again.
Mar. 30, 1955	Oahu, ½ mile off Waikiki Beach	G. Freund	Saw on top, then followed below surface with aqualung.
July 1956	Hawaii, Keahole Point, Kona	E. Y. Hosaka	Seen 0600, swimming slowly close to shore.
July or Aug. 1956	Lehua (off Niihau)	L. A. Faye	Large adult hauled out on rocks; photographed.
Dec. 22, 1958	Molokai, Moomomi Beach	R. J. Kramer	Swimming 50 feet off rocks in storm surf; headed west.
Mar. 27, 1962	Kauai, Polihali Beach, Kilauea.	?/ via Warden J. Yamada	Female had pup on beach. Pup captured, sent to aquarium; adult roamed to Hanapepe and Fort Allen for over 1 week.
March 1968	Kauai, various locations	?/ via biol. T. Telfer	Seen swimming offshore for 2 weeks.

HABITS

On the outer islands seals are normally seen only inside the reef or hauled out on the sand; it is very rare to see one swimming in deep water although they obviously do so. Although they are genetically tame they will display threatening behavior when annoyed or with pups. On many occasions I have been able to lie quietly at the side of yearling animals, who had certainly never encountered a human before, and touch them gently without encountering any reaction other than an initially curious stare and an occasional sleepy glance. On the other hand, old adults (many of whom, I am sure, had been molested by sailors) seldom tolerate a close approach and either attempt to escape into the water or to attack in a series of clumsy lunges.

Young monk seals are genetically tame and can be easily approached. This animal was startled from his sleep, but made no attempt to bite the photographer.

Richard Warner (pers. comm.) was once forced to fend off a repeatedly charging animal in the water by repeatedly kicking it in the face with his swim fin while stroking for shore.

No particular social observation has been observed and it has therefore been promulgated that the monk seal is "sexually promiscuous," meaning that, unlike sea lions and fur seals, the males do not form harems or breeding territories. Females with pups will have nothing to do with curious males and will engage in fierce, water-borne battles with them.

The seals appear to be most numerous on land during the winter months and on a daily basis they haul out most often in the afternoons. While many of the animals lie 20 or so feet from the water's edge, a number crawl into the shade of *naupaka* (*Scaevola takata*) bushes. Some of these animals remain on this higher ground throughout the night; Butler and Udvardy (1966) noted that the common housefly (*Musca domestica*) in some seasons bothered the seals so much that they retreated to the water's edge or out to sea until the late afternoon.

The mother seal is very affectionate toward her pup until she abandons it after weaning, and while moving about on land they keep in contact vocally (monk seals make a variety of bellowing sounds plus a strange bubbling sound that can be uttered with the animal's mouth shut). She can recognize her young by scent, if not too disturbed. Normally she will try to keep her body interposed between an intruder and the pup, or directly under her chin, but occasionally she becomes so enraged she will attack right over the body of the pup, which certainly cannot do that tiny animal much good.

I once found a day-old pup whose mother had, for one reason or another, disappeared. The pup had crawled up to the vegetation line next to a long redwood log and was vainly exploring up and down the length of the log looking for a nipple. After watching for sometime I approached and as I stood astraddle the pup and looked for its mother, it took my pants cuff in its mouth and began to suck. When I picked the pup up it immediately tried to nurse on my fingers, my chin, my shirt, or anything it could poke into its mouth. When I finally had to put the youngster down and leave, it crawled after me for some distance giving a weak bark; that was the only time I have seen an abandoned pup.

It is possible that the aforementioned mother fell prey to sharks; a quarter mile down the beach was a school of between 75 and 80 sharks in water 4 to 15 feet deep. The day before, I watched three seals very unconcernedly swim past this school and despite the fact that several sharks swam over to them, the seals evinced no concern and continued past with their heads out of the water. It is known that sharks do attack seals and many adult animals exhibit massive scars which make one wonder how they survived the wound. I have twice found yearling seals with one flipper recently bitten off and still bleeding scars on their sides but neither animal seemed critically hurt and both immediately returned to the sea. It would seem that if the shark does not kill the seal with the first bite the seal is agile enough to then elude his hunter.

FOOD HABITS

Kenyon and Rice (*op. cit.*) collected stomach contents from two monk seals and found them to contain the remains of conger eels (*Ariosoma bowersi*), moray eels (*Gymnothorax sp.* and *Echidna sp.*), flatfish (*Bothus mancus* and *B. pantherinus*), a scorpenid (*Scorpaenopsis gibbosa?*), a larval fish, and either squid or octopus (*Cephalopod*) parts. From these species they deduced that the monk seal is primarily a nocturnal bottom feeder, at least around the atolls. I have watched several species of wrasse fish (Labridae) swim constantly along behind monk seals in shallow water, feeding on seal feces as they were discharged and have never seen a seal pay the slightest attention to these fish even though they sometimes turned and swam right back over them. I have also thrown them recently killed fish during the day but, after looking to see the source of the splash, they completely ignored the bait.

In captivity, seals still show a preference for eels, but will feed on smelt (*Osmerus mordax*) and mackerel (*Trachurus symmetricus*) if nothing else is available. The captive seal in the Honolulu Zoo in 1951 did not eat for the first six weeks of captivity but finally took eels voluntarily (Park, 1952).

PARASITES

Kenyon and Rice (*op. cit.*) sent samples of all parasites collected on a male monk seal to experts for identification; at the present time only a synopsis of this information is available. *Contracaecum turgidum*, a nematode, was first described from the monk seal by Chapin (1925) and was again found in the seal taken in 1957. It is common to many pinnipeds of the Pacific Coast. One or more species of the acanthocephalan *Corynosoma sp.* were collected from the anterior portion of the small intestine; these are believed to be undescribed species but the genus is widely distributed in marine mammals. There were at least three forms of the cestode *Diphyllobothrium sp.*, one of which is known to be *D. hians*. These were found in various parts of the small intestine. None of the species mentioned above appears to be particularly debilitating to the seal.

THE FUTURE

The future prospects for the preservation of the population of the Hawaiian monk seal are exceedingly bright. The majority of the population lives on or about islands protected by either the federal government (the Department of Defense protects the Midway animals, and the Department of Interior protects all other islands except Kure) or the state government of Hawaii (which has regulatory power on Kure). Both federal and state laws make it illegal to injure, capture, or kill the monk seal and it is believed that very little, if any, poaching or harassment occurs. Since most of the breeding islands are within the boundaries of the Hawaiian Islands National Wildlife Refuge, which is patrolled and managed for sea bird and endemic land bird protection as well, there is little chance of these islands again becoming so changed by human forces that the seal cannot find a quiet stretch of beach for himself.

LITERATURE CITED

Anonymous
  1838 Ocean Island. Hawaiian Spectator 1: 336.

  1894 Occupation of Necker Island. Friend 52: 45.

  1950 Shucks, it was a Hawaiian seal, not sea lion, sighted near Hilo. Hono. Star Bull. Dec. 12.

  1950 Sea lion sighted off Hilos' shore Sunday morning. Hono. Advertiser, Dec. 13.

  1955 Hawaiian seal believed sighted off Waikiki. Hono. Star Bull., Mar. 30.

  1962 Zoo unable to take gift of baby seal. Hono. Advertiser, April 19.
Atkinson, A. L. C., and W. A. Bryan
  1914 A rare seal. Bull. N.Y. Zool. Soc. 16: 1050–1051.
Butler, G., and M. D. F. Udvardy
  1966 Basking behavior of the Hawaiian monk seal on Laysan Island. J. Wildl. Mgnt. 30(3): 627–628.
Dill, H. R., and W. A. Bryan
  1912 Report of an expedition to Laysan Island in 1911. U.S. Dept. Agri., Biol. Surv. Bull. 42: 30pp.
Jardine, Sir W.
  1839 The Naturalists Library. Mammalia. Vol. VIII. Am-

phibious Carnivora, including the Walrus and Seals. London.

Kellogg, R.
1922   Pinnipeds from Miocene and Pleistocene deposits of California ... and a résumé of current theories regarding origin of Pinnipedia. Bull. Dept. Geol. Univ. Calif. 13: 23–132.

Kenyon, K. W., and D. W. Rice
1959   Life history of the Hawaiian monk seal. Pacific Science 8(3): 215–252.

Kenyon, K. W., and C. H. Fiscus
1963   Age determination in the Hawaiian monk seal. J. Mammal. 44: 280–281.

Lyons, A. B.
1890   In bird land. Part of the journal of a visit to Laysan Island. Friend 48: 90–91.

Matschie, G. F. P.
1905   Eine Robbe von Laysan. Sitzburg Gesellschaft Naturforscher Freunde Berlin: 254–262.

Park, S.
1952   Many turtles, few seals left around islands. Hono. Star Bull. Jan. 15.

Paty, J.
1857   Journal of Schooner "Manuokawai." Hawaii State Archives. (Hand-written journal of an exploratory voyage to the leeward Hawaiian Islands in April and May, 1857.)

Rice, D. W.
1960   Population dynamics of the Hawaiian monk seal. J. Mammal. 41: 376–385.

Schauinsland, H.
1899   Drei Monate auf einer Koralleninsel (Laysan). Biologische Centralblatt Vol. XIX. (Also published separately by M. Nossler, Bremen: 104pp.)

Scheffer, V. B.
1958   Seals, sea lions and walruses. A review of the Pinnipedia. Stanford U. Press: 179pp.

Svihla, A.
    1959   Notes on the Hawaiian monk seal. J. Mammal. 40: 226–229.
Tinker, S. W.
    1941   Animals of Hawaii. Tongg Publ. Co., Honolulu: 190pp.

The Horse *and* The Mule

Equus caballus

Equus caballus
x *Equus asinus*

The horse and the mule played a vital role in the exploration and development of Hawaii in the 19th century, and the mule continued to carry out its role well into the 20th century despite increasing mechanization and road development. Hawaii's cowboys became famous the world over, and with their specially bred range ponies produced several world champion rodeo riders. Horses are big business in Hawaii today and are bred as polo ponies as well as for cattle herding and pleasure riding. It would probably be improper to say that there are feral horses and mules present today, but there are a number of "loose" animals of both kinds present, particularly on Hawaii. The criteria for this seemingly ambiguous statement apparently revolve around the recurring question of "Is damage done?" On Hawaii there are several herds of mules and a few horses running loose in Waipio Valley, and two or three animals in Waimanu Valley. The residents in nearby areas often claim one or another of these animals (even though their attempts to catch them are usually futile) until such time as a herd wades through a freshly planted taro patch or does other damage. All animals immediately become "wild" and the "former owners"

166

immediately and steadfastly deny any form of ownership or responsibility.

HISTORY

Richard J. Cleveland brought the first horses to Hawaii on his ship *Lelia Byrd* in June 1803. E. N. McClellan (Henke, 1929) writes that the *Lelia Byrd,* in May of that year, visited a small California bay 60 miles from the Mission of San Borgia; while there Cleveland purchased a pair of horses with the intent of making them a gift to Kamehameha I. His ship then sailed to St. Joseph's Mission where he purchased a mare and a foal; the ship sailed on May 28 for Hawaii and anchored in Kealakekua Bay on June 19. The ship sailed from there on the twenty-third and anchored in Kawaihae Bay for the apparent sole purpose of landing the mare and foal, "for which John Young was very urgent." The ship then proceeded to Lahaina, Maui, where, it is written, "Kamehameha I visited Cleveland on board the *Lelia Byrd* . . . before the horse and mare were landed. The King viewed the horse but could not be betrayed into any expression of wonder or surprise. This 'want of appreciation of the value of the present which they had taken so much pains to procure was naturally a disappointment to the donors.' "

When Bloxam visited the islands 22 years later, in 1825, he mentioned only that there were a few horses on Maui, but that horses were "very plentiful" on Oahu, and were "let out at a dollar per diem" (B. P. Bishop Museum, 1925).

Horses may have just been getting a start during Bloxam's visit, but they rapidly became abundant on most islands in short order. In 1852, Bishop estimated that there were 1,200 wild horses on Hawaii, plus 2,500 (tame and wild) animals on Maui, 200 on Molokai, 6,500 on Oahu, and 1,300 on Kauai and Niihau (Bishop, 1852). Henke (*op. cit.*) found a letter written in July 1851, to the king's delegate, attempting to purchase all the government horses on Kauai for $3,000. Two years after

Bishop's report, Hopkins (1854) wrote to the Royal Hawaiian Agricultural Society that "in making up a report on horses, the first thing we wish particularly to call attention to is the lamentable increase of the miserable creatures to be seen every day in the streets of Honolulu and in all the horse breeding districts on the Islands. Horses are evidently fast becoming a curse and nuisance to the country and to most of their owners, especially to the lower classes of natives. . . . About one-half of the horses on the Island are never used for any purpose but multiplication—are never bitted or backed—are born, live and die without being of any advantage to anyone, or having served any purpose, useful or ornamental, but the impoverishment of the land, and the propagation of the nuisance."

The report apparently had little impact on either the government or its citizenry because Henke (*op. cit.*) records an increase from the 11,700 previously mentioned, to 29,454 in 1879, to a peak of 30,640 in 1884. Further figures show 18,913 in 1895, 19,694 in 1905, 24,307 in 1920, and only 12,073 in 1928, when gasoline-powered vehicles and improved roads provided a mortal blow to much of the horse industry.

Henke (*ibid.*) also records the laying out of Kapiolani Race Track about 1872 and says that racing was very popular there, with King Kalakaua being one of the primary patrons. About this same time another race track was founded in Waimanalo and His Majesty King Kalakaua and selected guests were often taken there on the steamer *J. A. Cummins* from Honolulu.

In 1884, Aubrey Robinson imported the first Arabian horses and kept them on Kauai and Niihau, while William Hyde Rice imported Clydesdales, Belgian, and Percherons about this same time; the Percherons proved to be the most popular draft breed, and Percheron mares were kept on many ranches for the primary purpose of breeding with jackasses to produce large mules (Henke, *ibid.*).

In the early 1890s Nottage (1894) wrote that ". . . a good horse, cross-bred between a native and an imported animal, fetches from $70 to $80, though a good native pony can be purchased for $30 or $40." In 1928 the average horse had an estimated value of $100 (contrasted with $200 for the more popular working mule), while today the price for a "non-blooded" horse varies between $100 and $200. Polo ponies and thoroughbred horses range in price from $2,000 up to a recently imported $50,000 animal.

Other than the so-called feral animals of Waipio and Waimanu, it is doubtful that there are any truly feral herds of horses left in Hawaii; the last date the author has been able to find is for 1942, when the last of a wild horse herd was driven from Haleakala National Park (Yocom, 1967).

Although no specific date has been recorded for the first mule to enter Hawaii, we must assume that mules were being produced shortly after 1825, when the first donkeys arrived (Bloxam, *op. cit.*). They were certainly present in fair numbers in 1851 when Cummins and Meek protested about the inferior quality of all equines and incidentally mentioned the mule (Cummins and Meek, 1851). In 1853 the question of breed improvement was once again briefly mentioned (Lee, 1853), but it apparently was not until sometime in the 1880s, when the Percheron was introduced, that any real effort was made to breed up the large mules preferred by ranchers and plantation owners.

Mules were in great demand by sugar plantation owners in the late 1800s and early 1900s, but owners often refrained from buying animals because of their high import costs—individual animals were being sold for about $225 in 1906–7—which was almost double their cost at the turn of the century (anon., 1908). The anonymous writer who noted the high cost also pleaded for local ranchers to start doing more breeding here; he offered the theory that, since it takes about as long to raise a mule as a steer, and that the former sell for five times the value of the latter, there "can be little doubt that mule raising in this Territory will prove profitable. . . ." In the same article it was mentioned that agents had recently been sent to Kentucky and Tennessee to purchase six or eight (presumably large) jackasses.

About the only specific mention of numbers of mules and their importance to the development of the Hawaiian Islands is a livestock census taken in June 1900 indicating there were 6,506 mules present (anon., 1903), and some statements by Henke (*op. cit.*) showing 10,542 animals in 1920, but only 8,072 in 1928, at which time they were valued at $200 each. During this latter nine-year period, 3,567 of these animals were imports from out-of-state sources, indicating that our anonymous writer of 1908 must not have convinced his readers to the extent he had desired.

As mentioned before, it is doubtful that there are still any truly wild horses in Hawaii and, since the mule is infertile, and thus incapable of perpetuating its kind, there will very shortly come a time when we can definitely, and sadly say, "There are no wild horses or mules in Hawaii."

LITERATURE CITED

Anonymous
1903   Livestock statistics. Hawaiian Annual for 1903: p. 3.
_____
1908   Mule breeding in the Territory of Hawaii. Bd. Commis. Agri. & Forestry, Fourth Rept.: 183–185.
Bernice P. Bishop Museum
1925   Diary of Andrew Bloxam, naturalist of the "Blonde", on her trip from England to the Hawaiian Islands, 1824–25. B. P. Bishop Mus. Spec. Publ. 10: 96pp.
Bishop, C. R.
1852   Trans. Royal Hawaiian Agri. Soc. 1(3): p. 91.
Cummins, T. and J. Meek
1851   Report on horses. Royal Hawaiian Agri. Soc. 1(2): 77–78.
Henke, L. A.

1929   A survey of livestock in Hawaii. U. Hawaii Res. Publ.
       5: 82pp., illus.

Hopkins, C. G.
       1854   Report committee on horses. Trans. Royal Hawaiian Agri. Soc. 2(1): 105–106.

Lee, W. L.
       1853   Annual report of the president. Royal Hawaiian Agri. Soc., Trans. 1(4): 3–14.

Nottage, C. G.
       1894   In search of a climate. Sampson Low, Marston and Co., Ltd., London: 351pp.

Yocom, C. F.
       1967   Ecology of feral goats in Haleakala Nat. Park, Maui, Hawaii. Am. Nat. 77(2): 418–451.

The Donkey, Ass, *or* Burro

Equus asinus

The Somali, Nubian, or Abyssinian wild ass of northeast Africa is the progenitor of all donkeys, asses, and burros. These wild asses proved relatively easy to tame and archeological records show that domesticated asses were in use in the eastern Mediterranean area at least as early as 3400 B.C. (McKnight, 1958). Being so well suited to a dry, subtropical environment, their offspring became common beasts of burden throughout southwestern Asia, Mediterranean Europe, and North Africa. Having proved their worth there, they were among the first animals to be landed in the Americas, and were soon being raised in large numbers in Mexico; as the Spanish moved south to the Andes, and north into the southern and western portions of the United States, the burro, as it is known to the Spanish, followed. Although all three of these named animals refer to *Equus asinus*, they are not truly synonymous, at least in the United States. Generally the small shaggy-haired animal is referred to as a burro, the donkey is next in size, and the ass is largest of the three. Since the animals in Hawaii are fairly large, and the shagginess of the coat varies according to climate and season,

we shall refer to the feral population of animals as being donkeys.

HISTORY IN HAWAII

Andrew Bloxam (B. P. Bishop Museum, 1925) was the first person to mention the donkey in relation to Hawaii. He records that, in February 1825, Captain Charlton (Richard Charlton, British Consul for Hawaii) sailed from Valparaiso with "a most extraordinary cargo on board, consisting of donkeys and Jews' harps—harmony combined." The four animals mentioned landed in good condition and were purchased by the king (Bloxam, *ibid.*). No further mention was made of donkeys until 1847 (Brookshier, 1945). Apparently more animals were brought in during this period because in 1851 Cummins and Meek complained to the Royal Hawaiian Agricultural Society that "donkeys in crowds running at large" and inferior stallions were detrimental to improvement of mules and island horse stock (Cummins and Meek, 1851). Brookshier (*op. cit.*) records that 30 "Jackasses" were shipped to Portland in 1858, and that the ship *Kehrwieder* left Honolulu in 1863 with three asses bound for Apia, Western Samoa; this may have been the first introduction into those islands.

By this time, the donkey had been introduced to several if not all of the larger islands. They were commonly used on Hawaii for scaling Mauna Kea and Mauna Loa after horses proved unsuitable for traversing some of the intervening rugged terrain. Arabian coffee (*Coffea arabica*) was first brought to the Hawaiian Islands in 1813 by Don Marin (Neal, 1965) and groves of considerable size were started at about the 1,500-foot level above Kailua-Kona on the island of Hawaii in the mid-1800s. The donkey proved an ideal beast of burden for these rugged uplands and proliferated there, becoming known far and wide as the "Kona Nightingale," an aptly sarcastic reference to its early morning protestations against being rounded up for a morning's

An old Hawaiian *paniolo* (cowboy) and his "Kona Nightingale." Archives of Hawaii.

work. The more recalcitrant animals were killed and eaten; the product was referred to as "donkey venison."

Brookshier (*op. cit.*) also notes that the donkey was commonly used to transport rice to market on Oahu and that they were often loaded with three 100-pound bags of rice before being led over the steep Nuuanu Pali trail.

Henke (1929) records that U.S. Livestock Census figures for 1910 showed 2,847 "asses and burros" present, but only 2,144 in 1920. In 1928 they had an average worth of $15 each, while Brookshier (*op. cit.*) says the purchase price was about $35 in 1945, when he estimated less than 500 animals present.

In the 25-year period from 1921 to 1946, Bryan (1947) notes that 357 donkeys were eliminated from fenced forest reserves on

Hawaii as a part of a rehabilitation program in watershed regions.

Elschner (1915) records that feral donkeys were present on Eastern Island of the Midway group in 1915, but nothing is known of their fate; they are certainly not there today.

At the time of this writing domestic donkeys are still present on the islands of Kauai, Oahu, Maui, and Hawaii, and are used mostly by the sugar plantations for hauling selected cane cuttings to limited experimental planting areas; a few other animals are kept as pets or curiosities. The jeep has, for the most part, supplanted the Kona Nightingale in the coffee groves of Kona.

There is still a feral population of donkeys on the island of Hawaii; there are between 50 and 100 animals ranging parts of Huehue Ranch, and an unknown number on Hualalai Ranch. It is believed that some of these animals will be caught from time to time, and used as "beasts of burden" or for sport riding. Although cowboys see these animals continuously, virtually nothing is known of their requirements or habits in Hawaii.

DESCRIPTION

The most striking aspects of the general appearance of the donkey *et al.* are two distinctive types of markings. McKnight (1964) perhaps describes these best by noting that "nearly every animal looks as if the lower three or four inches of its muzzle (mouth, nose, etc.) has been dipped in a bucket of white paint. This feature is particularly pronounced on black burros, which look for all the world as if they were made up for a minstrel show. In addition, most burros have a long dark stripe extending down their backs from mane to tail, crossed at right angles by a shorter dark stripe over the shoulders. The two stripes together form a distinct cross, which is more noticeable on the lighter-colored animals."

While animals of all three strains may be found in various shades from bluish gray or whitish gray through brown to jet black, Gerald Swedberg (pers. comm.), who owns a formerly feral animal, says that the feral animals in Hawaii have sleek blue-gray coats in the summer and change to a woolly, shaggy brown coat in the colder winter months.

The size of these animals varies considerably and size, combined with color, have created different names for various strains. Such large forms as the Kentucky or Poitou reach a height of slightly over five feet at the withers, while the dwarf forms may be only two and a half to three feet high. The male donkey or ass, when crossed with a female horse or mare, produces the sterile mule, while the offspring of a female donkey and a stallion is called a hinny.

OTHER CHARACTERISTICS

The feral burro has often been described as being the hardiest and most adaptable of all feral animals in America and this statement probably applies to Hawaii as well. Although we do not have the great barren expanses of desertland found in much of the American Southwest, there are still considerable areas of naked lava flow, broken only by strips of unpalatable native grasses and scattered, low-growing shrubs, and it is on these areas that we find scattered groups of feral donkeys. No studies have been done on the food habits of the Hawaiian animals but, as McKnight (1958) mentions, their "voracious and non-discriminating appetite" makes them completely adaptable to most range conditions. Unlike some of the other feral animals, the donkey does find standing water a necessity. Davis and Golley (1963) have pointed out that while donkeys can tolerate the same water loss (25 percent) as camels, they cannot go for as long a period due to a thinner coat and a more stable body temperature. They do, however, have an amazing ability to drink back their water loss; they can recover a 25 percent loss of water in less than two minutes. This may have been a distinct advantage to the wild Nubian ass by making it less susceptible to predation at the rare and scattered water holes of its native range.

Little is known of the breeding habits of feral animals, but it is thought that in Hawaii they breed throughout the year. McKnight said that it appeared that the jacks (males) sought to gather harems of jennies (females), but because of the harshness and desolation of the donkey habitat in the U.S., plus a lack of interest among biologists, no life history studies have been done on the feral animals. For this same reason no pertinent studies have been done on parasites or disease in this species.

LITERATURE CITED

Bernice P. Bishop Museum
    1925   Diary of Andrew Bloxam, naturalist of the "Blonde",
           on her trip from England to the Hawaiian Islands,
           1824–25. B. P. Bishop Mus. Spec. Publ. 10: 96pp.
Bryan, L. W.
    1947   Twenty-five years of forestry work on the island of
           Hawaii. Hawaiian Planters' Record 51: 1–80.
Brookshier, F. A.
    1945   On the burro trail in Hawaii. Paradise of the Pacific
           57(12): 17–20.
Cummins, T., and J. Meek
    1851   Report on horses. Roy. Haw'n. Agri. Soc. 1(2): 77–78.
Davis, D. E., and F. B. Golley
    1963   Principles in Mammalogy. Reinhold Pub. Co., New
           York: 335pp.
Elschner, C.
    1915   The leeward islands of the Hawaiian group. Honolulu:
           68pp.
Henke, L. A.

1929   A survey of livestock in Hawaii. U. Hawaii Res. Publ.
        No. 5: 82pp.
McKnight, T. L.
    1958   The feral burro in the United States: distribution and
            problems. J. Widl. Mgnt. 22: 163–179.

    1964   Feral livestock in Anglo-America. U. Calif. Publ. Geog.
            16: 78pp.
Neal, M. C.
    1965   In gardens of Hawaii. B. P. Bishop Mus. Spec. Publ.
            50: 924pp.

The Pig

Sus scrofa

The origin of the pig that was first introduced to Hawaii by some early Polynesians is, and may continue to be, a mystery. In 1959, biologists of the State Division of Fish and Game collected several specimens of the "typical Hawaiian wild pig," and sent the skulls to mainland experts, who subsequently identified them as being indistinguishable from *Sus scrofa,* the wild boar of Europe, North Africa, and southern Asia as far south as Indonesia. Warner (1959) attempted to trace the origin of our pig but found only sketchy information; the species known as *Sus papuensis,* which is widespread over much of Melanesia and New Guinea, undoubtedly has *Sus scrofa* as its ancestor, and Buck (Warner, *ibid.*) reports a Samoan legend wherein a Samoan voyager visited the Fiji Islands and brought back young pigs on his return, thus introducing them to those islands. Then there is a Tahitian legend that says that when their ancestors first settled those islands no man had ever seen a pig or chicken, and that it was not until many years later, when the son of the chief of Raiatae went to Bora Bora, one of the Society Islands nearest Samoa, that the Tahitians encountered, and subsequently raised, pigs. It may be assumed that the pig was transported from Tahiti to Hawaii during some of the early

180

voyages. Warner is, however, quick to admit that there are re-searchers who disagree with portions of this interpretation, and agrees that the historical aspect of the introduction needs further study.

Despite our lack of knowledge about the origin of the original Hawaiian pig, we know that prior to the arrival of Captain Cook, they were not only abundant (at least in captivity), but also played important roles in the Hawaiian culture.

Sir Peter Buck felt that more pigs were raised in Hawaii than elsewhere in Polynesia, and indicated that they were raised not only for food but for payment of rent to overlords, and for re-ligious and magical purposes. In this latter regard, he noted that the Hawaiians gave the pig credit for considerably more intelligence than is normally given that animal; they were said to have the gift of identifying high-ranking persons who were living incognito. Supposedly, from some instinct of respect, they raised their snouts in obeisance when they came across such a person, and their diagnosis was considered infallible (Hiroa, 1964).

Luomala (1960) points out that throughout Polynesia, when an archipelago had both pigs and dogs, the pig outranked the dog as a gift either to human beings or to gods; she also notes that, as might be expected, humans in Hawaii outranked hogs and dogs as sacrificial objects for the gods.

Although the pig was to become a food eagerly sought by both sexes after the overthrow of the taboo system in 1819, pork before this time was taboo to women. Campbell observed that in 1809 "dogs' flesh and fish were the only kinds of animal food lawful" for women to eat (Campbell, 1816, Luomala, *ibid.*), and Cook's journal mentioned that a girl was beaten when people ashore learned that she had eaten pork with the sailors on board the ship.

Malo (1951) wrote that pork could only be eaten in the men's house; since this place was also the family shrine, where images and other sacred objects were kept, it was taboo to wom-

en of all ages, as well as to young boys who had not yet gone
through the rites of passage that would allow them to eat in that
area. It would thus appear that young boys of high rank, as
well as adult male commoners who were of insufficient rank to
warrant entry into this sacred place, were also unable to eat
pork.

Luomala, in her extensive study of the Hawaiian dog (*op.
cit.*), noted that "food was one of the principal means by which
Polynesians defined status and granted privileges to individuals
high in the ranking order. Religious and social sanctions maintained prize foods as sacred or taboo. Their consumption was
limited to certain social groups and usually only to the men in
them. Prized foods, no matter by whom raised or obtained, be-
longed to high-ranking people who had them collected from
the producers, both informally, according to fancy, and systematically, as in Hawaii during the Makahiki, and redistrib-
uted according to the ranking order of the society." She went
on to note that as a food item pork once again ranked above
dog, and reviews Ellis' 1853 writings that at a feast the highest
chief present was given the head or brains of a pig, while the
carver, a commoner, got the tail and the backbone.

Luomala further records that the eating of pork was taboo
during the Makahiki period (October into January), although
fish and dog meat were apparently not restricted. Vancouver
attended a feast at the conclusion of these annual rites and noted
that "the more common productions, such as fish, turtle, fowls
and dogs" were completely absent because the pork taboo had
just been lifted, and sacred foods like pork, plantains, and coco-
nuts, "consecrated for the principal chiefs and priests," were
then served (Luomala, *ibid.*). After Hawaiian historian David
Malo had written of a five-day religious ceremony and feast,
Sir Peter Buck counted Malo's figures for the number of pigs
baked, and ended with a total of 2,240 pigs cooked (Hiroa, *op.
cit.*).

In Kamakau's account of the 1779 visit and subsequent death

of Captain Cook, it was noted that Cook traded nails, barrel hoops, and other pieces of iron for pigs; a pig one fathom long was good for a piece of iron, and a longer pig would get a knife for a chief. It is evident that not only did the pigs belong to the chiefs, regardless of who raised or bartered them, but so did the items received in trade. Kamakau wrote that if a common man received anything (from Cook), a chief would take it, and if any item of trade was concealed and later discovered, the commoner was killed (anon., 1935).

In February 1778, one year before Cook's death, the famous navigator presented the natives of Kauai with a pair of pigs "of English breed" (Bryan, 1937). Certainly, the characteristics of these two pigs were quickly submerged by breeding with local animals, but, since they were only the first of many unrecorded introductions, the "Polynesian strain" began to suffer a loss of identity. Today, about the only animals that seem to be of almost pure Hawaiian stock are those of the dry upper reaches of Mauna Kea and Mauna Loa.

DISTRIBUTION

Wild pigs are presently found on the islands of Hawaii, Maui, Molokai, Oahu, Kauai, and Niihau. We know that domesticated or semiwild pigs were present on Laysan Island in 1891 (Walker, 1909), but the last of them were killed and eaten sometime before 1910. Elschner (1915) observed pigs inhabiting Sand Island on Midway Atoll in 1915, but there have not been any there for many years.

When Wilkes visited Kahoolawe in 1841, he found many wild pig tracks, but observed only one animal. McAllister visited this island in 1931 for an archeological survey and found no signs of pigs (McAllister, 1933). Thrum (1902) documented the fact that Kahoolawe was an early place of banishment for a number of Hawaiian males, and wrote that these prisoners caught wild pigs and also apparently kept tame ones, feeding the latter on *kūpala* (*Sicyos pachycarpus*?). Thrum also notes that census figures for 1823 indicate 50 people lived on the island, and we might assume that pigs were present then.

Almost nothing is known about the early distribution or abundance of pigs on Lanai. The population was very low in the early 1900s, and it is believed that Roland Gay shot the last pig sometime in the 1930s (G. Swedberg, pers. comm.).

With the exception of the island of Niihau, the majority of Hawaii's pigs live in either the wet forest or on high elevation arid lands. Although no concrete data is presently available, I suggest that the densest populations are in the vegetation zones called D_1, D_2, D_3, E_1, and E_2, by Ripperton and Hosaka (1942). The characteristics of these zones can be studied in Table 4. Pigs also occur in zones C_1 and C_2 but in lesser numbers. On Niihau pigs are numerous in the only zone available to them, zone A (or, as it is more commonly known, the "*kiawe* zone" [*Prosopis chilensis*]). Feral pigs also inhabited this zone on the west end of Molokai until the last of them were shot in 1946 or 1947 (Noah Pekelo, Jr., pers. comm.), and pigs still inhabit this zone from Mahukona to Kailua, Kona, on the Big Island, but appear here to be dependent on the availability of cattle troughs for drinking water. Actually pigs appear to be so highly adaptable that they can be found in any tropical to subalpine area that is not intensively used by humans.

DESCRIPTION

Lyman Nichols, Jr., a wildlife biologist who worked for the Division of Fish and Game, spent four years making observations on the pigs of the island of Hawaii, and he concluded that there are two "varieties" of pig on that island, the "mountain pig" and the "forest pig." As noted earlier, the pigs of the upper, more remote, slopes of Mauna Kea and Mauna Loa have been long isolated from the influence of escaped or released domestic swine. They appear to have reverted in form to the point that

they now very closely resemble the European or Asiatic wild boar. Nichols has also observed the progeny of wild boar in Tennessee and California, and notes (1962) that the only apparent differences between the Hawaiian mountain pig, and the boar of Europe and the U.S. mainland, are those of coat color and coat density. The adult European boar is typically colored a grizzled gray-black or gray-brown, with the lighter colors being pronounced on the face and muzzle, while the Mauna Kea animals are a solid black with occasionally one or more white feet. The mountain pig also exhibits a considerably sparser coat; this might be merely a result of Hawaii's milder climate.

Other characteristics which typify both the European boar and the Hawaiian mountain pig are: moderate to heavy coats of long bristles, each split into two or more prongs at the tip; an undercoat of fine, bronze-colored wool; a heavy crest, from the forehead down past the shoulders, of long, erect bristles; pointed, erect, well-haired ears; long, straight tail, well haired and with a tuft on the end; long legs; long, curved tusks on the boars; and thick "shields," composed of thick skin and connective tissue, growing over the shoulders. These shields, which have apparently developed as a means of protection when fighting, have been measured at over one-inch thickness in several mountain pigs. These animals also typically have high shoulders, thick chests, and sloping rumps, while both sexes have long, narrow snouts. Another characteristic found on all mountain pigs, and supposedly typical of the true wild boar, is the metacarpal gland found on the inside of the foreleg.

The mountain pigs of the island of Hawaii do not approach, in size, the great weights of the forest pigs of that or other islands. Nichols' study unfortunately took place during a period of extended drought when an estimated 80 to 90 percent of the mountain pigs suffered either extreme debility or death; the largest pig of this type that was collected (of 60 specimens) weighed 145 pounds, but he states that there were unsubstantiated reports of pigs being captured that weighed up to 200 pounds, and felt that this would not be an uncommon weight for boars during better years (Nichols, 1962).

The "forest pigs" of the island of Hawaii's lower slopes are the only other animals that have been fairly closely investigated, and there appears to be little difference between them and the feral pigs of the other islands (with the possible exception of Niihau animals, about which nothing is known). These animals have been more recently, and more commonly interbred with domestic breeds which have escaped or been released from captivity, and are somewhat more like domestic animals in appearance and size than the mountain pigs. One noticeable difference from the mountain pig lies in their coloration and coat. Nichols (*ibid.*) found that of all mountain pigs examined, 88 percent were solid black, and 12 percent were black with white on the feet. The forest pigs on the other hand are frequently black and white, brown, brown and white, or white (the author has seen a number of animals with red in the coat, and even a few tricolored animals). Besides color, the coat of the forest pigs is generally much shorter and sparser, the bristles are not as consistently split at the tips, and the wool undercoat is rare.

The forest pigs also exhibit a more blocky body conformation; they generally appear to have shorter legs, and do not have the high shoulders and sloping rump of the mountain animals. They also reach a far greater size; this is undoubtedly because of the influence of their domestic bloodlines as well as the generally greater abundance of nutritious foods in the forest. Forest pigs very commonly average 200 to 300 pounds, and a few are double that weight. Clarence Coelho and Charles Meyer took a 523-pound female on Molokai some years ago (Noah Pekelo, Jr., pers. comm.), and Nichols (*ibid.*) tells of a hunter in the Kohala Mountains on the Big Island who lugged out a carcass and hide weighing 348 pounds; this was not counting the head, entrails, and feet. Nichols then weighed a smaller animal the same way and found that the parts left behind were equivalent

190 HAWAIIAN LAND MAMMALS

to about 64 percent of the carcass and hide; assuming the same ratio of loss, the live animal would have weighed about 570 pounds. The same hunter then stated that he had killed even larger animals in the area, but had not been able to weigh them.

The young of the wild European boar are all born with "water-melon striped" coats, consisting of a light brown base color and longitudinal stripes of dark brown or black. Domestic pigs rarely, if ever, show this characteristic. Of 82 mountain piglets born under penned conditions, 13 animals (16 percent) showed this condition; the remainder were black, or black with one or more white feet. This same striping occurs, but to an apparently lesser extent, in some of the forest pig litters on all islands. This striping fades into the adult coat when the young are one or two months old (Nichols, 1964).

REPRODUCTION

With the exception of Nichols' study of the pigs of the northern half of the island of Hawaii, knowledge of this facet of the Hawaiian pig's life history is sadly lacking; it is also unfortunate that his information was gathered in years of unusual drought, since the resultant lack of "normal foodstuffs" and rainfall undoubtedly causes a variation in data from that of more "normal" years.

Nichols (1964) was able to observe the breeding and farrowing dates in five captive "mountain pig" sows. The gestation period varied from 109 to 123 days, averaging out at 118 days. This compares favorably with a range of 108 to 119 days for the European wild boar in Tennessee (Matschke, 1961, Nichols, *ibid.*) and 112 to 116 days for commercially raised swine in the U.S. (Cook and Juergenson, 1962). Although Blansford (1891) and Corbet (1966) both state that *Sus scrofa* in Asia and Europe do not breed until their second year, Nichols found that at least five gilts (females who farrow before the age of 15 months) were bred successfully at approximately five and one-half months of age. This may be indicative of a certain amount of domestic bloodline. A four and one-half month old boar was known to have successfully impregnated several sows; Nichols felt that these instances probably represented the minimum ages of sexual maturity rather than the average age. It is doubtful that males of this age actually get much opportunity to breed in the wild because of inability to compete with older and larger boars. Males in the pen were not seen fighting one another until they were ten months old, at which time their "shield" was just developing.

In 1964, 15 captive mountain pig litters were farrowed. The number of young per litter varied from 3 to 9, with an average of 5.5; this compared with an average of 5.7 small pigs per nursing sow observed in the wild during this same period. Cannibalism among the penned animals was fairly common and it was thought that the average number of pigs per litter might have been somewhat larger than the number observed (Nichols, 1964). Table 5 presents the typical weights of newborn mountain pigs; it can be seen that, while there is a considerable variation in weight, males generally outweigh females at birth.

Table 5. Weights of Hawaiian wild pigs at birth
(From Nichols, 1964)

Sex	Age	No. of Specimens	Weight Range: Ounces	Average Weight: Ounces
male	1 day	14	28–37	30.6
male	2 days	12	31–43	37.0
female	1 day	16	19.5–30.5	27.6
female	2 days	14	24–40	32.4

Little data are available concerning natural weaning times or rebreeding of the sows. Sows were observed weaning litters at five and one-half weeks, at four months, and at five and one-half months. Although domestic breeds generally come into heat three to five days after weaning their young (Cook and

Juergenson, *op. cit.*), the sow that nursed her litter for over five months was rebred on the same day she weaned her litter; one other sow was bred at five days, and another after fourteen to seventeen days.

The facts are definitely inconclusive, but indications are that there is, on the northern half of the island of Hawaii at least, a peak breeding season in October and November with another, smaller peak in February, March, and April. The peak farrowing season then occurs in February and March, with another smaller one in June, July, and August. An undetermined amount of breeding and reproduction occurs during all months of the year; until a relatively large number of samples are taken during all the months of the year it still remains to be proved that such cycles are in fact present.

When ready to farrow, wild pigs build a rather elaborate nest. They are usually made from piles of dry vegetation which the sows carry in from the surrounding area and place in the lee of rocks, trees, or dense shrubbery. They are then hollowed out to some extent so that they form a dry, sheltered "nest." Nichols (1962) described one such nest found in the dry algaroba (*Prosopis chilensis*) forest of the Puako area: "The sow had bitten off many young algaroba saplings, some of which were up to one-half inch in stem diameter, and all of which had bushy foliage. These she had carried from as far as 30 feet away and stacked in a circular form with one partially open side, the opening facing away from the prevailing wind. The walls of the windbreak were from one and one-half to two feet high when found, and were probably higher when the foliage was green and fresh. The floor of the nest within the windbreak was soft, dry dust, somewhat hollowed out into a bowl-shape from use, and the whole nest was located in a relatively thick patch of saplings beneath several large algaroba trees. It was well screened from observation, and must have given the piglets good protection from the wind."

The piglets remain with the sow until they are weaned, but

they can apparently subsist almost entirely on vegetation in less than two months if they are forced to; a number of pigs as young as one month have been seen feeding alone. After weaning, some of the litters drift away from the mother, while in other cases they may remain with her for some months. Corbet (*op. cit.*) noted that two litters of different ages commonly accompany the female European wild pig, and there is evidence to show that the Hawaiian animals do the same. Young pigs that separate from their mother often join up with others of similar size, and are frequently seen in groups of half a dozen or more, traveling and feeding together. Nichols (1962) felt that these groups may form into long-term associations, since many of the groups of young adult pigs he has seen have been composed of animals of approximately the same age.

MOVEMENT STUDIES

In four years, Nichols captured, tagged, and released 236 wild pigs. Although many were presumed to have died during the drought of 1962–63, 22 animals (9 percent) were recovered. The great majority of tagged animals were of the "mountain" variety, all of whom live on much more open range than do the "forest" variety; consequently we might assume that the tagged animals tended to range farther afield than do those of the dense fern forests. The longest distance traveled was by a boar who, after 13 months and 20 days, was recaptured 3.9 miles from the original tagging site. The longest time interval between tagging and recovery was 16 months and 18 days, and this animal was killed only 0.6 miles from the tagging site (Nichols, 1964). Another animal, on Kukaiau Ranch, was recaptured and released within 200 yards of the original tagging site, and nine months later was killed in this same area. Another animal, after three months, was also seen 200 yards from its original location. A fifth animal, after 11 months of freedom on Parker Ranch, was recovered less than 500 yards away (Nichols, 1962).

Although preliminary investigation tends to indicate that sows have a small home range and that boars travel farther afield, many hundreds of animals will have to be tagged and recaptured before any definite conclusions can be drawn.

FOOD HABITS

The pig can probably best be described as being a vegetarian omnivore, but it will feed on snails, insects, worms, ground-nesting birds, bird eggs, and rodents whenever the opportunity arises. Like most other aspects of the ecology of the Hawaiian pig, there is not sufficient evidence gathered to date to make any firm pronouncements about the effect of its food habits on the community in which it lives. Because of the great variety of biotic communities in which we find pigs, it would perhaps be improper or useless to put in one long list all of the plants and animals eaten. We know for example that the pigs of Puako eat cactus and algaroba, but this information is of no value to the biologist on Kauai who may be studying the effects of the pig on the Alakai forest bog, where these plants certainly do not exist. For range, forest, or animal management purposes it is important to delineate and define a circumscribed study area and then specifically study the problems therein; for the vast majority of the Hawaiian Islands' pig range this has not been done. Table 6 indicates the types of food utilized by pigs on the island of Hawaii, but must, at this stage of our knowledge, be considered as merely an introduction to the total question.

The ranch or pastureland mountain pigs primarily appear to be grazers, as evidenced by the high proportion of grasses and gosmore in their diet. In these areas, the rooting that takes place seems to be mostly in search of bracken fern roots, earthworms, and army worms. Nichols (1963) noted that army worms appear to be a choice food even though they only make up a small percentage of the total volume of the diet; they occurred in almost 50 percent of the stomachs examined.

Table 6. Average percentages of foods eaten by
pigs on Hawaii Island, by species and area
(From Nichols, 1963)

Mountain-ranch habitat (surrounding Mauna Kea) (24 specimens)
  grasses (leaves, seed heads, roots)   45%
  gosmore (blossoms, leaves, roots)[1]   34%
  bracken fern (roots primarily)[2]   16%
  army worms[3]   1%
  māmane (blossoms, leaves)[4]   1%
  earthworms,[5] clover, pukeawe,[6]
    unidentified animal remains   3%
                                                      100

Fern forest habitat (Kohala Mountains, Kulani Forest) (11 specimens)
  hapu fern (trunks, roots, leaf shoots)[7]   91%
  forest litter and mud   4%
  grass and sedge   2%
  unidentified plant material   2%
  army worms[3]   Trace
  earthworms[5]   1%
                                                      100

Wet forest habitat where fruit and grass are available (Maulua) (4 specimens)
  grasses   45%
  hapu fern (roots, trunks, leaf shoots)[7]   25%
  passion fruit (fruits, leaves)[8]   23%
  earthworms[5]   5%
  poha (fruits)[9]   2%
  army worms[3]   Trace
                                                      100

Mountain scrub-forest (Mauna Loa flats) (2 specimens)
  'ūlei (berries)[10]   75%
  grass   20%
  rat remains   5%
                                                      100

[1] *Hypochaeris radicata,*   [2] *Pteridium aquilinum,*   [3] *Cirphis unipuncta,*
[4] *Sophora chrysophylla,*   [5] *Pheretima sp.,*   [6] *Styphelia tameiameiae,*
[7] *Cibotium splendens, C. chamissoi,*   [8] *Passiflora sp.,*   [9] *Physalis peruviana,*
[10] *Osteomeles anthyllidifolia.*

In and above the high forests of Mauna Kea and Mauna Loa, where the amounts of grassland diminish with altitude, rooting is much more prevalent. Here the pigs appear to feed primarily on the roots of bracken fern, with perhaps some browsing on *pukeawe* and seedling *māmane*. To get at these roots, the pigs plow furrows and trenches that are a foot or more deep and up to 10 or 15 feet long. With their tough disced nose and short, powerful neck muscles, they are easily capable of rooting out and pushing aside boulders of up to 50 pounds as they follow an underground root system.

In the wet forest habitat the major food item is the tree fern; each mature tree fern produces from 50 to 70 pounds of a nearly pure starch (Neal, 1965), and the pigs break open the smaller trunks to get at this soft center food. They also eat the newly sprouted fronds and, on occasion, dig up the roots. When fruits, such as guava (*Psidium sp.*), Java plum and rose apple (*Eugenia sp.*), passionfruit (*Passiflora sp.*) and Methley plum (*Prunus cerasifera*), are falling, the pigs will seek these foods and feed almost exclusively on them until the supply is exhausted. It is my own impression that they will travel considerable distances from their normal home range in order to feed on these fruits, and that when the supply is exhausted they tend to return to their former range.

Pigs living in the *kiawe* zone graze when they can, but feed mostly on *kiawe* beans, and on the fruit of the "prickly-pear" cactus (*Opuntia sp.*). In specimens from the Puako forest, Nichols (1962) found that these "beans" made up almost 100 percent of the stomach contents of most animals examined; other items included small quantities of grass, cockroaches, and other insects.

BEHAVIOR

A full discussion of the behavior patterns of the wild pig would double, or perhaps triple, the size of this chapter, and so must await the eventual publication of a monograph on this species. I shall instead present a short synopsis of their habits and behavior from Nichols' 1962 report.

Wild pigs do not exhibit strong herding or grouping instincts except when very young. When groups are seen together, they are usually either a mother with several generations of young, or are fortuitous groupings that occur temporarily, such as might come together when a particular grove of trees is dropping fruit. When disturbed, the groups readily break up, with individuals going their own way. Except when a sow is in heat, the older boars prefer to remain separated from family groups, but they will on occasion form loosely attached associations with other males.

Wild pigs generally are most active during the late afternoon, night, and early morning hours, but in more remote areas some animals may be found abroad at all hours of the day. In the dryer areas, or on ranchlands, where water during the summer is only available in cattle troughs or reservoirs, the pigs prefer to drink soon after leaving cover in the afternoon and most of the activity around these areas is at that time; very little use of water has been noted during the morning hours, perhaps because of a sufficiency of morning dew on the vegetation they consume. Pigs in the forest generally find abundant and well-distributed watering places and do not follow this movement pattern. When ranchland pigs do move to water, they commonly travel along well-defined trails which converge, like the spokes on a wheel, to the closest water hole. After drinking, and occasionally wallowing, the animals move off randomly and spend the rest of the evening and night feeding.

Within several hours after sunrise, the majority of pigs move into some form of cover, and here many seek the shade and protection of "nests" or "lairs." These day-nests are different from those made by farrowing sows and are usually just rough hollows beneath fallen trees or overhanging rocks, or along the banks of dry stream beds. When they are available, pigs will use shallow caves. The floors of most nests are comparatively dry and are either deliberately scraped clean of loose debris and litter, or are accidentally cleaned through use. Where the floor is soft, the nests appear as bowl-shaped hollows, formed by the wriggling of their body as they shift about. Quite frequently, a group of up to eight or ten pigs will squeeze into the same nest, where they spend the day crowded next to one another.

Although the pigs prefer the dryest possible resting area they are not averse to using a mud wallow for short periods. In ranch and pastureland areas the pigs form wallows along the edges of reservoirs by wading into the soft mud along the edge and then rooting out a trough with their snouts. They then lie down and squirm around until almost buried. In the forests, patches of boggy ground, seep springs, and rain-created mud puddles are used for this purpose. Wallowing is probably done for several reasons; it cools during hot weather, it helps soften the normally dry scaly skin, it probably relieves irritation caused by lice, and it may have some as-yet-unexplained relationship with the sexual activity among boars. Wallowing is believed to have some territorial significance to the European wild boar, with a preponderance of wallowing in the autumn (Corbet, *op. cit.*).

In addition to using wallows for relief of lice bites, pigs frequently rub themselves against trees. In some cases, the trees may be so often used that the bark is rubbed off entirely. I have also noted telephone poles, particularly creosoted ones, being used for the same apparent purpose. Pigs will come for long distances to rub against a creosoted object and I assume that the creosote serves as a type of repellant to the lice. Since pigs' bodies are relatively inflexible they find it difficult to reach around to bite or lick irritated areas, and rubbing and wallowing are their only means of alleviating their discomfort.

Wild pigs are far more agile and swifter than are their domestic cousins. They move at a walk while feeding or traveling, but when disturbed, chased, or just in a hurry, they break into a fast trot that can carry them over the roughest terrain with surprising speed. When really chased they break into a headlong gallop that will often outdistance a young dog. Despite their tiny sharp hooves they can negotiate the roughest and boggiest of forest and move up and down 60-degree cliffs with apparent ease; in fact, the forest pigs seem to move into these densely tangled areas by choice. The only area that they cannot negotiate is the jagged, broken glasslike, *aʿa* lava flows; when a hunted pig reaches the edge of one of these flows he will stop and prepare to fight. Although the wild pig is a poor high jumper, it can make broad jumps of at least six feet; they commonly leap the six-foot-wide Kohala irrigation ditch.

Wild pigs have an excellent sense of smell and have scented humans from a distance of nearly a half mile when conditions were right. They also indicate the development of this sense in their rooting for underground foods, such as worms and fern roots. This habit of moving along with their snouts to the ground in their search for food often makes them oblivious to the odors wafting over their head which would normally spell danger—an approaching hunter or his dogs.

Hearing and eyesight both appear basically good, but pigs in most areas seem to depend so little on these two senses, particularly their sight, that they do not use them adequately. Consequently they often appear somewhat deaf and nearly blind. Under normal circumstances it takes no particular skill to stalk these animals in the forest since they seem to take no notice of sounds, such as footsteps, low talking, or breaking of twigs underfoot. Their eyes are so untrained that they seem unable to recognize slowly moving humans at any great distance, or motionless humans at distances of over 15 to 20 yards. In certain other areas, such as in the grasslands of Parker Ranch, the pigs use these latter two senses to great advantage; they can recognize an approaching man or vehicle from more than a mile away, and will start running on hearing voices or a motor, even though they cannot see it.

The voice of wild pigs is similar to that of domestic animals and normally consists of a variety of grunts as they feed, or shrill squeals when they are excited, badly frightened, or hurt. Sows commonly call their young with grunts, and boars grunt when pursuing sows. When fighting, boars emit loud squeals and also squeal when harassing a sow in heat. They are also known to emit a groaning bellow, much like the moo of a cow, but the significance of this is unknown. When extremely excited, as when fighting another boar or a dog, their grunts and squeals of rage are quite unnerving. Their normal alarm call is usually an explosive grunt, which may be repeated over and over as they run, but when suddenly confronted with danger close at hand, this call is reduced to a sudden, loud "woof" of surprise. A cornered pig may utter this sound at the instant of charging its opponent. Piglets under the age of two or three months are the most vocal of all and constantly "talk to themselves" in a series of surprisingly deep-throated grunts.

The aggressive nature of wild boar is well known throughout the world—Sterndale has recorded several instances in India of fights between a large boar and a tiger where the boar has won (Blansford, *op. cit.*)—and Hawaii's wild boar are no exceptions. Although they will normally run from danger if they can, they will not hesitate to attack if they are cornered or wounded or are unusually excited. A lone man runs little risk of attack unless he stumbles onto a sow with young, in which case the sow may attack. A person attempting to approach a wounded animal may almost invariably expect it to attack if it can. The commonest technique of hunting wild pigs in Hawaii is by using one or more dogs to locate, corner, and then hold the pig while the hunter rushes in, grabs it by a hind leg or the tail, and then stabs it through the heart, or cuts its throat. If the dogs release their hold, the hunter is in serious trouble, At least one hunter has been killed (and partially eaten!) in past years (Bryan, *op. cit.*), and a number have been seriously wounded. I recall selling a hunting license to a man who had to use both hands to hold his pen as he signed his name; both arms were bandaged to the elbow. I asked him what the trouble was and he casually stated that his dogs had let go of a boar just as he grabbed for it; the boar's tusks had severed all the tendons on both wrists, but he was undaunted and intended to go hunting again as soon "as I can close my fingers to hold a knife!" In areas where pigs have not been heavily hunted, a fight between a pig and a dog may attract other pigs which will charge in and join the fight deliberately; even small piglets have been known to fight and attack when cornered. A male pig's tusks are actually its lower canine teeth. The base of these tusks is located far back in the jaw—usually under the second molar—and grows slightly down, and forward, before erupting from the lower jaw just behind the third incisor. These teeth grow throughout life, forming an ever elongating semicircular curve. The upper canines are much shorter, and grow down and then curve sharply out and up. When the mouth is closed they fit against and to the rear of the lower canines; actually, they overlap the rear part of the lower tusks, but constant wear between the two forms a flattened surface on both teeth so that they fit flush together. This constant wear acts like a honing process and serves to keep the edges of the lower tusks sharpened. Angry or excited boars deliberately sharpen their lower tusks by rubbing them rapidly, and very audibly, against the uppers; it is a rather terrifying sound. The total length of these tusks may reach 11 or 12 inches on occasion, but the portion above the gumline rarely is more than three and one-half inches. Although sows have similar canine teeth, they never develop into the long, curving tusks of the male nor do the upper canines curve up and out. They can, however, inflict a terrible bite, and will make every attempt to do so where their young are concerned.

PARASITES AND DISEASE

Like other facets of the life history of the pig in Hawaii, information about parasites and diseases of these animals is rudimentary. Free-ranging animals appear to be afflicted with a number of organisms, many of which are potentially communicable to man and/or domestic animals, but because of a shortage of manpower in both the Division of Fish and Game, and in the pathology sections of the Departments of Agriculture and Public Health, detailed information about the prevalence of even one known disease is not available. Table 7 lists the parasites presently known to occur in both domestic and wild swine. For further information concerning these species the reader is referred to pages 87 through 94 in Dr. J. Alicata's *Parasitic Infections of Man and Animals in Hawaii* (1964).

Table 7. Parasites of swine in Hawaii
(After Alicata, 1964)
Asterisks (*) indicate known occurrence in wild pigs
on the island of Hawaii.

Name of Parasite	*Location*	*Intermediate Host (if any)*
PROTOZOA:		
Balantidium coli	large intestine	
Eimeria debliecki	small & large intestines	
Eimeria scabra	intestine	
Eimeria spinosa	large intestine	
ROUNDWORMS:		
Ascaris lumbricoides	small intestine	
*Ascarops strongylina**	stomach	Coleoptera: (probably coprophagous beetles)
*Choerostrongylus pudendotectus**	lungs	Oligochaeta: (earthworms, probably of the genus *Pheretima*)
*Globocephalus urosubulatus**	small intestine	
Hyostrongylus rubidus	stomach	
*Metastrongylus elongatus**	lungs	Oligochaeta: (earthworms, probably of the genus *Pheretima*)
Oesophagostomum dentatum	large intestine	
Physocephalus sexalatus	stomach	Coleoptera: (probably coprophagous beetles)

*Stephanurus dentatus**	adults in kidneys and kidney fat; immature forms in liver and other internal organs	
Strongyloides ransomi	small intestine	
*Trichinella spiralis**	adults in small intestine; larvae in muscles	(same in final host)
*Trichuris trichiura**	cecum	

TAPEWORMS:

*Taenia hydatigena** (cysticercus)	attached to liver, mesentary, and omentum	Artiodactyla: *Sus scrofa, Ovis aries*
Taenia solium (cysticercus)	larvae in musculature and viscera	Artiodactyla: *Sus scrofa* Primate: *Homo sapiens*

FLUKES:

*Fasciola sp. (gigantica?)**	liver	Gastropoda: *Fossaria ollula, Pseudosuccinea columella*

ARTHROPODS:

*Haematopinus suis**	external	
*Sarcoptes scabiei suis**	external	

Nichols (1963) also found the common flea, *Pulex irritans,* infesting one animal. He at the same time noted that the hog louse (*Haematopinus suis*) was present on every pig from every area, and that infestations varied from light to heavy.

The first laboratory-proved case of human trichinosis was found in Hawaii in 1936. Between this time and 1964, there were 112 cases of human trichinosis reported (Alicata, *op. cit.*), and in an examination of 133 human diaphragms from autopsy cases in Honolulu, 7.4 percent showed encysted trichina larvae (Alicata, 1942). Dr. Alicata found that most of the 112 infected persons had eaten, or were suspected of having eaten, improperly cooked wild pork or products made from wild pork. During Alicata's 1936 survey of trichinosis, he found that of 47 domestic hogs and 40 wild pigs from the island of Hawaii, 1 (2.1 percent) domestic animal and 6 (15 percent) wild animals were infected. No trichinae were found in 92, 130, and 30 domestic hogs examined from the islands of Maui, Oahu, and Kauai, respectively; no wild pig samples were taken from these areas for observation (Alicata, 1938). In contrast to Alicata's Hawaii Island findings, Nichols had 48 wild pigs examined and found only 1 case; this animal came from the dryland forest of Puako (Nichols, 1962, 1963). There is no doubt that the meat from wild pigs constitutes a health menace unless proper precautions are taken in the cooking of it.

Nichols took blood samples from the majority of pigs that he collected, and these were serologically tested by the Department of Health until April 1963, when that service was discontinued. Prior to that date, a number of samples indicated that some wild pigs were either carriers or were infected, or had been exposed to such diseases as leptospirosis, brucellosis, and scrub typhus; a number of pigs also showed an unexplained reaction to typhoid antigens O and H, and paratyphoid antigens A and B (Nichols, 1963). Obviously, investigation into these questions should begin immediately.

Other abnormalities noted include stomach ulcers, mechanical injuries to the mucosa and walls of the stomach, ovarian cysts, and cysts or tumors of the prostate. One sow had large tumors on her brisket and in her lungs and stomach (Nichols, 1962).

LITERATURE CITED

Alicata, J. E.
    1938   A study of *Trichinella spiralis* in the Hawaiian Islands. U.S. Pub. Health Serv., Pub. Health Rept. 53: 384–393.

1964 Parasitic infections of man and animals in Hawaii. Hawaii Agri. Exp. Sta. Tech. Bull. 61: 138pp.

Anonymous
1935 Kamakau's account of Captain Cook. Paradise of the Pacific 47(11): 12–21.

Blansford, W. T.
1891 The fauna of British India, including Ceylon and Burma —Mammalia I & II. Taylor and Francis, Red Lion Court, London: 617pp.

Bryan, L. W.
1937 Wild pigs in Hawaii. Paradise of the Pacific 49(12): 31–32.

Cook, G. G., and E. M. Juergenson
1962 Approved practices in swine production. Interstate Printers and Publishers, Danville, Ill.: 329pp.

Corbet, G. B.
1966 The terrestrial mammals of western Europe. G. T. Foulis and Co., Ltd., London: 264pp.

Elschner, C.
1915 The leeward islands of the Hawaiian group. Honolulu: 68pp.

Hiroa, Te Rangi (Sir Peter Buck)
1964 Arts and crafts of Hawaii. B. P. Bishop Mus., Spec. Publ. 45. Honolulu: 606pp.

Luomala, K.
1960 The native dog in the Polynesian system of values. In: Culture in History (S. Diamond, Edit.). Columbia Univ. Press, New York: 190–240.

Malo, D.
1951 Hawaiian Antiquities. B. P. Bishop Mus., Spec. Publ. 2, 2nd Edit.: 278pp.

McAllister, J. C.
1933 Archeology of Kahoolawe. B. P. Bishop Mus. Bull. 115: 61pp.

Neal, M. C.
1965 In gardens of Hawaii. B. P. Bishop Mus. Spec. Publ. 50: 924pp.

Nichols, L., Jr.
  1962 Ecology of the wild pig, W-5-R-13, Job 46(13), State
        of Hawaii, Div. of Fish and Game, Honolulu: 20pp.,
        mimeo.

  1963 Ecology of the wild pig, W-5-R-14, Job 46(14), State
        of Hawaii, Div. of Fish and Game, Honolulu: 11pp.,
        mimeo.

  1964 Ecology of the wild pig, W-5-R-15, Job 46(15), State of
        Hawaii, Div. of Fish and Game, Honolulu: 11pp.,
        mimeo.

Ripperton, J. C., and E. Y. Hosaka
  1942 Vegetation zones of Hawaii. Haw'n. Agri. Exp. Sta.,
        Bull. 89: 58pp.

Schwartz, C. W., and E. R. Schwartz
  1949 A reconnaissance of the game birds in Hawaii. Bd.
        Commis. Agri. and Forestry, Honolulu: 168pp.

Thrum, T. G.
  1902 Kahoolawe, an early place of banishment. Hawaiian
        Annual for 1903: 117–122.

Walker, F. D.
  1909 Log of the Kaalokai. Hawaiian Gazette Co., Ltd.,
        Honolulu: 64pp.

Warner, R. E.
  1959 Ecological investigations of the Hawaiian pig, W-5-R-
        10, Job 46(10), State of Hawaii, Div. of Fish and Game,
        Honolulu: 5pp., mimeo.

The Axis Deer

Axis axis

In late 1957, the Division of Fish and Game initiated its first life history study of a Hawaiian mammal. For three and one-half years Dr. William Graf, professor of Wildlife Management at San Jose State College, and Lyman Nichols, Jr., wildlife biologist for the Division of Fish and Game, intensively studied the populations of axis deer that roamed the islands of Lanai and Molokai. In 1967, Graf and Nichols published, in the *Journal of the Bombay Natural History Society,* a 105-page paper entitled "The Axis Deer in Hawaii." This article provided, from the information available at that time, a very detailed story of one of Hawaii's most picturesque animals. Like all animal biographies, bits of information gleaned on later dates have helped fill in some of the gaps and have either strengthened or weakened some of the hypotheses originally formulated. Gerald Swedberg, biologist with the Division of Fish and Game, has very carefully gathered this more recent information and, using Graf and Nichols' works as a base, has put together a "popularized" account of this deer. It is from this paper (in press) that the Division of Fish and Game has kindly allowed me to write this chapter. Scientists wishing greater details are, of course, referred to the aforementioned writings.

HISTORY

The ambassadors and consuls who represented the Hawaiian monarchy in foreign countries sent back gifts to keep the good will of their monarchs. According to contemporary newspaper articles, the Hawaiian consul from Hong Kong presented a small number of axis deer (*Axis axis*)* to King Kamehameha V.

Four bucks and four does were provided from the upper Ganges River in India and were then shipped from Calcutta to Hong Kong. Several animals died en route, but a Mr. Magniac (a member of the house of Jardine, Matheson, and Co., Hong Kong) replaced the dead animals† with others of like sex and then transshipped the eight deer to Honolulu, consigned to Dr. Hillebrand. One male died en route, but shortly after the ship docked in Honolulu a male fawn was born. The ship carrying the deer was the *Loch Na Garr* and docked in Honolulu in December 1867. In January 1868, the deer were taken to Molokai aboard the king's yacht *Ka Ma I Ie* to be released.

The release area was in or near the native forest on the slopes above Kaunakakai. This forest had apparently been heavily

---

* There is some contention among taxonomists and physiologists as to the true position of the axis deer in the deer world. Some persons feel that it is so strongly related to the European-type deer that it should more properly be called *Cervus axis;* until a positive stand is taken by a majority of zoologists we shall continue to use the term *Axis axis.*

† It is not known where Magniac got the replacement deer. Tinker (1941) refers to axis deer from Japanese parks being shipped to Molokai for release in 1868, and they may have been the deer in question, but since Tinker also mentions that the deer were kept at the Damon Estate in Moanalua, Oahu, prior to being shipped to Molokai, while newspaper articles of the time refer to a direct transfer from ship to ship, it seems probable that this was either a second shipment during the same year or that Tinker's information is erroneous. Though a shipment of axis deer may have been obtained from Japan, they are not native to that country; their native range is strictly India and Ceylon.

grazed by cattle and had become an open parkland forest with considerable grassland. Tinker quotes George Munro as saying the ridges in the release area were covered with grass at that time. It can be assumed that the numerous, steep gulches of the area remained vegetated with native shrubs and trees.

For many years following the release, the deer were allowed to reproduce without restriction. According to Colin Lennox (1950), the herd had increased to between 6,000 and 7,000 animals by 1898. In 1900, two professional hide hunters were employed by the Molokai Ranch Company to eliminate the deer from the forest. By 1903 only a few deer remained in the forest area, and a few had moved down into the kiawe (*Prosopis chilensis*) forest belt, which was then developing on the lower slopes of the island in the dry areas. George Cooke, former manager of Molokai Ranch, estimated that between 4,500 and 7,500 deer were removed. The stragglers in this portion of the forest were subsequently eliminated by island residents after the area had been placed in forest-reserve status in 1912.

There is no information about what happened to the deer on the eastern end of the forest. The extermination campaign was not carried on there, probably because of the diverse land ownership. Efforts to eliminate the deer probably did not extend beyond the head of Pelekunu Valley.

In 1920, 12 axis deer were transplanted to Lanai by George Munro, and became established in the Palawai plateau. There they multiplied and concentrated in the cactus (*Opuntia megacantha*) zone which was later knocked down for the planting of pineapples; when this occurred, the deer were forced into the lower, dryer, kiawe zone. Some effort was made to exterminate them in the 1930s, but these efforts were never pressed and the program was eventually discontinued.

The history of the deer on Oahu is uncertain. In view of the transfer of the original eight deer from Oahu to Molokai, more deer must have been shipped to Oahu, but no one knows from where the animals came. Prior to 1898, a herd flourished in the region of Diamond Head. This herd was decimated by the first American soldiers, who camped at Kapiolani Park, and this herd was totally exterminated at some later date.

A sizable herd existed for many years in Moanalua Valley, Oahu, where they were afforded protection by the owners of the valley. This population originated with the escape of a buck and two does from captivity about 1910. Although these deer had free access to the upper end of the valley, they remained in the dry *koa haole* (*Leucaena glauca*), *klu* (*Acacia farnesiana*), and *kiawe* habitat in the region of the present Camp Catlin and ammunition-storage area. In 1940 the owners of the valley removed approximately 300 deer because of their incompatibility with other activities. New housing developments, illegal hunting, and probable harassment and predation by dogs have all served to reduce the population to the point of near extinction; there have probably been less than 20 animals present in the last seven or eight years.

A pair of axis deer were released on the windward side of Oahu, at Kaneohe Marine Corps Air Station, in 1954 (anon., 1954), and survived there for several months before disappearing. Four or five years later several third-hand reports were made of a herd of deer in the forest above Waiahole, but the absolute presence of these animals has never been proven.

Two male and three female deer were introduced to the "Red Hill" area of Maui in September 1959, and an additional buck and three does were let go on Kaonoulu Ranch on that island in July 1960. Little effort has been made to understand the impact of these animals on that island. The population was estimated to be 85 to 90 animals in 1968.

DESCRIPTION

The color pattern of not only the young but the adult axis deer is similar to that of the familiar spotted fawn of the Americas. The fallow deer (*Cervus dama*) and the Japanese *sika* deer

(*Cervus nippon*) are also spotted, but only in their summer coats, leaving the axis deer as the sole member of the deer family that retains its spots from its first day to its last. The coat is a general light brown over the back and sides, and white on the belly and on the inside of the legs. The brown portions of the body are covered with bright white spots, with the exception of the upper neck, the head, and the lower legs. A dark, chocolate-brown stripe, with two rows of spots, extends along the middorsal line from the neck to the tail. There is little if any difference between summer and winter pelage colors.

Mature bucks differ from does and fawns in that they are much darker in color over the head and neck, with some very old ones being almost charcoal colored. Bucks have blackish facial markings, while does and fawns do not.

The hair of the coat is short, soft, and supple, giving the animals a very sleek appearance. Angry or excited bucks may erect the hair on their back and sides, giving the appearance of being somewhat larger than they really are. Under some conditions of excitement, the tail is raised and the hair fluffed out, showing a large white "flag." A gradual molt takes place in the spring or early summer, but this molting seems to be a mere thinning, with little difference occurring in color or texture.

Mature bucks generally weigh more than does, and compare favorably in size with American mule deer (*Odocoileus sp.*). There is no obvious difference between the weights and measurements of Molokai or Lanai deer. The average "field-dressed" (only internal organs removed) buck—from 26 specimens—weighed 120 pounds. These specimens showed a dressed weight range varying from 74 to 170 pounds, indicating live weights varying from 94 to 224 pounds. It is statistically conceivable that an occasional buck may weigh from 240 to 250 pounds.

The average dressed weight of 38 does was 70.5 pounds with a range of 55 to 97 pounds; this indicated live weights ranging from 74 to 127 pounds.

Table 8 was constructed by collecting 26 male and 38 female deer, weighing them whole, then field dressing them and weighing them again. It provides a handy reference for the hunter who brings back a field-dressed animal (which, by the time he has dragged it out of the field, weighs at least 500 pounds) and who wants to know how much it weighed "on the hoof."

Table 8. A comparison of the dressed and live weights of axis deer

Dressed Weight	Approximate Live Weight*	
	BUCKS	DOES
40 pounds	53 pounds	58 pounds
50	66	70
60	79	84
70	92	98
80	105	112
90	118	126
100	132	140
110	145	154
120	158	168
130	171	——
140	184	——
150	197	——
160	211	——
170	224	——
180	237	——
190	250	——

* rounded to the nearest pound

A closer examination of this chart shows that males lose an average of 24 percent, and females 31.6 percent, of their live weight in field dressing them.

Mature bucks stand about 36 inches high at the shoulder, while does average 30 inches. The ears, averaging five to five and one-half inches long, are some two to three inches shorter than those of the black-tailed deer of Kauai; however, the axis deer's tail, averaging 10 to 12 inches, is somewhat longer than that of its Kauai relative. The hunter who is seeking a set of trophy antlers would do well to remember that, from the tip of its nose to the notch of its ear, a buck's head length averages about 12 inches. When scanning a herd for trophy animals, it is an easy method of comparison, and any buck with antlers more than two and one-half times the face length can be considered a respectable head.

The axis deer, like other members of the family, have a series of glands with external orfices. The metatarsal (on the outside of the tarsus, below the hock) and interdigital (between the toes of the hooves) glands are not so well developed—and not so odoriferous—as those of the mule deer, while the infraorbital (below the eyes) glands are extremely noticeable, particularly when flared open (especially by bucks when excited.)

Only bucks carry antlers. Antlered females have been reported, but if any existed, they would be abnormal specimens.

Antler growth in male fawns is first noticeable at about seven months of age, and the spike antlers are fully developed at about 14 months. In the second year light-beamed antlers develop with either two or three points per side. Antlers of mature bucks typically have three points to a side; a heavy brow tine, a short, inward-pointing tine about two-thirds of the way up the beam, and the long, spearlike tip of the beam, which usually points slightly forward and inward. Less than 1 percent of deer examined at hunter check stations had one or both antlers with four tines. Various abberrations from the norm do occur, but these are usually caused either from damage when in the velvet stage, or from senility. In adult bucks, antler growth takes slightly longer than four months from the beginning bud to the stage of velvet shedding. Bucks carry hard antlers for almost eight months of each year.

There are no longevity records for wild axis deer, but a captive animal on Molokai, at the age of 11½ years, showed no sign of senility, and his antlers increased in size each year. Dover (1932) records "chital"—as the deer is known in much of India —as averaging 10 to 15 years in Calcutta zoos, but also notes that one lived for almost 19 years in a Paris zoo. It appears that when the animals do start to become senile, their antlers tend to decline in size and length, and often only exhibit two points, the brow tine and the regressing main beam tip.

The majority of bucks have hard antlers in the months from April through December with a peak occurring in August, but a fair percentage of the male population can be found in various stages of antler development the year round.

Antler measurements of 98 deer taken during the 1959 hunting seasons on Lanai and Molokai show that antlers measuring over 22 inches in length, or 15 inches from tip to tip, are a better

An axis buck in aggressive posture; note that the ears are turned back, the neck and back hairs are raised, and the infra-orbital scent gland (below the eye) is open. Penned animals will attack humans at this time. Also note the dried "velvet" hanging from the now-hardened antlers. William Graf.

than average trophy, while bucks with lengths of more than 30-inch beams, and spreads of more than 24 inches, are in the record class.

The dental formulae (see Appendix C) of most deer, like those of sheep, goats, and cattle, characteristically lack the upper canine series. The axis deer, on the other hand, has a pair of small, tear-shaped teeth in the upper jaw, just above the outer pair of incisors. These are usually shed before the animal reaches one year of age, but can sometimes be found in the cartilage of the upper jaw of adults. They appear to be totally nonfunctional.

REPRODUCTION

The breeding and fawning seasons of axis deer are not nearly as clear cut as those of mainland deer, and some breeding and fawning occurs every month of the year. A peak breeding period apparently coincides with the period when a majority of bucks have matured antlers, from April through August. The gestation period of one captive doe is known to be 229 days. Examination of field records indicates that slightly more than 60 percent of fawns observed were born during the five-month period from November through March, while the remainder were born sometime during the other seven months.

Bucks appear to be capable of breeding at any time of the year, even though they may not outwardly exhibit rutting characteristics. Velvet-antlered bucks and bucks that had recently shed their antlers were seen in the field, attempting to breed does; specimens were then shot, and their reproductive tract examined microscopically. In all cases, active and mature sperm were abundant, indicating that they could impregnate a receptive doe at any time.

Most axis deer reach sexual maturity in their first year. Spike bucks have frequently been seen pursuing does, but they are usually chased away by larger bucks. A ten-month-old pet buck showed signs of sexual excitement and maturity. Numerous yearling does have been observed with fawns, and several pregnant ones have been collected. One doe, estimated to be eight to ten months of age, was pregnant, and another of the same apparent age had a ripe follicle in the ovary, indicating that it would probably have become pregnant if bred.

Does normally give birth to a single fawn. Only two possible observations have been made of does with twins in the field, and only one definite record of a zoo deer bearing twins has been made. Where forage is good, indications are that does average one fawn every 12 months. Of 31 does examined, 29 exhibited either some stage of pregnancy or were lactating, indicating a pregnancy rate of 94 percent.

For a detailed discussion of breeding and rutting behavior (which becomes quite complicated), the reader is referred to Graf and Nichols' 1967 article.

BEHAVIOR

Axis deer have very acute senses and are unusually alert. They are able to hear and smell an intruder at considerable distances, but sounds do not seem to frighten them as much as scent. Their vision is keen.

When badly frightened, axis deer usually break into flight, which frequently takes the form of "blind panic." Older bucks appear to have a more stable disposition and are less prone to panic when frightened. When in this state of excitement, does and fawns are apt to run blindly into obstacles or over cliffs.

On Molokai, the deer are fairly gregarious, and are often found in groups of 10 to 20 or more animals. The Lanai deer are rarely seen in herds, being most often encountered in small groups of three to six, with single animals or pairs being common.

The axis deer is one of the most vocal of deer and is commonly referred to as the "barking deer." At least four different calls are heard frequently, and have been roughly interpreted. The most common call is the high-pitched "bark" of curiosity or mild alarm. A group of deer who sense something out of the ordinary, but not particularly frightening, will often bark back and forth for several minutes, while at the same time intently watching their surroundings. This bark is a high-pitched "yowp!" Another call is similar, but lower in pitch. It is apparently an expression of fear and surprise; it is usually emitted only once, by the first deer in the group to recognize danger. Immediately following this yelp the group will flee in panic, even though it seems that all members may not have recognized the source of the danger. Male deer, when in the rut, occasionally emit a low-pitched groaning roar, or "howl," which is entirely unlike any normal vocal expressions. Fawns call with a variety of "mewing" sounds, but does have not been heard to answer.

The axis deer is a fleet and graceful animal; its common gaits are the walk, trot, and run. While feeding or moving cross-country, they normally walk, with occasional spurts of trotting. Their normal running gait is a limber, low, stretched-out run. This is not the bouncing run of a mule deer, but is more like that of a greyhound. They have been clocked at 50 miles per hour over open ground, for short distances, and will, when hard pressed, drive smoothly between the strands of a cattle fence without slowing. They do not appear to be accustomed to jumping and almost invariably crawl through or under fences. I once watched a large buck try to climb a woven-wire fence when he could not find any way under it, and he got hung up on the top until I approached to within five feet, when his panic put him over. Despite their speed, they cannot maintain the pace for very long and their dash rapidly slows to a tired gallop, then to a trot, and then they quickly seek thickets in which to hide and rest.

These deer show a high degree of mobility in their feeding behavior and are constantly on the move. They are of a nervous temperament, which increases noticeably the farther they are from cover. It is very rare to find a deer more than 100 yards from some sort of cover during the daylight hours.

An hour or two before sundown, deer begin emerging from the heavy cover where they have spent the day, appearing hesitant at first, but becoming bolder and more confident as darkness approaches. Feeding is carried on mostly during the late evening, night, and early morning hours. As daylight approaches, they move back toward trees and dense vegetation, and by two hours after sunrise they are seldom found in the open. During the day they stay in these more densely vegetated areas, resting and occasionally browsing. Preferred resting sites are under *kiawe* trees on the rims, sides, and bottoms of gulches, or in dense brush and forest on the ridgetops. In general, they move and feed up the slopes during the evenings and night, and reverse direction, moving downhill, again at dawn.

When traveling to and from feeding, resting, or watering areas, the deer usually follow well-used trails which form a network within and just above the *kiawe* forests. While actually feeding they wander randomly over the slopes, but if frightened they try to follow trails, and will nearly always run in an upwind direction.

Weather affects their daily movements to some extent. During and after rains they keep to cover and do not feed in the open as much as they do on clear days, and when winds are strong they tend to stay away from open and exposed ridges. On foggy or overcast days, deer usually feed later into the morning, and begin feeding again earlier in the evening.

DISTRIBUTION AND HABITAT

As noted earlier, deer have been introduced to the islands of Molokai, Lanai, Oahu, and Maui. With the exception of the deer that inhabit the rain forest on the eastern end of Molokai, we can say that these animals generally occupy a similar habitat on each of the islands. This area coincides nicely with the A and C vegetation zones that were described by Ripperton and Hosaka (1942), with some overlapping into the B zone occurring. Zone A is more commonly called the *kiawe* zone and zone C the guava zone; these names do much to describe the more conspicuous elements of the vegetative pattern. The *kiawe* zone can be summarily characterized as occurring from sea level to about 500 feet on lee sides or low windward lands, with a mean annual temperature of 75 degrees, but occasionally exceeding 90 degrees, a rainfall of 20 inches or less, and with ground cover sparse and semidesertlike. Annual grasses and herbs are scarce except after infrequent rains. The guava zone reaches from sea level to about 2,500 feet, has a mean annual temperature of about 70 degrees, and averages 40 to 60 inches of rain which originates with the northeast tradewinds. This zone was originally forested, has good soil, and both temperate and tropical plant species are adapted to growing here. The vegetation of zone B is similar to that of the *kiawe* (A) zone, but plants are more numerous and vigorous due to a rainfall averaging 20 to 40 inches.

An examination of the deer distribution maps show that, on Lanai, deer totally circumvent the island; the only areas not occupied are the pineapple fields and the small remaining rain forest. The lowland areas of the northern section of this island contain the heaviest concentration of deer.

On Molokai, the deer population is stretched across the entire 37-mile leeward coast, from Laau Point to the headlands of Halawa Valley. They apparently survive in the rain forest above Halawa only as a relic from times past, when cattle grazing had created an open parkland forest. Graf (1959) found that the deer in this area did not enter unbroken rain forest, but were highly partial to the glades and meadows found along the ridges. As these areas are becoming smaller, from infringement by reseeding trees and ferns, the deer population appears to be diminishing. The major population of Molokai deer is on the

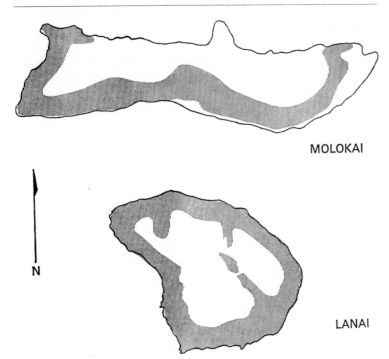

MOLOKAI

N

LANAI

Fig. 2. Distribution of axis deer

extreme western third of the island; in this area they are also found along the dry windward coast.

There have been no follow-up studies of the deer released on Maui, but the animals that are there are known to be keeping to these same two vegetative zones. The remnants of the Oahu herd are, as mentioned earlier, confined to a tiny area which is comprised of typically A-zone vegetation.

FOOD HABITS

The stomachs of 48 deer have been analyzed for food contents. Of these, 14 samples were from deer taken at various locations within the low, dryland habitat (zone A) of Lanai. An additional six deer were collected from the upper habitat (the lower portion of zone C) along the lower fringes of the eucalyptus-*ohi'a*-fern forest which covers the higher ranges of Lanai.

On Molokai, samples were obtained from 23 deer from the zone A habitat, and five samples from the wet forest habitat (upper zone C) on the island's east end.

Deer were collected during all seasons (with the exception of the Molokai east-end deer, which were taken only during the summer), but since there were insufficient samples from each season to analyze seasonal preference, the information represents a gross, year-long diet.

Analysis shows that both browse and grass are taken regularly and that *kiawe* and *klu* are two of the most important food items on the lower Lanai habitat (62.7 percent of volume), with *kiawe* and lantana being the primary foods on the lower areas of Molokai (51.3 percent of volume). Both the leaves and the seed pods (or "beans") of the *kiawe* and *klu* are eaten in quantity, as are the pods and leaves of the *koa haole,* a lesser food. The beans of all three species are taken in either the green or the dry state.

In the upper, wet forest habitat on Lanai, the most important foods are guinea grass, *'ūlei, pukeawe,* molasses grass, and *koa haole;* these five species contributed 78.7 percent of the total volume of food consumed. In the upper areas of Molokai, *Drymaria* and *hilo* grass made up 84.8 percent of the animals' diets. Although the 10 plant species listed above account for almost 70 percent of the total volume eaten, another 46 species of plants are known to have been consumed. A checklist of all species is presented in Table 9.

For a more detailed account, and breakdown of plant species consumed, the reader is referred to Swedberg's paper.

Water, either fresh or brackish, is a necessity for axis deer; in dryer parts of both islands the major populations of deer concentrate around available water holes during the summer. During the winter and early spring the deer find natural water

Table 9. Common and scientific names of plants eaten by deer
on Lanai and Molokai

COMMON NAME	SCIENTIFIC NAME
Ageratum	*Ageratum conyzoides*
apple of Sodom	*Solanum sodomeum*
Australian saltbush	*Atriplex semibaccata*
Bermuda grass	*Cynodon dactylon*
buffel grass	*Pennisetum ciliare*
Chinese violet	*Centella asiatica*
cocklebur	*Xanthium strumarium*
Cyperus	*Cyperus polystachyus*
Drymaria	*Drymaria cordata*
dwarf koa	*Desmanthus virgatus*
ena ena	*Gnaphalium luteo-album*
eucalyptus	*Eucalyptus spp.*
Euphorbia	*Euphorbia lorifolia*
feather-finger grass	*Chloris virgata*
Galinsoga	*Galinsoga parviflora*
golden crown beard	*Verbesina encelioides*
gosmore	*Hypochaeris radicata*
gouldia	*Gouldia spp.*
guava	*Psidium guajava*
guinea grass	*Panicum maximum*
hilo grass	*Paspalum conjugatum*
ilima	*Sida fallax*
Indigo	*Indigofera suffruticosa*
Jamaica vervain	*Stachytarpheta jamaicensis*
Japanese tea	*Cassia leschenaultiana*
kakonakona	*Panicum torridum*
kamote	*Jussiaea suffruticosa*
kiawe	*Prosopis chilensis*
klu	*Acacia farnesiana*
koa haole	*Leucaena glauca*
kukaipuaa	*Digitaria sanguinalis*
lama	*Diospyros sandwicensis*
lantana	*Lantana camara*
miki palaoa	*Cassia occidentalis*
molasses grass	*Melinus minutiflora*
morning-glory	*Ipomoea pentaphylla*
natal redtop	*Rhynchelytrum repens*
olopua	*Osmanthus sandwicensis*
pamakani	*Eupatorium adenophorum*
Panicum	*Panicum spp.*
pigweed	*Portulaca oleracea*
pili grass	*Heteropogon contortus*
popolo	*Solanum nodiflorum*
pualele	*Sonchus oleraceus*
pukeawe	*Styphelia tameiameiae*
sandalwood	*Santalum ellipticum*
sandbur	*Cenchrus echinatus*
sedge	*Fimbristylis diphylla*

(cont.)

(Common Name)	(Scientific Name)
slender amaranth	*Amaranthus gracilis*
smooth cat's ear	*Hypochaeris glabra*
Spanish needle	*Bidens pilosa*
uhaloa	*Waltheria indica var. americana*
'ūlei	*Osteomeles anthyllidifolia*
wild zinnia	*Zinnia pauciflora*
wild pea-bean	*Phaseolus lathyroides*
wiliwili	*Erythrina monosperma*

holes in the rocky bottoms of gullies, and this factor, combined with a greater abundance of sprouting forbs and green grass, allows the animals to move farther afield during these seasons. On the north shore of Lanai the deer are often forced to seek ground water seepages at the edges of the beach; it has been noted that on the south and west sides of Lanai, where water is available from pipeline units, that deer can be commonly found at higher elevations.

Little is known of the mineral requirements of axis deer on either Lanai or Molokai. It seems that sufficient minerals are supplied by vegetation consumed to maintain the animals in good condition. As an experiment, salt blocks were provided in the Lanai deer habitat, but these were completely ignored.

PARASITES

Deer have been collected from all habitat areas and have been carefully examined both in the field and in the laboratory for the presence of parasites. The only ectoparasite found has been a biting louse (*Bovicola sp.*), which is commonly found on the wild goats of Lanai.

A trichostrongylid worm, *Cooperia punctata,* which usually occurs in the small intestine, was the only internal parasite found during the course of study. Only two or three deer were found with light infestations, but this nematode is common in Hawaiian cattle and sheep. Liver flukes have been reported from deer living in the rain forest on Molokai's east end, but none were found during the life history study.

LITERATURE CITED

Anonymous
1954 Partridges join game reserve. Honolulu Advertiser, Dec. 27.

Dover, C.
1932 The duration of life of some Indian mammals. Bombay Nat. Hist. Soc., J. 36: 244–250.

Graf, W.
1959 The Axis deer *(Cervus axis)* in the rainzone of Molokai Island. Amer. Philos. Soc., Yearbook: 236–238.

Graf, W. and L. Nichols, Jr.
1967 The Axis deer in Hawaii. Bombay Nat. Hist. Soc., J. 63(3): 629–734.

Lennox, C. G.
1950 Factors considered by Board of Commissioners of Agriculture and Forestry in approving Project to introduce deer to Hawaii. Terr. Bd. of Agri. and Forestry, Honolulu: 7pp., mimeo.

Ripperton, J. C., and E. Y. Hosaka
1942 Vegetation zones of Hawaii. Hawaiian Agri. Exp. Sta., Bull. 89: 58pp.

Swedberg, G. (Edit.)
1968 The Axis deer *(Axis axis)*: Its history and management in Hawaii. Hawaii State Div. of Fish and Game, Honolulu: 66pp. (In Press).

Tinker, S. W.
1941 Animals of Hawaii. Tongg Publ. Co., Honolulu: 190pp. (Second Edition).

The Columbian Black-tailed Deer

Odocoileus hemionus columbianus

The black-tailed deer in Hawaii belong to a race of the mule deer, *Odocoileus hemionus columbianus,* according to Cowan's revision (1936). Prior to that revision, many zoologists separated the races of this species into two: the mule deer of the interior range (*Odocoileus hemionus*), and the black-tailed deer (*Odocoileus columbianus*). Where these two animals came together, or overlapped in range, offspring were often called hybrids. Since Cowan's study, it is now generally accepted that the blacktail is merely a racial variety of the mule deer; in this book I shall continue to use the vernacular name "blacktail," for it is by this name that the Kauai animals are most commonly known.

HISTORY

The black-tailed deer was introduced onto the island of Kauai on June 11, 1961, by the Hawaii Division of Fish and Game.*

* According to Clark (1939), Capt. Alexander Adams brought two deer (believed *Odocoileus*) from North America about 1816, but both were killed for food to restore the health of Billy Pitt, former adviser to Kamehameha I.

226

The primary purpose of the introduction was—and still is—
the hope that, by providing a sporting and aesthetically pleasing
"big-game" species, the hunting public would eventually come
to prefer this type of animal to the forest-damaging feral goat,
which could then be eliminated from many, if not all areas of
present establishment, without arousing the ire and subsequent
political pressure that would occur if no substitute species were
provided.

Mr. John McKean, chief of game operations of the Oregon
Department of Fish and Game, agreed to supply Hawaii with
the initial breeding stock. Each year, well-meaning Oregonians
turn in a number of fawns that are seemingly "abandoned";
these fawns were kept and raised by an Oregon staff member in
a pen just north of Corvallis, Oregon. After being weaned, the
animals were fed on a diet of dry alfalfa and Fishers Calf Ration.

Prior to shipping the animals, the Department of Veterinary
Medicine of Oregon State University conducted tests on the
young animals to assure that they had no disease. Blood samples
were drawn for leptospirosis, brucellosis, and anaplasmosis testing. All samples proved negative. Just before shipping all deer
were dusted for external parasites with a 4 percent Malathion
dust, drenched with purified fine-particle phenothiazine to
eliminate internal parasites, and given a subcutaneous injection
of 1 cc. of Dictycide to eliminate the possibility of lungworm
infection.

The first shipment of five young bucks and five young does
arrived in Honolulu on June 10, 1961; they were trucked out
to Barbers Point Naval Air Station and flown the next day to
Kauai, courtesy of the U.S. Navy. They were then trucked from
Bonham Air Base to the release pen, situated next to Trail No.
4, Polihale Ridge, in the Puu Ka Pele Game Management Area
and Forest Reserve. This pen was situated about two miles west
of the Waimea-Kokee Road, on the western slope of the island
at an elevation of just over 2,000 feet.

The deer were kept in this "gentle release" pen for nine days, during which time a Division of Fish and Game staff member camped next to them, made observations on their food choices and general health, and saw to it that they were amply supplied with Fishers Calf Ration, and dry and green alfalfa. This was done to prevent digestive troubles which might have occurred if the animals had been subjected to a sudden change in food; the vegetation was, needless to say, completely different from any that these animals may have found in their Oregon pen. Only one temporary case of diarrhea occurred. By the ninth day the animals concentrated on eating the natural forage and lost interest in the commercial feed. When the pen walls were dropped on two ends (to prevent feral dogs from trapping them in a corner), the animals browsed around the area of the pen before making short, exploratory trips down both sides of Polihale Ridge. Four animals returned that night and slept in the opened pen.

The same procedures of acquisition, testing, and shipment were followed the next year, and on June 4, 1962, two bucks and eight does were landed at Bonham Air Base, once again through the kind auspices of the U.S. Navy. They were placed in the same holding pen and held there until June 12, when they were released.

In November 1965, five more does were procured and released, and in April 1966, thirteen does and two bucks were released in the same area. This last shipment brought the total number introduced to nine males and thirty-one females. In this same five-year period two bucks and one doe were known to have been killed; one after being struck by a car on the Kokee Highway, and the other two by poachers.

By June 1965, there were an estimated 100 black-tailed deer on Kauai (Swedberg, 1965). In June 1966, there were an estimated 120 to 160 animals, and it was believed that this number remained almost constant throughout the next year (Swedberg, 1966 and 1967a). The apparent lack of increase is believed due to heavy poaching activity; there are innumerable third-hand reports of families dining on local venison. As of 1968, no hunting season has been declared.

DESCRIPTION

The black-tailed deer varies considerably in weight and antler conformation throughout its mainland range. Since no hunting season has yet been held, there is practically no data available on the average configuration of the Kauai deer, but there is presently little doubt that the island animal closely resembles its Oregonian brethren. In time, it is entirely possible that these animals will exhibit heavier weights, better antlers, a higher percentage of twinning and fawn survival, and an extended breeding and fawning season. This would of course be due to the more equitable climate (severe, unseasonal cold and unusually harsh winters create great, usually detrimental, variations in the above-listed characters), the possibly higher nutritive value of the varied Hawaiian vegetation, and the maintenance of smaller herds (less deer per acre) by carefully managed hunting. In lieu of Hawaiian data, the typical Northwest Pacific Coast deer will be described.

SIZE AND WEIGHT. Adult deer stand from about two and one-half to three feet high at the shoulder and only the males bear antlers. The spotted fawns range from 21 to 26 inches high at the shoulder. The average fawn weighs from six and one-half to seven pounds at birth and gains an average of 0.44 pounds per day during the first two or three weeks of life (Brown, 1961). At the age of six months, the females average from 50 to 55 pounds, and the males average about 10 pounds more. Brown (*ibid.*) states that bucks tend to increase in weight throughout life, but does reach maximum weight in about three or four years, then hold their own for several years or start to decline in weight. Does in Washington run between 103 and 146 pounds, with an average of 124 pounds at their prime; bucks range from 130 to 190 pounds at this same age, and after five or six years may scale over 200 pounds.

TAIL. The tail, from which the black-tailed deer gets its name, is from six to ten inches long from its base to the tips of the hairs at its end, and may be from three to five inches wide, with the buck's tail slimmer than either the fawn or the doe tail. The outer (dorsal) surface varies from black to several shades of brown; generally the black is relegated to the distal half, with the brown of the basal part growing paler toward the outer margins. The under (ventral) side of the tail is white and this color sometimes extends completely around the tail near the base. There is a white rump patch, which appears almost as an extension of the white belly pelage, and in many animals this circular patch sets off the blacktail to good advantage; in other animals this lighter area is almost hidden by the tail hairs.

PELAGE. When the spotted fawn first sheds his coat (usually in September or October) he assumes the winter pelage of gray. The yearling male may then show blackish markings on the face which the young female does not have. Other than this character, both sexes retain this gray dorsal and side color, but show a white belly region and a light patch under the throat. The summer coat begins its first appearance about the first of May, but complete shedding may not take place until the end of June or early part of July. This summer coat is a glossy reddish brown, but the white belly does not change color. Replacement of the summer coat begins in August or September.

EARS. The ears of the black-tailed deer are large in comparison to its head and body, with each ear being seven to eight inches long. They are often but not always tipped and edged with white. Being highly maneuverable, they convey various moods and potential activities of the deer. When alerted or alarmed the ears are raised high and cupped forward; when merely seeking a questionable sound from the rear or side, the animal may only move the ear on that side until it is pointing at the sound source. If then unsure, the whole head is turned and both ears focus sharply in the questioned direction. In attitudes of aggressiveness or defense the ears are placed in a drooped position, often below the horizontal. It has been noted that the animal with the ears lowered the most is ordinarily most successful in dominating the others; "it is as if the degree of ear lowering were an index to self-confidence" (Linsdale and Tomich, 1953). The ear-flicking habits of the deer are often the only thing that gives their presence away. An animal bedded down under the deep shade of a tree on a bright afternoon is usually impossible to see, but the author has found that, by sitting quietly on a vantage point and gazing broadly at the terrain, rather than attempting to focus sharply on shapes in the bush, the flicking of the ears of resting deer soon becomes apparent although the animals' bodies cannot be seen.

ANTLERS. Black-tailed bucks produce dichotomously branched antlers; that is, they branch into two, and these two prongs may then branch again. Unlike the mature, healthy axis deer, which characteristically produces three-tined antlers, the epitome of blacktail perfection is an equally matching four-point system, although it is not uncommon to find animals with two, three, five, six, or even more points.

Brown (*op. cit.*) has traced initial antler development in simple terms; "male fawns show changes in their skull structure . . . very early in life. By the time the fawn is two to three months old, the knobs on the skull from which the future antlers will grow, can be felt. At six months, these knobs may be as much as $1\frac{1}{2}$ inches in length and project upward from the skull enough to be plainly visible at close range. However, these are not actually antlers, but are the pedicels from which the antlers will grow. During this first year of life, they do not break the skin.

"When the fawn is about ten months old, the first true antler starts to develop. This first antler may be anything from a small nubbin, less than one inch in length, to a branched antler seven or eight inches long. Normally a yearling buck will have spikes three to six inches in length.

"In its second year a buck may again have spikes, but ordinarily this age group produces a forked, or two-point, antler. Both two-point and three-point antlers are common in the three-year-old group. A few three-year-olds may produce small four-point antlers. Also, the antlers of deer in this age group generally have a small brow tine. Three-point antlers seem to be the most common for deer in the four-year age class, but both two-point and four-point antlers are well represented."

Obviously, the number of points on the antlers cannot be used to accurately distinguish age. The configuration is, instead, a result of genetic inheritance combined with environmental and mechanical factors, such as abundance of food supply and minerals, and possibility of bumping or bruising of the velvet antlers, or injury to the gonads.

In Hawaii, antler growth begins about the first of April and continues, in the velvet stage, until about the first of August, when the bucks begin to strip the velvet from their antlers. Wislocki (1943) did an extensive study on the structure and growth of antlers in the white-tailed deer (*O. virginianus*) and explained that "antler growth is primarily initiated and controlled by the hypophysis, although the subsequent internal reconstruction and hardening of the antlers, as well as their ultimate shedding, are regulated by the testes, either alone or in conjunction with the pituitary." Obviously, the physiological transformations that occur under the velvet skin of the developing antlers are detailed and involved. For that reason we shall not go into details of growth in this chapter. Suffice it to say that the velvet skin covering the growth is highly specialized; it is covered with short (3–4.5mm.) buff-colored hair and has an extensive network of blood vessels feeding it. The bucks are very careful about not damaging their antlers when in velvet, but when injury does occur there is considerable bleeding, probable pain to the animal, and occasional malformation of the antler at the point of injury. In August—about one month later than in the mainland—the swelling at the tip of the antler recedes, the velvet shrinks tightly against the now-hard antler, and the blood vessels of the velvet cease functioning. Removing the velvet is a rapid process, seldom taking more than a few hours, although dried skin in deep grooves near the base may hang on loosely for several days, and rubbing of the antlers to polish them may continue for weeks.

Shortly after the end of the breeding season the bucks begin to cast their antlers. In Hawaii this action takes place during January, February, March, and occasionally April. When the antlers finally drop—and they often fall off within minutes of each other—there is usually some slight bleeding from the depression at the tip of the bony pedicel, but this is minor and scabs soon form. When freshly cast off, antlers have a paperlike translucent ring at the lower edge of the burr, where the base separates from the epidermis, but exposure to weather soon causes the disintegration of this substance.

Deer, rodents, and birds chew or peck on the fallen antlers (probably for the mineral content) and a study by Linsdale and Tomich (*op. cit.*) in California showed that of 203 partially destroyed antlers, deer were responsible for 188 of the gnawings. Separation of the animals causing the damage is easy; birds peck at the cortex at the base, rodents gnaw indiscriminately, and deer grasp the tips of a tine and rasp the opposite surfaces so that they appear flattened or constricted.

REPRODUCTION

Black-tailed deer are capable of breeding as yearlings, but it is believed the majority of animals, bucks in particular, do not breed until they are just over two years old. There is considerable literature to prove that females six to seven months of age have bred, but it would appear that good range conditions are a must, if this is to happen. I know of no specific information on the time of sexual maturity in males and Brown (*op. cit.*) mentioned that male fawns under observation displayed no interest in breeding-season activities. Yearling males exhibit considerable interest in does during the breeding season and are probably capable of breeding a doe, if they can steal one away from the older, more aggressive, and ever watchful bucks.

It would appear that both sexes reach their peak of productivity in the ages from three and one-half to six and one-half years, and then begin a gradual decline. Unless the nutritive values of the Hawaiian vegetation are considerably lower than those of mainland plant species—a facet not yet explored—we might expect the Kauai does to produce a larger number of twins, but this possibility remains to be proven.

The gestation period varies somewhat according to the general health of the doe, and the severity of the preceding winter months, but may be assumed to be somewhere in the neighborhood of 200 to 210 days. The animals in Brown's study varied from 199 to 207 (*ibid.*) and ten observations by Cowan (1956) ranged from 183 to 212 days.

Blacktails are known to have been kept in captivity at least 16 years (Cowan, *ibid.*) but it is extremely unusual for a wild animal to live longer than 10 years. Those who survive the hunting seasons and do not succumb to predation, parasites or disease, eventually die of starvation when their teeth wear down.

HABITAT AND DISTRIBUTION

The site chosen for the deer release was in the Puu Ka Pele Game Management Area and Forest Reserve, comprising some 9,000 acres of land on the far western slopes of Kauai. It is split, from west to east, by seven nearly parallel valleys that begin just above sea level and slope upward until reaching the road from Kekaha to Kokee. Almost immediately east of the road is the steep-walled Waimea Canyon which, in its central reaches, is almost 3,000 feet deep. Due north of the Puu Ka Pele plateau are chasmic valleys, such as Honopu and Kalalau, which drop abruptly to the sea. To the south of Puu Ka Pele is another Game Management Area, Kekaha, which encompasses another 5,000 acres of land, most of which drops gently from about the 1,700-foot elevation to the sugar-cane fields that begin about three miles north of the town of Kekaha. This area is dissected with many deeply eroded gulches, which terminate at a low cliff adjacent to the cane fields.

Swedberg (1967b) describes the area: "Except for the cliff region, the Puu Ka Pele area is covered by thick vegetation made up partly of native Hawaiian forest, mainly koa (*Acacia koa*), ohia (*Metrosideros collina*), and kukui (*Aleurites moluccana*). The remaining portion of the forest is made up of exotics such as silk oak (*Grevillea robusta*), and several species of eucalyptus. The understory is also of mixed native and exotic species, the exotics being primarily those which were brought to Kauai for their soil-holding qualities, or those which are escaped ornamental species, such as lantana (*Lantana camara*). The Division of Forestry tree planting program call for clearing 1,175 acres . . . for planting to southern pine species.

"To the north of the Puu Ka Pele area lies a portion of . . . Forest Reserve, which is similar . . . but with steeper cliffs and a greater percentage of native vegetation. To the south . . . the vegetation is primarily exotic, mainly silk oak, with an understory of molasses grass (*Melinus minutiflora*), lantana, and some native shrubs . . . such as aalii (*Dodonaea eriocarpa*) and pukiawe (*Styphelia tameiameiae*)."

Movements of black-tailed deer on their native range have always been rather limited; by moving deer into totally unique and strange environmental situations we might expect one of two things to happen. Deer might either be extremely wary and reluctant to leave the immediate vicinity of the release site, or they might all scatter in short order and wander for miles before settling down into a chosen territory. In Hawaii it appears that the majority of animals took the former course with only a few bolder animals (usually bucks) taking the latter alternative. Within one month of the initial release, a buck and a doe had moved about four miles northwest of the release site to an elevation of approximately 3,600 feet, while the rest of the animals remained within one mile of the release pen. Four months after release, one buck was seen in the Niu Valley area, five miles to the south. This animal remained there in a *koa haole* (*Leucaena glauca*) thicket for at least ten months. In 1964 and 1965 other deer moved to the lowlands of the Kekaha Game Management Area but the bulk of sightings continued to be made within two miles of the release site. As the population increases in this area we can expect to find an ever increasing arc of expansion. The most distant sightings have been in early 1967 when several deer were seen in the bottom of Waimea Canyon, near its mouth, a linear distance of about seven and one-half miles.

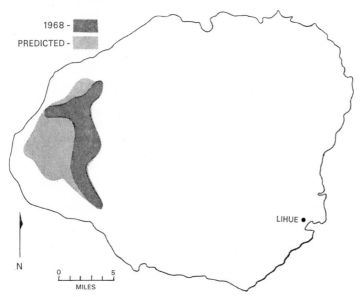

Fig. 3. Distribution of black-tailed deer on Kauai

As of 1968, the 150 to 200 deer present on Kauai apparently live in widely scattered herds over some 21,000 acres of land.

FOOD HABITS

Because of the small size of the population and the fact that no hunting season has yet been held, no quantitative data are available on the food habits of the blacktail. Swedberg (*ibid.*) has compiled the list of plant species noted below, from the stomach contents of four dead deer and from field pen observations.

COMMON NAME	SCIENTIFIC NAME
aalii	*Dodonaea viscosa*
blackberry	*Rubus penetrans*
cotoneaster	*Cotoneaster pannosa*
eucalyptus	*Eucalyptus spp.*
Florida beggarweed	*Desmodium tortuosum*
koa haole	*Leucaena glauca*
koa, Hawaiian	*Acacia koa*
lantana	*Lantana camara*
lilikoi	*Passiflora spp.*
molasses grass	*Melinus minutiflora*
nutgrass	*Cyperus rotundus*
paperbark	*Melaleuca leucadendron*
paspalum	*Paspalum urvillei*
pine (slash & loblolly)	*Pinus elliotti & taeda*
plum	*Prunus spp.*
poha	*Physalis peruviana*
pukeawe	*Styphelia tameiameiae*
rose	*Rosa spp.*
sensitive plant	*Mimosa pudica*
silk "oak"	*Grevillea robusta*
spanish needle	*Bidens pilosa*
strawberry guava	*Psidium cattleianum*
ti	*Cordyline terminalis*
yellow foxtail	*Setaria geniculata*

In 1963, 1964, and 1965, several reports were made of deer

damaging either seedling pines (*Pinus elliotti*), shoots of young fruit trees, or truck garden vegetables. Investigation of these reports proved that a very few deer had, in fact, caused minor damage as described. Division of Fish and Game personnel issued packets of "deer repellant," consisting of a mixture of two-thirds powered blood and one-third powdered bone meal, to the complainants with instructions to hang small sacks of the compound from the tree limbs and to scatter some on the ground. The repellant apparently worked and no more damage reports came from these areas. Repellants are usually ineffective on wild deer.

PARASITES AND DISEASE

In 1966 a buck shot by poachers was found dying and was autopsied by a local veterinarian. No internal or external parasites were found.

In 1967 a doe which had been attacked by dogs and found dying from shock was autopsied. No external parasites were discovered, but several tapeworms, identified as *Echinococcus granulosus*, were found in the small intestine. Since this parasite requires a member of the dog family as an intermediate host, it was recognized that the doe must have fed on a plant that had been previously defecated on by dogs. Infection of other deer by this parasite would probably be uncommon.

No bacterial or viral diseases have been observed as yet.

LIFE CYCLE (*From Swedberg, 1967b*)

From 1961 to 1967, observations on the Kauai black-tailed deer indicate that, while the majority of animals follow the normal (mainland) seasonal cycle shown below, individual animals—such as several bucks with hard antlers seen attempting to court does as late as March 7—have responded to Hawaii's more temperate climate.

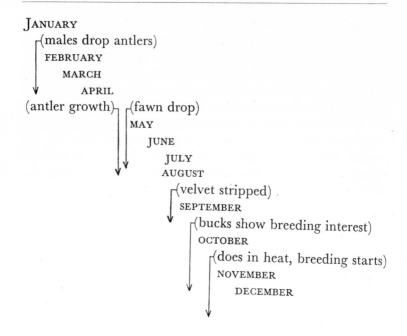

JANUARY
(males drop antlers)
FEBRUARY
MARCH
APRIL
(antler growth) (fawn drop)
MAY
JUNE
JULY
AUGUST
(velvet stripped)
SEPTEMBER
(bucks show breeding interest)
OCTOBER
(does in heat, breeding starts)
NOVEMBER
DECEMBER

THE FUTURE

To date the blacktail population has expanded to include almost exactly the range initially predicted. It is a certainty that population numbers will continue to increase throughout these 21,000 acres, and it is also a certainty that a number of animals will wander farther afield than they have to date. It is the author's very strong contention that any animal that strays outside the Game Management Area should be considered fair game the year round, and should be vigorously hunted. Although it is doubtful that very many animals will ever wander into the high native forest, I do not believe we want even one animal in the Alakai forest and "swamp" region; this area is too precious in its present form (as a preserve for rare and unique birds and flora) to tolerate the presence of any more herbivores.

If the projected dam, to be located between Kokee State Park and the Alakai Swamp, is completed, and water supplies are furnished to the Hawaiian Homes Commission lands of Kekaha, it is very likely that vast acreages of croplands will spring up in the center of the present blacktail population. When this occurs it is certain that damage complaints will be made and that the deer population will be drastically reduced, perhaps to the point of extinction.

LITERATURE CITED

Brown, E. R.
1961   The black-tailed deer of western Washington. Wash. State Game Dept. Biol. Bull. 13: 124pp.

Clark, B.
1939   Telling the Kamaaina. Hono. Star Bull., April 13.

Cowan, I. McT.
1936   Distribution and variation in deer (genus *Odocoileus*) of the Pacific coastal region of North America. Calif. Fish and Game, Vol. 22(3): 255–246.

1956   The Deer of North America. Edited by W. P. Taylor. The Stackpole Co., Harrisburg, Pa.: 668pp.

Linsdale, J. M., and P. Q. Tomich
1953   A herd of mule deer. U. Calif. Press, Berkeley and Los Angeles: 567pp.

Swedberg, G.
1965   Introduction of exotic game mammals. Portion: Black-tailed deer—Kauai. W-5-R-16, Job 54(16), State of Hawaii Div. of Fish and Game, Honolulu: 3pp., mimeo.

1966   Introduction of exotic game mammals. Portion: Ecology of the blacktail deer—Kauai. W-5-R-17, Job 54(17), State of Hawaii, Div. of Fish and Game, Honolulu: 5pp., mimeo.

1967a Introduction of exotic game mammals. Portion: Ecology of the blacktail deer—Kauai. W-5-R-18, Job 54(18), State of Hawaii, Div. of Fish and Game, Honolulu: 4pp., mimeo.

1967b The blacktail deer introduction to Kauai. State of Hawaii, Div. of Fish and Game, Honolulu: 9pp., mimeo.

Wislocki, G. B.
1943 Studies on growth of deer antlers. II. Seasonal changes in the male reproductive tract of the Virginia deer (*Odocoileus virginianus borealis*) with a discussion of the factors controlling the antler-gonad periodicity. Essays in Biology in Honor of Herbert M. Evans (Berkeley, U. Calif. Press): pp. 631–653.

The American Pronghorn

Antilocapra americana americana

On November 30, 1959, 56 pronghorn "antelope" were trapped by the Montana Department of Fish and Game. These animals were destined to become the first wild population of pronghorns established outside the continental limits of North America. On December 10, 1959, they were landed on the Lanai, where their offspring survive somewhat uncertainly today.

Except for the history of the introduction and a smattering of information gleaned from the first hunting season for this species, most of the information in this chapter is drawn from Arthur Einarsen's classic book *The Pronghorn Antelope and Its Management,* written in 1948. This book is a truly monumental and definitive study of the life history of a single species, and it would be presumptuous of the present author to do more than abstract and rearrange small portions of Einarsen's work to fit the Hawaiian situation. Any opinions given about the Hawaiian animals are my own and should not reflect on Einarsen's study.

DESCRIPTION

The pronghorn, or American "antelope," was first assigned this erroneous latter name by early explorers of North America who

HAWAIIAN LAND MAMMALS

were familiar with the external appearance of either the African or Indian species. Our pronghorn is not a true antelope, all of which belong to the family Bovidae, but is instead the sole living representative of the family Antilocapridae. This family was apparently native solely to North America with fossils representing long extinct relatives of the pronghorn having been found in geological formations dating back some 20,000,000 years. According to Bailey (1931) there are four distinct subspecies: *Antilocapra americana americana* (the Hawaiian introduction), the Oregon pronghorn *A. americana oregona,* the Mexican pronghorn *A. americana mexicana,* and the pronghorn of Lower California *A. americana peninsularis.* These other "antelope" are differentiated from the type species primarily by coloration of the hide or slight differences in horn, skull, or tooth structure.

Like its namesake, the pronghorn "antelope" is cloven hooved, has a multichambered stomach, and is a cud chewer, but unlike the true antelope, or any other member of the hollow-horned bovids, the horns (borne by both sexes) are flattened, have one prong, and are shed each year. The adult measures about four and one-half feet from nose to tail tip and stands about three feet at the shoulder. The adult Oregonian male averages about 114 pounds with the female running smaller at 92 pounds. Twenty-five animals weighed during Hawaii's first hunting season showed our bucks to average slightly less, at 108 pounds, and does slightly more, at 95 pounds (Medeiros, 1967). Perhaps of future significance is the fact that the maximum recorded weight of a female in Oregon was 105 pounds, whereas one of five females taken on Lanai seven years after introduction was 120 pounds.

The pelage, or coat, is similar in both sexes with the upper parts and upper sides of the animal being buff colored; the belly, lower sides, inside of the limbs, upper chest, sides of the face, lips and chin are cream white. There is a rump patch of white which can be spread at will into a sparkling white rosette or relaxed to become inconspicuous.

A pair of musk glands are located near the base of the rosette, but the exact function of these glands is not yet understood. They occasionally show up on individual animals as a yellowish, greasy patch just below and to either side of the tail.

The tail is mostly white but a rufous area on top extends forward, partly dividing the white rump patch. There is a short mane on the neck which is rufous colored and tipped with black; the ears are whitish inside but are edged and tipped with black. There are two, easily visible, cresentic bands of white crossing the throat region.

The muzzle in both sexes is black; in adult males this coloration continues up the ridge of the nose, between the eyes, to the base of the horns. Another clearly distinguishable sexual characteristic of males is the black spots located at the angle of the jaw just below the base of the ears.

The young are similar in color to the adults but the white of

Hair on rump patch in normal position. Note dark spots at location of musk glands.

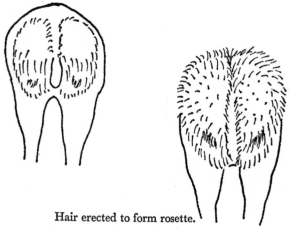

Hair erected to form rosette.

Fig. 4. Rosette pattern of the pronghorn

the sides and the rump are at first obscured; these juveniles also generally appear to be slightly paler in color than the adults.

In North America, the summer coat appears to be darker, with more pronounced markings than the winter coat, but no pelage description has yet been made for the Lanai animals. Walker (pers. comm.) reports that the Lanai animals were molting in the first week of March.

There are two facets of the pronghorns' physical characteristics that are quite unique and fascinating: the hair and the horns. While the pronghorn has a coat of true hair, each hair except on the lower legs, is pithy and contains large air cells. By means of this hollow hair, the animal is very effectively insulated against any extreme of heat or cold. By flexing a thin muscle layer which lies just under the skin, the pronghorn can maintain its coat at a definite angle. To keep cool, the hairs are erected, and any vagrant breeze can pass freely to the skin; as cold weather overtakes them the hair is laid flat, like overlapping shingles, to exclude the cold and retain body heat. Consequently, the underhair which is so thick and fine in other mammals of the colder regions is sparse in our pronghorn and of little significance as a protective measure. These hairs are brittle, continually shed and loosely attached to the hide; hunters who shoot moving animals almost invariably find large areas of fur scraped off as the animals fall. This is one reason for Einarsen's comment (*op. cit.*) that "a skilled hunter will select his prey and stalk it until within shooting range, then kill it with one bullet." The hair on the legs is different from the body hairs in that it is firmly attached to the skin, is shorter, finer, and denser in structure. This is an obvious adaptation for withstanding wear which occurs as the animal moves through the low, often dense vegetation of its range.

The horn core of the pronghorn is a part of the bony structure of the skull and can be likened to a knife, with the external horn (which is really specialized hair) forming the sheath. The new horn sheath forms under the one about to be discarded, and its tip is fastened to the horn core. This bony core, which is apparently fed through the circulatory system, has a tip of plastic-like material which develops rapidly after the former sheath is shed. This tip takes on the symmetry of the finished horn by growing upward, while at the same time becoming covered with a membraneous material which moves down until it comes in contact with the coarse hairs at the base of the core. In this process of downward growth the fine hair mat on the core is covered and this material also becomes a part of the sheath. Although this growth occurs in both sexes, the process generally takes longer in does and young animals, and occurs to a lesser extent. Some females do grow horns comparable to the males, and these make equally unique trophies.

HISTORY IN HAWAII

Lyman Nichols, Jr., was resident wildlife biologist on Lanai in 1959 and was fascinated by the similarity of some 35 square miles of unoccupied, open grass range on Lanai to that of the pronghorn country oᶜ eastern Colorado and Wyoming. He mentioned this to other employees of the Division of Fish and Game, and after consultation with other biologists, state officials, and the management of Dole Corporation (who owns the island), it was decided that the Division of Fish and Game would introduce a trial herd of pronghorns to this "vacant big-game mammal's niche." The Montana Department of Fish and Game offered to supply the basic stock, and on November 30, 1959, captured 56 pronghorns; these animals were carefully checked for disease or parasites; none was found so the herd was shipped by truck to Seattle and then by freighter to Honolulu. They arrived in Honolulu on December 9, with 12 animals lost en route.

The 44 survivors were doused with Malathion to kill any possible ectoparasites and then trucked to Hickam Air Force Base for the night. Four of these animals were given to the

Honolulu Zoo, and the remaining 40 were flown by Air Force plane to Lanai; two more animals died en route. The survivors were released into a small holding pen at the 1,700-foot level of the Mahana section. When they were all grouped into a single herd, the pen walls were dropped and the pronghorns moved out onto the large grassy plateau on the northeast end of the island.

Unfortunately, one major factor in planning for the release had been overlooked; we had forgotten that these Montana pronghorns had never really seen the ocean even though they had just crossed 3,000 miles of it. They were thirsty, and like all members of their far-sighted kind, insatiably curious. They headed for this huge blue "lake" and bypassed all the artificial water units that had been installed for them, never having experienced these either. Sometime during the afternoon and night they found their way through the heavy *kiawe* forest (*Prosopis chilensis*) bounding the coast and ended up on the narrow sand beach between the forest and the sea.

Nichols (1960) documents the subsequent tragedy:

The next day, they were found wandering disconsolately up and down the narrow beach, searching vainly for drinking water, and unable to return to the cooler, open country above because of the solid forest which they refused to enter. A crew of volunteers was immediately rounded up, and the antelope, now suffering from lack of water, were herded up the beach to an open ridge that led to the higher rangeland and water units. During the drive, some of the animals became confused and took to the water, swimming out over the reef towards the open sea; however, the surf turned them, and they returned to the shore with no losses. A few became lost in the trees and did not make it up the ridge with the main herd. Most of these were subsequently chased—or captured and carried—up to the open range of the release area, but at least two died on the beach, probably from the effects of drinking salt water.

The majority regained the release area and found the water units. They remained there for a number of days before commencing to wander. By January 20th, the known number of survivors had been reduced to 18. A number had died from the effects of having their eyeballs punctured by the thorns on the algaroba trees while they were at the beach, and others had wandered from the herd and could not be found. Most of the 18 were suffering from the scours, probably brought on by the severe change in diet, and it is possible that some losses were caused by this.

No more losses were known to have occurred through the remainder of January or in February or March, and the animals all remained in a single herd, where they recovered their health and spirits. In April the herd began to split up and move about; between then and the middle of June three more animals disappeared forever, but of the six adult does who survived the initial release, three gave birth to twins and two to single kids, so by July when the herd re-formed on their original range there were 23 left.

The animals were left much to their own resources in the next six years; the Division of Fish and Game was badly under-staffed and only cursory attempts were made to census and understand the environmental changes these animals were forced to undergo. In these years the herd grew and split up, with small groups rambling off and exploring other areas. As an example of the inadequacy of the observations, in the prehunt-ing season census by helicopter in late July 1966, only 25 males (and 71 females) were found, but 27 bucks were killed just one month later.

As of 1968, the pronghorn population is believed to be in the neighborhood of 150 animals.

DISTRIBUTION AND ABUNDANCE

For some unknown reason, the pronghorns of Lanai have broken up into several smaller herds. Since June 1960, when the entire herd had once more concentrated in the Mahana section in the 1,600- to 1,700-foot altitudinal level, the animals have ranged all the way down to the 700-foot level, just above the *kiawe* trees, and have wandered beyond the originally predicted range. This is unusual since they had to traverse several thick windbreaks and steep gulches, obstacles ordinarily not attempted by the mainland pronghorn. The reasons for such variations are presently unknown, but deserve careful study if the herd is to persist and increase in future years. Several possible reasons come to mind. One, which has been demonstrated in cattle populations on other islands, is a lack of available phosphorus on the supposedly preferred range. According to the nature of the deep lateritic soils, the phosphates may be so tightly bound that the plant community cannot make use of

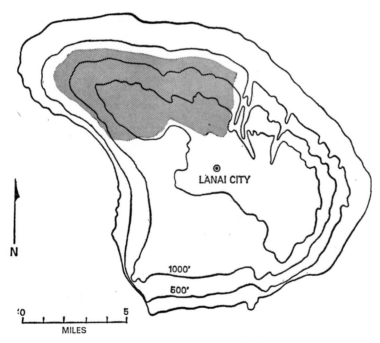

Fig. 5. Distribution of pronghorn on Lanai (1968)

them; in consequence, the range animals suffer. If there is a lack of calcium phosphate or phosphoric acid in the animal's diet a condition known as aphosphorose occurs and is shown by symptoms like perversion of the appetite, abnormality in gait, sexual apathy, disturbance of the oestrus cycle, and easily broken bones. Seven of the 33 animals taken during the first season had brittle bones (in fact, the hunters reported that the bones broke in their hands while they were dragging the animals back to their vehicles) which the state veterinarian attributed to an overabundance of fluorine.

While I do not question the field diagnosis I think it is prudent to quote Einarsen (*op. cit.*), who says, "The length of tendons and ligaments [of the legs] is so nicely adjusted that only in the rarest instance can a bone be so forced beyond its usual position as to result in damage." Einarsen then describes a test between a cow's foreleg bone, and one of the pronghorn. The cow's bone— supporting in life a weight seven times that of a pronghorn— failed at 41,300 pounds of weight load per square inch while a comparable section of pronghorn did not fail until 45,300 pounds pressure per square inch were applied.

Since over one-fifth of the animals examined exhibited an unnaturally brittle bone structure, and since the herd has not increased at a normally expected rate, these physiological circumstances may indicate a mineral deficiency which the animals, by wandering into unusual habitat, may unconsciously be seeking to overcome.

Another, unproven, factor which may be influencing the distribution and eventual abundance of the population relates to the recent history of stock raising on that island. Henke (1929) says that sometime between 1861 and 1880, a sheep ranch was started on Lanai and population estimates ranged up to 50,000 animals grazing there prior to 1910. There were still 20,588 sheep on the island in April 1911, while Judd (1930) says there were at least 10,000 goats running free in 1910. This same year (1910), the Lanai Company, Ltd., took over. They stopped sheepherding, switched to cattle production, and hired George Munro as manager. Munro was aware of the damage already done to Lanai by the sheep and goats and in fact noted (1955) that others had described the Lanai forest as "a moth-eaten remnant" as early as 1870. He attempted to get rid of the goats, but unfortunately failed. He did eventually eliminate the sheep —in 1920 there were only 860 left—but in the meantime the company had vigorously raised cattle. Henke (*op. cit.*) records the Lanai Company as grazing 5,536 animals in 1923 and selling an additional 4,462. In 1928 they sold all their 6,764 animals and went out of the cattle-raising business. All of this on a total land mass of 141 square miles.

Needless to say, the vegetation of Lanai had suffered greatly; with every rain, tiny but ever growing rivulets were cut around the sparse, chewed-up clumps of grass and in the hot windy summers "the red flag flew"—referring to the giant clouds of red dust which boiled off the uplands of both Lanai and Kahoolawe and trailed off to sea in a southwesterly direction. I have talked with sailors who used to navigate by using the red winds as a position locator. Through the efforts of Munro and later managers, windbreaks were planted across many of the areas that were denuded, but regrowth was a slow process; even today there are replanting projects sponsored by the Dole Corporation.

Forbs and grass (*Paspalum sp.*) had finally been re-established on much of the formerly barren area and it was here that the pronghorn was initially released. Because this area is no longer flat, rolling native grassland, but has become pocked with erosion gullies and denuded of many of its native species, we cannot expect it to return to its original configuration and we do not know what exotic species will eventually dominate. It is obvious today that molasses grass (*Melinis minutiflora*) is succeeding the Paspalums in some areas, and *koa haole* (*Leucaena glauca*) is forming larger and larger thickets. Whatever successions ultimately occur cannot be predicted now, but they almost certainly will not prove favorable habitat for the pronghorn if allowed to develop in an uncontrolled manner.

FOOD HABITS

Pronghorns are browsers rather than grazers and Einarsen (*op. cit.*) has observed that plants need not be abundant to provide good pasturage; in some Oregon habitat there may be only one plant per square yard with the intervening space just gravel or bare rock. Browse plants are followed in importance by weeds (forbs) and, finally, grasses. In the mainland, various species of sagebrush (*Artemisia sp.*) are a favorite food, particularly in winter; the absence of this plant in Hawaii has not seemed to have had any effect on our animals.

The only vague knowledge of the Lanai animals' food habits presently rests upon two reports: the gross examination of the stomachs of 14 animals taken in the 1966 hunting season, when Medeiros (1967) reported that large amounts of *kao haole* (*Leucaena glauca*) leaves and stems were found along with seeds, fruits, and leaves of lantana (*Lantana camara*), plus some unidentified grass and seeds, and that the stomachs of two bucks contained chunks of pineapple (*Ananus comosus* var.), and a later observation (R. Walker, pers. comm.) showing animals to be browsing on *ūha'loa* (*Waltheria americana*), Spanish needles (*Bidens pilosa*), Flora's paintbrush (*Emilia sonchiflora*), and redtop grass (*Agrotis alba*).

If another public hunting season occurs, there can be no excuse for not taking stomach samples from every dead animal and analyzing the contents, not only for percentage volume but for species composition. Only by doing this, and by conducting a simultaneous botanical range survey, can biologists compare and determine the impact of the population on the range and at the same time predict the future ecological vegetative changes which will occur.

REPRODUCTION

Einarsen (*op. cit.*) has written an incisive description of reproduction occurring in the Oregon pronghorn herds and there
presently is little doubt that the Lanai animals follow the same
life pattern.

Most pronghorn does are capable of being bred for the first
time when they are 15 to 16 months old. Due to a complicated
courtship pattern that involves both physiology and habit patterns, Einarsen felt that if the first mating with an individual
female was unsuccessful the buck would not attempt to breed
her a second time; he further deduced that if the ovum failed to
develop, a second period of oestrus did not occur.

The gestation period is from 230 to 240 days and either one
or two kids are produced. There is a wide year-to-year variance
in the doe/kid ratio within the same herd; it is therefore imperative that annual kid censuses be taken prior to the hunting
season.

In the mainland, a fair number of kids die shortly after birth
from inclement weather or predation, but since Hawaii generally has fine weather in May and June when most of the kids
are born (Walker, 1963, records one kid born in December),
and there are no counterparts to the desert coyote (*Canis latrans*)
on Lanai, we would expect to see the herd grow at a much faster
rate than in the mainland. For management purposes, the fact
that most kids are born within a 10 to 15-day period is of para-
mount importance; should a period of wet, windy weather
occur at this time it is conceivable that the entire yield of kids
could be lost for that year.

When the doe is ready to deliver she seeks a kidding ground
separate from the rest of the herd. This is generally in a basin
surrounded by low hills where the ground vegetation averages
9 to 18 inches. The ground cover provides protection and cam-
ouflage for the kid while the hill provides a vantage point for the

doe. The doe lies down to deliver; after drying the kid she walks away for a quarter or half mile and takes up her vigil. If she gives birth to twins she usually delivers them 50 to 400 feet apart. The kids stay where they are born the first day, and while they can rise, appear to be very weak and uncoordinated. They lie with their heads outstretched on the ground, blending well with the terrain because of the wavy pattern of their juvenile pelage. After four days the kid can outrun any man and after the sixth day it can outrun the average dog. About this time the kids begin to pick and nibble at the vegetation; by the time they are three weeks old they feed continuously in this manner but continue to nurse. They are totally weaned about the end of August and weigh from 45 to 55 pounds at this time.

Mainland pronghorn seldom live more than six or seven years in the wild but even old does continue to bear young. The commonest cause of natural death appears to be simply senile decay or wearing down of teeth leading finally to starvation.

HABITS AND BEHAVIOR

Almost everyone is aware of the speed and endurance of the pronghorn but the rough, winding jeep trails of Lanai do not allow a vehicle to be driven fast enough to present the challenge a pronghorn will accept. These animals obviously enjoy a good race and, in the mainland, will run as much as a quarter of a mile out of their way to challenge a car. Speeds to 60 miles per hour have been recorded many times and some observers report animals passing in front of a car doing 60. They normally maintain a herd speed of 25 to 35 miles per hour when not frightened. They can travel at least five to seven miles nonstop at this lower speed but tire rapidly after a mile or so at full speed. Although the cheetah is recorded as the fastest animal it is doubtful that one could catch a pronghorn who had a 100-yard headstart, nor could it maintain the pace long enough to wear down a pronghorn.

The 3-inch-long erectile white rosette hairs on the rump are spread like a fan when the animal is greatly disturbed or alarmed. This signaling device works quite well on the open plains and one often spots a pronghorn herd only because of the observation of a distant white flash. This flash recalled the techniques of signaling with mirrors and gave rise to another name for the pronghorn—"the heliographer." Einarsen also mentions another characteristic that is noticeable at a great distance: at the end of a run, all members of the herd simultaneously shake their bodies and wriggle their skins. The herd is then immediately obvious for a second or two before blending once more into the background.

Another interesting aspect of pronghorn behavior is its insatiable curiosity. With eyes the size of a horse's their range of vision is astounding; they can spot the tiniest object out of place in their environment at a distance of three or four miles. In pioneer days hunters took advantage of this curiosity by stalking as close as they dared, then lying on their backs and kicking their feet in the air until a curious pronghorn approached to within rifle range.

When alarmed or anxious, adult pronghorns give an explosive snort through the nostrils which can best be described as sounding like "cha-oo"; in fact Einarsen says the Klamath Indians named the animal after its call. Adults are otherwise silent. The kid makes a high-pitched quavering sound; this call apparently stirs great anxiety in the adults and is probably not used except in times of danger.

Pronghorns in Oregon shed their horns during October and November, leaving only the horn core which does not have a prong. By January the horn sheath of a buck averages two and one-half to three inches (the doe's horn is usually less than one-inch long at this stage), and by July the growth appears to be complete. During this same time the herd stays fairly grouped together and the animals live in harmony. Einarsen says that there is no deference shown to older animals either because of their age or tribal position. In late July the males have garnered their strength, their horns are firmly set, and does with their new kids have rejoined the herd. A restlessness then begins to overtake the males and individual bucks begin to strike odd poses and perform strange antics. Einarsen writes:". . . a buck striking such odd poses at once becomes the wonder of the entire herd, and he arouses among his fellows about the same degree of concern as a man having an epileptic fit on a city street." These antics are merely a manifestation of the onset of the rutting season and soon most of the bucks enter into this ritual display. By late August the males have begun to fight among themselves and attempt to collect does for their harem. The victors will initially round up a harem of 10 to 15 does, but as the rutting season progresses this number usually dwindles to seven or eight as fresher bucks steal some away. By late October the rutting season is over for the year and the harems begin to break up; the animals then regroup at water holes and the herd slowly re-forms.

The herd may drift off to new areas but since this movement seems to be influenced more by external factors—diminishing water supply, molestation, etc.—than by any innate migratory "impulse," it is doubtful that the Lanai herd have felt any constriction in their present range.

PARASITES AND DISEASE

As noted earlier, the animals first introduced were carefully checked for parasites in Montana and were again dusted for ectoparasites in Honolulu. A postmortem examination of 14 animals shot in 1966 showed neither endoparasites nor ectoparasites present. Because the only other species of herbivores on the island are also almost free of disease, it is improbable that the pronghorn will develop any organism of a debilitating nature in the future.

THE FUTURE

The pronghorn on Lanai, after nine years' residence, must still be considered as a trial introduction. The herd has not increased at the projected rate but little time or effort has been available to determine why.

Einarsen said, "Antelope survival hinges on a knowledge of their daily habits. This knowledge can only be gained by field workers assigned to the area and giving full time to the job.

"Unfortunately, absentee or uncoordinated management has been responsible to a large degree for the extirpation of pronghorns from vast stretches of suitable range."

Not only is knowledge of the life history of the Lanai pronghorns very sketchy but information about vegetative succession stages on the range is nonexistent. Certainly every conservationist wants to see Lanai re-establish a vegetative cover sufficient to reduce or eliminate the further degradation of the soil, but with proper management this need not occur at the expense of good pronghorn habitat. Not only can these animals provide extremely interesting biological information about adaptive powers of a temperate-zone animal to a subtropical habitat but they can provide Hawaiian hunters and photographers with superb trophies and happy memories of pleasant days on the uplands of Lanai.

LITERATURE CITED

Bailey, V.
　　1931　Mammals of Mexico: No. Am. Fauna series, No. 53; p. 22.
Einarsen, A. S.
　　1948　The pronghorn antelope and its management. Monumental Printing Co., Balt.: (Sponsored by the Wildlife Management Institute): 238pp., illus.

Henke, L. A.
    1929   A survey of livestock in Hawaii. Univ. Hawaii Res.
           Publ. No. 5; Honolulu: 82pp., illus.
Judd, H. P.
    1930   The goat menace on Hawaii. Friend 100: 193–194.
Medeiros, J.
    1967   Results of 1966 Lanai antelope season. Hawaii State
           Div. Fish & Game, P. R. Project W-5-R-18, Job 53(18):
           5pp., mimeo.
Munro, G. C.
    1955   Letter to the editor—"Make Lanai a hunter's paradise."
           Hono. Advertiser, May 2.
Nichols, L., Jr.
    1960   The history of the antelope introduction on Lanai Is-
           land, Hawaii. Aug. 20, Hawaii State Div. Fish & Game:
           4pp., mimeo.
Walker, R. L.
    1963   Experimental introduction of exotic game birds and
           mammals. W-5-R-14, Job 50(14), State of Hawaii, Div.
           of Fish and Game, Honolulu: mimeo.

The Water Buffalo

Bubalus bubalus

The water buffalo existed for only a short time in a wild state in Hawaii but certainly warrants mention in any book on the mammals of Hawaii. Today there are only six of these animals in the state, but in times past the "carabao," as it is called in the Philippines, played an important role in the developing economy of Hawaii.

HISTORY

The domestic water buffalo of today is derived from the arna, or Indian wild buffalo. The original range of the arna is not quite certain but is presently restricted to northeastern India, Burma, northern Ceylon, southern Indo-China, and the Malay Peninsula (Carter *et al.*, 1945; Garland, 1922). The domestic buffalo differs but little from the wild buffalo and was domesticated at an early time in human history. We know they were used by the Egyptians in the 5th century, and that they were introduced into Greece and Hungary about the same time. In A.D. 600 they were introduced into Italy and Sicily by the Romans. The author has observed that a short-horned breed of buffalo is prevalent in Yugoslavia and is much more commonly in use than either oxen or bullocks along the river banks of that country. An unsuccessful attempt to introduce water buffalo into western Europe was made by Napolean on his return from Egypt. He introduced them into Landes, a district in France bordering on the Pyrenees and the Bay of Biscay where much of the land was so swampy that peasants tending their herds walked on stilts, but the venture failed, probably due to the coldness of the winter climate (Garland, *ibid.*).

At other, unknown dates, the carabao was introduced into much of China, Japan, the Philippines, many islands of the Far East, and Australia.

The history of the introduction of carabao to Hawaii is uncertain. Oberline (1940) says that "the first pair of water buffalo came to Honolulu in the early 1880s, brought here by Walter Hill for a Chinese rice farmer named Ah In. . . . the original animals . . . came from Southern China." This statement may have been based upon a news release appearing in the *Saturday Press* on January 22, 1881, which announced that "the four small Chinese buffaloes that were brought here by the *Quinta*, are to be used in the rice fields, as they are in China" (anon., 1939). The first Chinese arrived in Hawaii in 1852. They originally came to work in the sugar-cane fields, but by the late 1850s some of them had started to grow rice on a small scale. We know that they originally used oxen to plow the fields, and that they shortly changed to horses for this task, as the oxen were too slim footed and heavy, and became bogged down in the paddy fields (Coulter and Chun, 1937). By the early 1870s the rice industry was getting into full swing, and, relating the industriousness of the Chinese with the skill and knowledge they possessed in this field, it is inconceivable that they waited over ten years to introduce an animal that they considered necessary to success. If, in fact, 1881 was the date of the introduction, it is certain that many more were imported in short order; Coulter and Chun (*ibid.*) state that six or seven carabao were kept on each of the larger rice plantations, and note that, in 1892, there

were between 160 and 200 plantations or farms engaged in producing rice.

It would appear that Hawaiian carabao reached its population peak about the turn of the century. Henke (1929) cites U.S. Livestock Census figures for 1910, 1920, and 1928, and shows population dwindling in these years from 399 to 193 to 150. In 1928 an adult animal was valued at $40 (Henke, *ibid.*); in 1963 and 1964 the University of Hawaii paid $200 per animal.

In the 1930s rice production in Hawaii was at a point of crisis because of an inability to compete with mainland rice prices, and many farmers switched to taro growing; the carabao, though still useful, was not in as much demand, and many of the animals were kept merely for nostalgic reasons or as curiosities.

Carabao were at one time found on all the rice-producing islands, which were Kauai, Oahu, Molokai, Maui, and Hawaii. Tinker (1941) records that, with the failure of a taro-growing venture in Pelekunu Valley on Molokai in 1921, carabao were turned loose to fend for themselves, and they "increased in

Chinese farmer and his water buffalo near Pearl Harbor; *circa* 1900. Archives of Hawaii.

number and ferocity." He further says they were often hunted and, in 1932 at least, shot for meat by workmen who were dismantling the wrecked steamer *Kaala* on that coast. The last of these Molokai animals were shot in 1936 (Noah Pekelo, Jr., pers. comm.) and the carabao of Waipio Valley on Hawaii were removed only a few years later. There is no record of the extinction of carabao on Maui.

This impressive beast certainly struck the imagination of many of Hawaii's more romantic souls, and poems both humorous and solemn are recorded in the pages of *Paradise of the Pacific* magazine, along with some fine photos and one water color by Staats Cotsworth. The reader is referred to Merrit (1924), Gesseler (1930), Westgate (1932), and Gallet (1935) in the literature citations at the end of this chapter.

As of 1968, the only carabao known to exist in the Hawaiian Islands are a pair being used on Kauai at the University of Hawaii's Rice Research Center, two animals at University of Hawaii's Peace Corps Training Camp in Waipio Valley, one old bull kept as a tourist attraction of the windward side of Oahu, and a cow in the Honolulu Zoo. Attempts are being made by the present zoo director, Jack Throp, and University of Hawaii officials, to import new breeding stock from Guam, but because of federal quarantine restrictions the possibility of further importations is doubtful.

DESCRIPTION

Excepting that the arna is generally larger, there is little to distinguish the domesticated buffalo that was introduced to Hawaii from the wild one. Phillips (1945) wrote that eight different breeds are recognized in India; comparison of the photographs accompanying his article show that our Hawaiian animal has little in common with them. The animals discussed by Phillips often had dewlaps, and their horns were less massive and often tightly coiled, which is unknown in the Hawaiian animals.

Bubalus is a genus of the subfamily Bovinae (which includes domestic cattle) but is easily distinguished from other members of this group. A cross-section of the horns at their base show them to be distinctly triangular rather than circular; the back part of the skull is also much more rounded than in other bovines. For many years the African buffalo was considered a member of the same genus but has now been relegated to its own genus, *Syncerus*.

The wild buffalo attains a magnificent size, larger specimens standing from five and one-half to six feet at the shoulder. Prater (1933) reported one weighed 2,001 pounds, although 1,600 to 1,800 pounds would be the more usual size. A bull carabao that died in the Honolulu Zoo in 1955 at an estimated age of 30 stood five and one-half feet high and was ten and one-half feet long (anon., 1953). There seem to be two general shapes to the black horns of the Hawaiian animals; some horns take a scimitar shape by almost immediately beginning their curve outward and backward toward the neck, while other horns proceed straight out from the skull for some distance before beginning the backward curve, which may be directed either upward or downward, but always to the rear. The flattened front surfaces of the horns have cross wrinkles and are not swollen or humped like those of the African buffalo. Although the cow's horns are generally less massive, the finest pair of horns on record belong to a cow; the length along the outer curve of one horn was 6 feet 5 3/8 inches. This horn is in the British Museum (Garland, *op. cit.*). In southern Thailand I once saw a bull with horns so long and upward curved that it would have been possible to string a hammock between them. As I started onto the field to measure them, people yelled at me to stop; this particular bull had killed three people in past years and did not like strangers. He went unmeasured.

In color, the adult Hawaiian carabao is slaty black; many are a dirty white from the hoof to just above the knee. A few show a white patch between the horns. The hair, which sometimes displays a reddish tint, grows sparser with age and in some animals disappears completely except around the face, knees and feet, and the end of the tail. The hair is directed forward from the haunches to the back of the head; a whorl in the hindquarters marks the point at which the hair of this region commences to be directed backward.

Hornless animals occur from time to time and albinos are quite common. In Southeast Asia, albinos are not considered as valuable as the darker-pigmented animals because the natives say they get sore eyes, are weaker, and have poor flesh. The University of Hawaii's oldest carabao pair produced an albino in 1967 but the animal was sickly and died of unknown causes three days later. Another interesting characteristic is the variable eye color. Many animals have the brown color usually expected in bovine animals, but Pitman (1914) recorded seeing large numbers of buffalo in India which had an "abnormal pale blue iris to the eye." Some animals had one normal brown eye and the other blue, while the eyes of others had a mixture of the two. The albinos have unpigmented pink eyes.

REPRODUCTION

The wild arna move about in small herds and during the rutting season the master bull drives the younger bulls away temporarily and takes possession of the cows (Prater, *op. cit.*). Since we have not had a herd of carabao in Hawaii for many years, it is not known if the domestic animals follow this pattern. We have observed that during the time the cow is in heat the bull stations himself between the cow and any intruder. He will attack his handler if too persistent an effort is made to separate the pair. The rutting season occurs in May, June, or July, and one or two calves are born ten months later. Any attempt to separate or otherwise meddle with the calf will bring on a violent attack from the mother. Garland (*op. cit.*) states that both sexes are sexually mature at age four. He also indicates that the cow may have five or six calves during her life but I suggest that this number is closer to ten or twelve since she is fertile until at least age 19 and perhaps longer.

HABITS

As the water buffalo's name implies, the animal loves water and mud and prefers to live on the shaded, grassy banks of a shallow stream, but it is not restricted to these areas if shade and sufficient water for a wallow are artificially provided. It lives almost entirely on grass or on aquatic plants, which it will immerse its head to obtain. The carabao has no sweat glands and is quite conscious of the heat; when working on a hot day the animal often becomes unmanageable and vile tempered unless it is allowed to wallow for a few minutes or is periodically doused with water. As Garland points out, one reason for preferring cattle to buffalo as cart haulers in the drier parts of India is the likelihood of the buffalo dashing into the nearest water, taking cart, contents, and driver along.

As far as I know, the carabao makes only one sound, one so highly unlikely for an animal of this size that you look around for the source of the noise. Instead of a bellow, roar or grunt, the carabao emits a querulous single note which sounds like a nasally emitted *nnerr*. This has also been described as resembling the quack of a duck, but on a lower register. The sound is easy to imitate, and a carabao will perk up its ears at 200 yards even though you might think the sound would not carry 50 feet.

A carabao's nature is two sided; it is often very timid and gentle to people it knows, but that person must exercise respect for its idiosyncrasies. No carabao can be trusted, no matter how often the attendant has had contact with it. In 1964 a man on Oahu, who owned the last major herd on the island, and who had cared for these animals for years, was tossed four times and gored in the thigh by a bull before he escaped to the safety of a tree (anon., 1964). The ferocity of a wild or feral water buffalo is matched only by that of the African buffalo. Indian royalty formerly staged battles between water buffalos and tigers. Not to be outdone, the Javanese, during "Tahun Baru," the Mohammedan New Year, staged fights between a bull or a cow with a calf, and two tigers. Buffalos usually won (Garland, *op. cit.*). A Caucasian in the wilder areas of Asia must be extremely cautious in approaching carabaos, even if the native boys who usually tend them are near; the animals do not get overly excited if a strange Asian comes near, but many a white man—the author included—has had to run for his life.

LITERATURE CITED

Anonymous
    1939   Reprint of "Notes of the week," Sat. Press (Honolulu), Jan. 22: p. 19. *from* Paradise of the Pacific 51(10): 16.

_____

    1953   Water buffalo dies of old age as zoo "curiosity." Hono. Star Bull. March 31: p. 1.
    1964   Man gored, treed by water buffalo. Hono. Advertiser, Nov. 17: p. A2.
Carter, T. D., J. E. Hill, and G. H. H. Tate
    1945   Mammals of the pacific world. Macmillan Co., New York: 227pp.
Coulter, J. W., and C. K. Chun
    1937   Chinese rice farmers in Hawaii. U. Hawaii Res. Publ. 16: 72pp.
Gallet, H.
    1935   Page the water buffalo. Paradise of the Pacific. 47(11): p. 1.
Gesseler, C.
    1930   The carabao. Paradise of the Pacific. 43(12): plate between pp. 42–43.
Garland, H. P.

1922   The water buffalo. Garland Mfg. Co., Saco, Maine: 51pp., illus.

Henke, L. A.
1929   A survey of livestock in Hawaii. U. Hawaii Res. Publ. 5: 82pp.

Merrit, R. C.
1924   To a water buffalo. Paradise of the Pacific. 37(1): 30.

Oberline, A.
1940   Just a relic of another era. Paradise of the Pacific. 52(11): 32–34.

Phillips, R. W.
1945   The water buffalo of India. J. Heredity 36: 71–76.

Pitman, C. R.
1914   The colouration of the eyes of the domesticated buffalo. Bombay Nat. Hist. Soc., J. 22: 390.

Prater, S. H.
1933   The Indian wild buffalo or Arna (*Bubalus bubalus*, L.). *In*: The wild animals of the Indian empire. Bombay Nat. Hist. Soc., J. 34(4); p. 31 of supplement.

Tinker, S. W.
1941   Animals of Hawaii. 2nd Edit. Tongg Publ. Co., Honolulu: 190pp.

Westgate, I.
1932   The carabao. Paradise of the Pacific. 45(9): p. 7.

The Feral Cattle

Bos taurus

Cattle were first brought to Hawaii by Capt. George Vancouver on his second voyage around the world. The breed is not known but they were believed to be of Spanish descent and probably resembled the longhorn, although there is evidence that they were of a black color. The bloodlines of those originally imported have long since vanished and the feral cattle of today show characteristics of many of the various breeds that have since been introduced.

HISTORY

R. C. Wyllie, in an address to the Royal Hawaiian Agricultural Society, in August 1850, was among the first to record the landing. He wrote that "on the 19th of February, 1793, he [Vancouver] landed a bull and a cow from California for Kamehameha I in the canoe of Krimamahoo, off the coast of Hawaii. On the 22nd of February, 1793, he landed five cows, two ewes and a ram, in the bay of Kealakekua for Kamehameha I; on the 15th of January, 1794, he landed a bull, two cows, two bull calves. . . ." Wyllie went on to note the record that Vancouver "landed first a bull and a cow, they were too weak to stand up;

271

he hired a canoe to take them on shore where they could get grass. The bull died in a few days; the remaining cattle, healthy but thin were landed at Kealakekua. The loss of the bull was a misfortune which prevented any increase. He had but one hope. Two of the young cows proved to be with calf and if one should bring forth a male, the increase might be effected. Fortunately his hopes were realized."

Kamehameha put a *kapu* (taboo) on the animals that lasted for almost 30 years. An account in the August 11, 1859 *Advertiser* says the animals were released on the upland slopes of Hualalai, and "here they rapidly increased and becoming a flock were removed to the Waimea plains, from whence breeding very fast, they spread inland and wandered off among the hills and valleys of Mauna Kea and became so numerous that when the tabu was removed about 1830, the interior plain and three mountains of Hawaii were full of them, and they were in some seasons hard pushed for feed, though generally very fat. . . ."

Despite the *kapu* on the animals, white visitors and residents made use of the cattle long before the king's ban was lifted. Delano, who visited Hawaii twice, noted in 1806 that "they had very recently brought to this island [Maui] one of the bulls that Captain Vancouver landed at Owhyhee. He made a very great destruction amongst their sugar canes and gardens, breaking into them and their cane patches, and tearing them to pieces with his horns and digging them up with his feet. He would run after and frighten the natives, and appeared to have a disposition to do all the mischief he could, so much so that he was a pretty unwelcome guest among them. There was a white man at this village, who told me that they had not killed any of the black cattle that Captain Vancouver brought there; and that they multiplied very much. This agreed with what I heard when there in 1801. I understood that the bull which they now had at Mowee, was the first of the cattle that had been transported from Owhyhee to any other place. I have within this year or two been told by several captains who have lately been to these islands, that they have increased so much, that they frequently kill them for beef" (anon., 1938).

When Bloxam (B. P. Bishop Mus., 1925) visited the islands in 1825, he noted seeing a few cows on Maui and said that "cattle, goats, and horses were very plentiful" on Oahu. When visiting the uplands of Hawaii, he saw cattle and wrote: "There are few natives who live near their haunts and even those are terribly afraid of them, so that there is nothing to hinder their increase." Another member of Bloxam's party recorded (anon., 1826), on the hike up to Mauna Kea that ". . . five hours walk brought them to the hut of a rough but useful European . . . whose employment it is to catch and kill the wild cattle and cure beef, which he does very skillfully."

Hall (1904) implied that the *kapu* did not really last 30 years, and said, instead, that by 1815 the cattle were recognized as a menace to forest growth and that slaughter was no longer forbidden although the herds continued to increase.

According to Eben Low, who was one of Hawaii's greatest cowboys and ranch managers, three expert Mexican cowboys, Kossuth, Lozuida, and Ramon, were brought to Hawaii and sent to Waimea in 1832 to teach the Hawaiians the art of cowpunching. Curtis J. Lyons (Henke, 1929) described them: "They brought with them the saddle, richly adorned, of stamped bull hide leather, and broad winged stirrups. They brought along the jingling spurs, the hand wrought bit and the hair rope with alternate strands of black and white. They made the lasso or lariat evenly braided from four strands of well chosen hide. They taught their worthy successors, the Hawaiian cowboys, how to throw the lasso, guide the horse by causing the rein to bear on the horse's neck and how to conquer the wild herds of Mauna Kea."

In 1834, the famous botanist, David Douglas (after whom the Douglas fir [*Pseudotsuga menziesii*] was named) attempted to hike across the island of Hawaii, but was killed by falling (or by be-

ing pushed) into a pit constructed to capture wild cattle; there
was a bull in the pit which battered him to death. Some people
who knew Douglas said that he had a morbid fear of cattle and
would have never voluntarily approached the pit, but must
instead have been robbed and pushed or thrown in by the man
who reported his death. There is today, a plaque and monu-
ment near the site of his death in the upper lands of Laupaho-
ehoe; the location is known on maps today as Kaluakauka,
meaning "The Doctor's Pit" (Bryan, 1934).

From 1811 to 1835 a number of shipments of Hawaiian cattle,
hides, and meat were made to settlers in the Pacific Northwest,
according to Towne and Wentworth (1955), and it is certain
that many captured animals were shipped to other major islands
in the chain. Henke (*op. cit.*) writes that "according to John
Manini of Waianae, Oahu, his granduncle, Paul Marin, had a
Longhorn cattle ranch in the Waianae region about 1840" (it
was this same gentleman who introduced Bermuda grass and
cactus to Hawaii, presumably for cattle forage), and when
Valdemar Knudsen started his ranch at Kekaha, Kauai, about
1860, he wrote that there were already many longhorns present
(Henke, *ibid.*). In February 1847, a Kauai rancher tried to sell
the government some 200 head of adult cattle at $8 a head, plus
yearlings and calves at $3 each. The government and the king
were joint owners of all wild, unmarked cattle and they sold or
leased the right to slaughter to private parties.

In opposition to Towne and Wentworth's previous statement,
Thrums Annual for 1909 (page 108) states that the first beef to
be exported from Hawaii was 158 barrels in 1849.

Angus and Hereford breeds were introduced in small numbers in 1850 (although Herefords were not brought here in
large numbers until the 1890s) and were shortly followed by a
number of other breeds such as Dexter, Devon, and shorthorns.
Henke (*op. cit.*) records the estimated cattle population in
1851 as:

Hawaii (tame)	8,000
Hawaii (wild)	12,000
Maui	3,500
Molokai	200
Oahu	12,000
Kauai/Niihau	5,000
Total	40,700

Tame, semiwild, and wild cattle apparently ranged at will around the environs of Honolulu, and after a man was killed in 1850 while trying to tie down a young wild bull in downtown Honolulu, the newspaper *The Polynesian* wrote the following editorial: "Upon the practice of leading wild bullocks through the streets of Honolulu for slaughter, we would express our most decided reprehension. There is scarcely an individual resident of Honolulu who has not been annoyed by this dangerous custom, or who has not at some period of his residence been obliged to jump a wall, rush through a convenient gate, or run for his life when meeting these furious animals. And we have knowledge of ladies and children being thrown into a dangerous fright while attempting to enjoy a walk or ride toward evening, in the streets of Honolulu or on Nuuanu Road . . ." (Baker, 1944).

In 1853, cattle were worth $5 a head on Oahu, but only half that much on the outer islands because of the difficulty of transporting them to market (Lee, 1853). By 1859, wild cattle were hunted almost solely for their hides (although packers on Hawaii's Waimea Plains, in 1858, advertised and guaranteed, for 12 months, their salt meat product), and it was noted that, "being unbranded, the hides have greater value than tame hides."

Theo. H. Davies was the agent for the Waimea Grazing and Agriculture Company and he paid hunters at the rate of $1.25 for each bull hide and $1.00 for each cow hide, properly dried and delivered to certain points on the mountain. From there they were carried by cart to Waimea and eventually Kawaihai, where they were shipped to Honolulu. During the first half of 1859, 222,170 pounds of hides were exported, mostly to the United States, for a selling price of about 25 cents per pound (Henke, *op. cit.*). Although the comment was made (apparently by Davies) that "the wild cattle have greatly diminished in numbers and in a few years will be very rare," the reduction did not occur, and the hide hunters continued their business. In 1869 Davies, still acting as agent for the Waimea company, asked the Minister of the Interior to renew their lease on the rights to taking cattle, and was answered in April 1870 that "for $2,000 per annum he may have the privilege of killing the wild cattle running on the Island of Hawaii—those cattle being the joint property of the crown and government" (Henke, *ibid.*).

A tallow-making plant was set up at Kawaihai sometime between 1850 and 1875 and was eventually moved up to Waimea. Since the meat was of little value for export, once the hides were removed the owners took to dumping the entire carcass in the tallow-rendering vats.

An anonymous writer, in 1886, noted that in the ten-year period between 1876 and 1885, 793 cows and 158 bulls were imported to Hawaii; presumably these were animals of superior bloodlines. Cattle ranching was becoming a big industry in Hawaii, particularly on the "Big Island." Nottage (1894) noted the technique used on the outer islands to load cattle for the Honolulu market: "At one place we called at, we took on 30 head of cattle. It is a cruel sight to witness. The beasts are driven down to the shore, and the cowboys then proceed to lasso them. This they do with marvelous skill, and then gallop off to the sea. Another horseman rides behind the lassoed ox, and between them he is driven and dragged into the water. The man who has lassoed him now swims his horse to the boat that is lying off, and, passing the rope on board, turns his horse's head again to the shore. The ox, after a few frantic struggles, allows himself to be hauled alongside, when he is made fast to the side of the boat, so that his head is kept above the water's edge. When seven on each side of the boat are thus made fast, the boat is hauled back to the steamer by a long warp. The poor beasts struggle most violently, and are much distended with the amount of water they have swallowed. Now comes the task of swinging them on board, and though it is done most skillfully, still it is dreadfully cruel. To allow them to lie down, as they often want to do, would mean death; and as there is no freight paid on dead beasts, their tails are twisted, until they are nearly wrenched off, in order to make them get on their feet again." A nearly identical system was still in use in Kailua, Kona, as late as 1947 (Clarke, 1947).

There are few references to the wild cattle population during

Loading Kona Coast cattle for shipment to Honolulu. Cattle were tied to the gunwales of the longboat by their horns. Archives of Hawaii.

the 1890s, but Judd (1939) records a group of Honolulu hunters killing about 100 wild animals on Kauai in one week, at about this time. Mr. William Hall (1904) wrote an article in the *Planters' Monthly* noting the susceptibility of Hawaiian forests to injury by cattle (trampling of the undergrowth causes the soil to dry out and the shallow-rooted trees cannot obtain the necessary moisture for survival) and at the same time quoted the manager of Parker Ranch, A. W. Carter, as estimating 10,000 wild cattle present on Mauna Kea that year.

Wild cattle were hunted heavily for the next several decades but we unfortunately do not have much of a history of this period. Bryan (1947) records the killing of 738 cattle from fenced forest reserves during the period from 1921 to 1946, and Judd (Tinker, 1941) reported that the last of the wild cattle were eradicated from the upper slopes of Mauna Kea in 1931. There were still several small herds roaming the southeast slopes of Mauna Loa, but Bryan, who estimated their numbers at about 200, noted that these were no longer of the longhorn variety, "but are of a little better stock" (Tinker, *ibid.*).

The other islands had apparently solved most of their wild cattle problems sometime before the early 1930s since a chart from the Territorial Forester's office for the period from 1933 to 1940 shows only 72 animals killed on islands other than Hawaii; 42 on Oahu, 16 on Kauai, 12 on Molokai, and 2 on Maui. Noah Pekelo, Jr., (pers. comm.) says that the last of the longhorns on Molokai was shot in 1934. Although Lanai was operated as a cattle ranch from 1910 to 1928 there were never any feral cattle on that island until after the latter date. In 1952, a hunting season was held to rid the island of an estimated 50 animals. The Hawaiian Pineapple Company gave up their rights of ownership so that the public could hunt; in two week-ends 35 parties of hunters bagged 12 animals (anon., 1952) but there is no record of how many animals were eventually taken from the island. There may have been a few feral cattle on Kahoolawe from time to time, but because both water and food had to be imported for the few cattle there in 1931 (McAllister, 1933), it is doubtful that untended strays survived for very long.

With the coming of World War II, hunting was severely restricted, and permits were not issued to hunt the wild cattle. In 1948, a group of hunters met with Colin Lennox, the director of the Territorial Board of Agriculture and Forestry, and requested an opening of the season. One hunter said that there were wild cows in "all sections of the island" and complained that he had been "treed" more than once. Mr. L. W. Bryan agreed that there were still wild cattle present (anon., 1948). A liberal season was opened shortly thereafter, but in May 1954, the Hawaii Cattlemen's Association sent a resolution to the Board of Agriculture and Forestry requesting changes in the regulation—the old rules allowed only four hunters to a party, and this was not considered a large enough group to carry out all the meat from the rugged and remote areas which the cattle inhabited, and, more important to the cattlemen, considerable rustling was taking place on weekdays under the guise of legal hunting (anon., 1954).

Except for an occasional stray, the last major herds of feral cattle in Hawaii appear to be in the Honaunau Forest Reserve (which, ironically, is almost immediately above Kealakekua Bay, where the first animals were landed), or in the "Lands of Kapua-Honomalino" above the 3,000-foot level (Herbert Kikukawa, pers. comm.). This is a privately owned area several miles to the south of Honaunau.

In a report to the trustees of the Bishop Estate (1959), Carlson and Bryan noted that "extensive damage by pigs and cattle" occurred from 1941 to 1946, but it was thought that the population reached a peak from 1947 to 1957. An aerial census conducted in 1956 showed an estimated 1,000 animals at large, but by 1958 it was reported that over 600 head had been shot by hunters, and about 300 more animals taken by employees of McCandless Ranch. The report went on to say that feral cattle had been excluded from the area by 1890, but a buildup gradually occurred within the area until 1950, when a series of earthquakes destroyed the stone walls and allowed more cattle into the area from the outside. Late in 1957, Bryan (anon., 1957) estimated that not more than 100 wild cattle were left in the area, "and they are getting wilder and smarter."

There are still a number of feral cattle in this area and small numbers of them will probably remain at large for many years. At the time of this writing, sport hunters are being offered the opportunity to shoot a "Vancouver Wild Bull" on private lands for a fee of about $100. A number of semitame animals are once again wandering loose on the eastern end of Molokai; because members of the herd are infected with tuberculosis (which, being communicable to humans, has meant a decline in hunting pressure on these herds), the state, with the cooperation of local ranchers, is trying to kill all of these animals.

LITERATURE CITED

Anonymous

1826   Voyage of H.M.S. Blonde to the Sandwich Islands in the years 1824–25. Davison Co., London: 260pp.

———

1886   Improvement of cattle in the Islands. Monthly 5: 131–133.

———

1938   Bull in a sugar-cane field. Paradise of the Pacific 50(2): 34.

———

1948   Hunters brief Colin Lennox on Big Island's wild cattle. Hono. Advertiser, March 5.

———

1952   Twelve head of cattle are "bagged" on Lanai. Hono. Star Bull., Aug. 23.

1954 Changes in wild cattle hunting restrictions asked by ranchers. Hilo Tribune Herald, May 3.

1957 Hunters bag 15 cattle. Hilo Tribune Herald, Oct. 9.
Baker R. J.
1944 The case of the wild bullock. Paradise of the Pacific 56(10): 24–26.
Bernice P. Bishop Museum
1925 Diary of Andrew Bloxam, naturalist of the "Blonde", on her trip from England to the Hawaiian Islands, 1824–25. B. P. Bishop Mus., Spec. Publ. 10: 96pp.
Bryan, L. W.
1934 Kaluakauka. Paradise of the Pacific. 46(12): 28–30.

1937 Wild cattle in Hawaii. Paradise of the Pacific 49(9): 9, 30.

1947 Twenty-five years of forestry work on the island of Hawaii. Hawaiian Planters' Record 51: 1–80.
Carlson, N. K., and L. W. Bryan
1959 Hawaiian timber for the coming generations. Report for the Trustees of the Bishop Estate, Honolulu: 111pp.
Clarke, M.
1947 The Humuula, Kamaaina ship. Paradise of the Pacific 59(12): 28–31.
Hall, W. L.
1904 The forests of the Hawaiian Islands. Planters' Monthly 23: 367.
Henke, L. A.
1929 A survey of livestock in Hawaii. U. Hawaii Res. Publ. 5: 82pp.
Judd, H. P.
1939 Cattle hunting on Kauai. Paradise of the Pacific 51(1): 17–18.
Lee, W. L.
1853 Annual report of the President. Roy. Haw'n. Agri. Soc., Trans. 1(4): 3–14.

McAllister, J. G.
   1933   Archeology of Kahoolawe. B. P. Bishop Mus., Bull.
          115: 61pp.
Nottage, C. G.
   1894   In search of a climate. Sampsom Low, Marston and
          Co., Ltd., London: 351pp.
Tinker, S. W.
   1941   Animals of Hawaii. Tongg Publ. Co., Honolulu: 190pp.
Towne, C. W., and E. N. Wentworth
   1955   Cattle and men. U. Okla. Press, Norman, Okla.: 384pp.
Wyllie, R. C.
   1850   Transactions of the Royal Hawaiian Agricultural Soci-
          ety 1: 36:49.

The Feral Goat

Capra hircus

Of the 27 states of the United States that have wild goat populations, Hawaii can claim the dubious distinction of harboring
the largest percentage. After nearly 200 years of supporting tens
of thousands of goats, whose populations have created many of
the more severe erosion problems, it is at last possible to say that
the state, through management of hunting seasons, finally has
the animals in their jurisdiction under control. Unfortunately,
the lands under federal control, such as Kahoolawe and Volcanoes and Haleakala National parks, are still severely over-
populated and undercontrolled. It has been convincingly demonstrated on all islands that the goat is a much sought game
animal, and that only through strict regulation of bag limits and
season lengths have certain populations of goats been able to
maintain themselves. It is the desire of state game biologists to
eventually provide less damaging game species, such as pronghorns, axis and black-tailed deer, and mouflon sheep, for the
hunters' pleasure, and then to eradicate the goats. Although
precise figures are not available, somewhere between five and
ten thousand hunter days are spent annually in pursuit of goats
and it would be impossible to eradicate the goat without incur-
ring the wrath of many devoted and rugged hunters unless

some other animal were provided in its place as a substitute.

HISTORY

The first goats, of an unknown breed, were introduced to the island of Niihau on February 1, 1778, by Captain Cook. This original group consisted of one billy and two nannies. Bryan (1930) says that when Cook returned to the island the following year, he found that the herd had increased to six but "the ownership of this small band was being claimed by two rival chiefs. A contest took place between these two chiefs to settle the ownership. The fight waxed so warm that after it was over all six of the goats were found to have been killed during the excitement."

Captain Vancouver came along four years later and landed a male and female on Hawaii and another pair on Kauai. The next year, 1793, he landed "several" on Maui (Bryan, *ibid.*).

There is little mention of goats in the literature of the next 50 years—excepting Bloxam's 1825 notation of numerous goats at Lahaina, Maui, and on Oahu (B. P. Bishop Mus., 1925)—but these animals must have been quickly transported to all the major islands where, it is imagined, they were left to browse in a semiwild or wild state. In the ten-year period from 1844 to 1853, 245,862 goat skins were exported from Hawaii (Henke, 1929). We know that the skins of this era were worth about 15 cents each, since Marques (1905) noted the value of 26,519 skins in 1850 as being $3,977.

Judd (1916) notes that goats were found running free on Kahoolawe before 1863, and Baker (1916) tells how King Umi's *heiau* (temple) on the saddle between Hualalai and Mauna Loa was converted into a trap and corral for goats sometime around 1867. The goat population in this latter area must have been enormous for the Hawaiians to have desecrated such an important, 250-year-old shrine.

Although we know that sheep were introduced to Lanai some-

time after 1861, it is believed that goats were responsible for most of the damage to the then unique Lanai forest. We have no information as to when the first goats were introduced to that island, but by 1870 Lydgate described the forest as "a moth-eaten remnant" (Munro, 1955).

Marques (*op. cit.*) said that Angora goats were introduced into the islands sometime in the 1890s, and stated that their primary purpose was to produce mohair for the weaving of saddle girths and cowboys' ropes.

Over the 66-year period from 1844 to 1900, a total of 1,581,000 goat skins were exported from the islands—an average of almost 24,000 per year (Henke, *op. cit.*).

By 1905, Marques wrote that of about 10,000 goats on Oahu only about 500 were domesticated; he also said that there were about 2,000 goats on Molokai, but there had been 10,000 a few years before. In 1904 an anonymous reporter for the board of Agriculture and Forestry wrote: "The forest problem on Lanai is essentially one of protecting the remaining native forest against the destructive ravages of the goats, which now run wild in large numbers, over the rougher and higher parts of the island. . . . That a start ought to be made speedily there is no question, for the destructive erosion of the mountain caused by the goats, is becoming more and more serious every month that it is allowed to go on" (anon., 1904). Four years later, Judd (1930) estimated 10,000 goats as still remaining on Lanai. He also estimated that there were 100,000 feral goats on Hawaii; and he erroneously reported that goats had been eradicated from Niihau and Kahoolawe. C. S. Judd, on the other hand, estimated 5,000 goats present on Kahoolawe just one year later in 1909, and goes on to say that from 1906 to 1916, 4,300 goats were slaughtered on this tiny island (Judd, 1916). From 1918 to 1928, the lessees of the island killed another 13,000 goats, at which time they thought they had exterminated them (Henke, *op. cit.*); a visit to the island today shows that, unfortunately, they had not.

The Niihau goats were not exterminated until 1911 (Forbes, 1913); no goats have been allowed free range on that island since that year, and Niihau is today the only one of the large islands of the chain that does not have a population of feral goats.

From 1924 until 1930, Bryan (*op. cit.*) estimated that 40,000 goats were killed on the Big Island, but also suggested that there were as many as 75,000 remaining. He was not far wrong because, in 1947, when summing up 25 years' work in the forestry program on that island, he lists 134,551 goats killed in or near forest reserves during the period of 1921 to 1946 (Bryan, 1947). Untold thousands of animals were also killed by private hunters and ranchers in other areas on that island. In an eight-year period from 1933 through 1940, foresters on other islands killed 21,000 animals in forest reserves (Tinker, 1941).

Mr. Munro spent 34 years on Lanai and made a valiant attempt to eliminate the goats there. He never quite succeeded, but he did reduce the population to such a low point that it has been possible to keep the herds under control. The Lanai herds have been kept at a level of somewhere between one and two thousand animals for the past ten years and, starting in 1967, the Division of Fish and Game started a year-round season with the intent of exterminating the herds. Hunters have made deep inroads into the population since that time and it is hoped that within one or two years the last of the goats will be killed.

Oahu, with its large hunting population, has reduced its goat herds to about 100 animals. All of these live in the more rugged parts of the Koolau and Waianae ranges; as the herds increase and move onto the more accessible ridges they are immediately reduced by shooting, and the survivors once again retreat onto the sheer cliffs. Most of the goats in the Koolau Range were killed in the early 1950s in the area above Waimanalo, but a few still survived there until at least 1963.

There are perhaps 2,800 goats on the island of Kauai, of which about 2,000 are to be found in either Waimea Canyon or on the Na Pali Coast. Four to five hundred of these latter animals are shot annually, which just about equals the numbers that are born each year. Hunters apparently keep the other 800 animals in relatively static balance.

Molokai has a population of perhaps 800 animals. With the exception of the animals on the cliff between Halawa and Wailau Valley, hunters keep the rest of the herds at relatively low levels.

No information is available about the present overall population of goats on Maui, but when Yocom studied the feral goats in Haleakala National Park in 1963, he estimated that at least 600 goats lived in, or immediately adjacent to the park. National Park records show that from 1946 until 1964, 11,870 goats were killed by rangers, either in or adjacent to the park boundaries.

At Hawaii Volcanoes National Park, on the Big Island, rangers' files show that 17,389 goats were removed in the five-year period from 1927 through 1931 (Yocom, 1967). These animals were removed by means of drives conducted by the territorial foresters. There is no data available for the next six years; for three of these years local riflemen took an unknown number until Office Order No. 288 ordered a stop to their hunting (hunting by private sportsmen is contrary to National Park regulations). In 1938, 5,085 goats were removed from the park by Civilian Conservation Corps enrollees under the direction of park rangers. At the end of that year, the assistant park naturalist, Samuel Lamb, wrote an optimistic article, parts of which I quote: ". . . an area of approximately 70 square miles . . . was thoroughly combed during the spring and summer months. The final count shows that a total of 5,085 goats were rounded up, this represents 70 goats per square mile or one goat to every nine acres. . . .

"It is a well-known policy of the National Park Service to preserve its lands in as nearly a natural state as is possible. Since goats are not native to Hawaii, they are an unnatural element. Also that they are very destructive to the native forests has often been shown. Over much of the area driven, all forms of plant life have been reduced to a minimum, giving a very desertlike appearance to the landscape. Now that the goats have been brought under control it is believed that some sort of vegetative cover will return over large areas. This will help to stop the erosion that has been in progress for many years as well as helping to bring about habitat conditions suitable for some of Hawaii's native birds.

"Now that these lands in the National Park are surrounded by goat-tight fences it is believed that the number of goats can be kept very low. Follow-up drives can be conducted from time to time and Park Rangers on patrol, working in pairs, will be able to kill off small bands as they become established.

"That the eradication of these exotic animals in the Territory of Hawaii is an important step in conservation cannot be denied. Similar drives, conducted on territorial lands by CCC workers, constitute an important contribution to the future welfare of the island's forest. It is hoped that the work can be carried on for years to come" (Lamb, 1938).

In the 25-year period (from 1939 to 1963) following this statement, 25,254 more goats were removed from National Park lands on Hawaii (Yocom, *op. cit.*).

It is this writer's personal contention that more than 5,000 goats still reside in the National Park. I recall hiking through a portion of the park one day in February 1965, shortly after a much publicized drive had removed about 1,200 goats, and counting more than 1,000 animals along a 6-mile course—and I was not searching for animals. In April 1968, rangers staged a drive near the rugged Hilina Pali, and received good publicity about the approximately 300 goats they captured, but one ranger admitted that they had seen "as many as a thousand . . . but some of them refused to be herded by helicopter or horseman" (Morse, 1968). These animals were sold at auction for $2.85 per goat; they were in turn sold in sugar-plantation camps, where they brought a price of from $7 to $10 each.

DESCRIPTION

The goat was one of the first hoofed animals to be domesticated, and the animal known as *Capra hircus* today seems to be a mixture of at least three different wild goats from different parts of the Old World. The domesticated progeny of these animals were, over many thousands of years, interbred and occasionally back-crossed in such a random manner that it is almost impossible to determine the relationships of the existing forms.

Marques (*op. cit.*) wrote in 1905 that the majority of goats of that time were predominantly black or brown or intergrades of those colors; goats with white patterns were only then appearing, and Marques believed this was due to crossing with the Angora breed which had been introduced only a few years earlier. He was perhaps the first person to record some of the effects of geographic isolation in Hawaii by also observing that, while the lips of the goats on Maui invariably had the upper protruding over the lower, the lips of the goats on Oahu were either equal or had the lower protruding beyond the upper. In the more than 60 years since Marques' observations, the various island herds have shown even more effects of isolation.

Graf (1963) recognized at least five different goat populations from the islands of Molokai, Lanai, and Hawaii, and Yocom's 1963 study of the Haleakala goats revealed significant color differences in each of his six study areas (Yocom, *op. cit.*). This indicates that there is generally no free movement from one population to another, even in areas where two or more herds could, if they desired, range together.

Graf noted that not only are the goats of Molokai's eastern rain forest readily distinguishable from the multicolored, scimitar-horned goats of the rest of the island but that there are two distinctive populations among these black-coated, smooth-haired, and short-bearded animals. Both subgroups have curling horns, similar to those on sheep, but the animals of the southeast sector of the forest have horns that are triangular in cross-section, with a relatively open curl, while goats from the northeast sector have horns that are circular in cross-section and are tighter in curl. The southeast sector goats also have a two- to three-inch grayish-white mane, running from the root of the tail to the base of the head, which the northeastern animals do not possess. Graf notes that while there is nothing to physically prevent these goats from mixing with those of the coastal cliffs, there appears to be little, if any, overlapping of range.

Graf found another predominantly black-goat population in the Keauhou area of Hawaii, but these animals had longer beards, and horns that were intermediate between curling and scimitar shapes. On Lanai, the goats are of a predominant buck-skin color, with a dark dorsal stripe down the spine and a dark cross extending down over the shoulders.

Graf generally lumped the rest of the goats seen into a category he referred to as "the common goat," which on the surface has no particularly distinctive characters except those of variation in color pattern, and very wide, flat-spreading horns. This common goat was the animal that Yocom was confronted with in his Maui study; by very careful recording of the individual color patterns of the animals of each herd he was able to tell that there were differences in proportions of basic colors from one herd to the next. As noted earlier, this indicates very definite separation of populations.

There are considerable differences in animal size as well as coloration in the various herds, but few quantitative studies have been done. Yocom notes that on Haleakala, from October 1963 through February 1964, the average weight of females collected was 66 pounds. Males collected over the same period averaged nearly 70 pounds, but one male weighed 105 pounds. According to National Park rangers, billies of up to 200 pounds had been shot in that area (Yocom, *op. cit.*). This latter size would not be unusual for some of the older billies on Lanai, or for the Molokai east-end goats, but most of the arid-land goats elsewhere in the islands probably average a live-weight of between 50 and 100 pounds. In looking through my field notes I find that in the Waimea Canyon goat season of October 1960, 196 goats were taken. Of this number, only 17 were brought to the check station with head and feet still intact. The other 179 animals averaged 28.8 pounds—they had no intestines, head or feet. Males averaged 34.2 pounds and females, 22.2 pounds.

Because of the wide variation in body weights of different goat populations it would be illogical to give generalized body measurements for the broad category of "goats," but hunters might be interested in knowing that Yocom records a spread of 38 inches as being the largest recorded trophy from the Haleakala region. I have seen horns of equal or larger measurements on goats of the Kailua-Kona region of Hawaii, but in general any animal with a tip-to-tip measurement of more than 26 inches can be considered worthy of hanging on a trophy-room wall.

REPRODUCTION

The gestation period of the domestic goat is known to be five months, and we have no reason to believe that the feral goat is different. Females are capable of being bred at five months, and in the smaller herds it is not unusual to see females of this age being chased. Males can breed at one year; Yocom doubted that much breeding was done by males of this age in the wild, but he was observing animals living on open areas where older and larger billies could and did chase off the youngsters. On the other hand, several others and the writer have watched older billies chase forest-dwelling females so persistently that the small young nannies took refuge under fallen logs or overhanging fern trees. The larger billies were then stymied while smaller males climbed under or into the refuges and bred the young females.

Breeding occurs year round; there may be seasonal peaks, but no quantitative data have been gathered to support this possibility.

It is impossible to determine, for the whole state population, a normally occurring sex ratio. This is because of the big variation in the length of hunting seasons; and regulations concerning the sex ratio "in the bag" cause wide year-to-year fluctuations in the sex and age make-up of individual herds. The only valid method of determining the average number born, and the sex ratio at birth, would be to collect a group of females in their fourth month of pregnancy and examine their fetuses.

FOOD HABITS

Because of the diverse vegetation on the different islands, and particularly in the areas of goat habitation, a list of plants eaten would certainly include hundreds of species. With the exception of a limited food-habit study made by National Park rangers in Haleakala in 1947 (Yocum, *op. cit.*), I know of no significant studies. It is possibly safe to say that they will nibble on any greenery within their range, but it is also known that each geographically separated population has certain favored plants, which they will often seek to the exclusion of adjacent vegetation. Further information in this field of study is urgently required.

Free water does not seem to be necessary for any of our feral herds, nor do most animals take it even if readily available. Yocom (*ibid.*) records seeing goats browsing around springs in Haleakala, but he never saw them drinking, and I have watched goats in Honopu Valley on Kauai standing in water and eating aquatic plants, but I have never seen one dip its muzzle for a drink. Goats on the arid lands of Kahoolawe seem to thrive in areas far removed from the seasonal water holes of the upper plateau, as also do goats that are on the coastal areas of the Big Island.

PARASITES

Very little work has been done in the study of parasitism or disease in feral goats. Alicata (1964) indicates that no information is available about protozoan infections, and states that neither tapeworms nor flukes have been found. He lists as present, the stomach worm *Haemonchus contortus*, the stomach and intestinal worms *Ostertagia circumcincta* and *Trichostrongylus colubriformis*, and the whipworm *Trichuris ovis*. Externally, the sucking louse *Linognathus africanus* and the biting louse *Bovicola caprae* have been identified.

DAMAGE BY GOATS

There is no doubt that the feral goat is presently the most destructive creature in the Hawaiian ecosystem (excluding, of course, man); cattle and sheep were possible contenders for this distinction in the past, but these animals are now restricted to certain areas of the island of Hawaii—or, in the case of the sheep, to Kahoolawe and Hawaii—where they continue to cause damage.

Yocom (*op. cit.*) noted that while erosion is a natural phenomenon in the crater of Haleakala, goat herds past and present have increased the rate. He lists ten categories of destruction, and this same destructiveness can apply to every goat herd in the islands; for that reason I list them below.

"Increased erosion has been brought about by:

a. Overgrazing of native plants.

b. Elimination of some native plants, thus eliminating ground cover.

c. Disturbance of the soil by sharp hooves.

d. Complete elimination of plants from saddles, hogback ridges, goat trails, and along the rim of the crater by feeding or loitering herds of goats.

e. Pawing of the ground by billies before lying down.

f. Increased erosion by rainfall of soils disturbed by goats.

g. Increased erosion by wind of soils disturbed by goats.

h. Slides started by grazing goats.

i. Slides started by goats of all ages playing on the exposed cinders and basalt.

j. Slides started by rocks dislodged by feeding goats."

Damage to native plant communities also indirectly occurs when goats eat introduced vegetation (such as blackberries) and later defecate the hard-shelled exotic seeds in other areas. When the seeds sprout an unwelcome form of plant competition occurs with, unfortunately, the invader often winning.

In 1966 the State Division of Fish and Game built a goat-proof exclosure on Short Mohihi Ridge on the eastern side of Kauai's Waimea Canyon. They intend to maintain this exclosure for some years and to photographically record vegetative changes both within and without the pen, in an effort to more fully understand the changes in cover attributable to goats. Within one year it became obvious that "natural erosion is being accelerated by feral goat activity" and this damage was, in that area at least, most pronounced on the crown of the ridge (Walker, 1968). This area has a herd of approximately 170 goats which are kept from increasing (or decreasing) by well-regulated hunting seasons; studies such as this will eventually provide important information about the ability of the range to recover when feral goats are excluded.

THE FUTURE

As previously mentioned, goats under the control of the state can presently be considered as being within manageable limits. The goats on Oahu will probably continue to exist in small numbers for many years, but their population will never again be allowed to expand to the point of posing a threat to the watershed areas of the Waianae Range. The goat population on

Molokai is fairly large (800 to 1,000 animals), but is kept at about this number by the hunters residing on that island. It is hoped that the Lanai goats will be exterminated within the next several years. In view of the Department of Defense's prohibition against landing on Kahoolawe, the two or three hundred goats on that island are relatively undisturbed, except for the occasional practice bomb. They will probably continue to exist on that island for many years.

The goats on Maui, with the hopeful exception of those in the National Park, will probably continue to exist for many years, but there is little indication that those on state lands are doing noticeable damage, and animals on private lands are adequately controlled by the landowners. On Hawaii, the major problem is in the Hawaii Volcanoes National Park; if we are to judge the future from the half-hearted efforts of the past, we can sadly predict that goats will continue to thrive there for many years to come. A statement made by a park ranger not long ago about "building and maintaining some goat-proof fences . . ." sounds very much like the prognostication made by Mr. Lamb just 30 years ago.

The inability of the National Park Service to control goats on their present parklands has had a definite effect on a proposal by this agency to acquire portions of Kauai for National Park status. Waimea Canyon and the Na Pali Coast fall within the proposed boundaries of the projected park and as mentioned earlier, there are some 2,000 goats on these lands. Over the nine-year period from 1959 through 1967, almost 9,000 hunter days were used by sportsmen to harvest at least 3,585 goats, an average of 448 goats per year (Telfer, 1968). Because National Park policy does not permit "open access hunting" by private individuals, who have to literally risk their necks to bag a goat— some conservationists who would otherwise have strongly favored a National Park continue to oppose the idea until park rangers can give more than lip-service to the statement that they could, and would, control the number of Kauai goats—

the conservationists would prefer to keep the lands under state control. The National Park administration does not seem to find it within their ability to eliminate 600 animals on open and relatively flat country; thus it is questionable if they could kill over three times that number, all of whom inhabit some of the ruggedest and steepest cliffs of the Hawaiian Islands.

LITERATURE CITED

Alicata, J. E.
    1964   Parasitic infections of man and animals in Hawaii. Hawaii Agri. Exp. Sta. Tech. Bull. 61: 138pp., illus.

Anonymous
    1904   First report of the Board of Commissioners of Agriculture and Forestry of the Territory of Hawaii. The Bulletin Publ. Co., Honolulu: p. 44.

Baker, A. S.
    1916   Ahua a Umi. Thrum's Hawaiian Annual for 1917: 62–70.

Bernice P. Bishop Museum
    1925   Diary of Andrew Bloxam, naturalist of the "Blonde", on her trip from England to the Hawaiian Islands, 1824–25. B. P. Bishop Mus., Spec. Publ. 10, Honolulu: 96pp.

Bryan, L. W.
    1930   Hawaii's wild goat problem. Paradise of the Pacific 43(12): 77–78.

    1947   Twenty-five Years of Forestry Work on the Island of Hawaii. Hawaiian Planters' Record 51: 1–80.

Forbes, C. N.
    1913   An innumeration of Niihau plants. B. P. Bishop Mus., Occas. Papers 5(3): 17–30.

Graf, W.
    1963   The effect of isolation on house mice (*Mus musculus*) and the feral goat (*Capra sp.*) on the Hawaiian Islands. Amer. Philos. Soc., Yearbook: 326–329.

Henke, L. A.
  1929   A survey of livestock in Hawaii. U. Hawaii Res. Publ.
         No. 5: 82pp.
Judd, C. S.
  1916   Kahoolawe. Thrum's Hawaiian Annual for 1917: 117–
         125.
Judd, H. P.
  1930   The goat menace on Hawaii. Friend 100: 193–194.
Lamb, S. H.
  1938   Goat drives in Hawaii National Park. Paradise of the
         Pacific 50(12): 91.
Marques, A.
  1905   Goats in Hawaii. Thrum's Hawaiian Annual for 1906:
         48–55.
Morse, G.
  1968   Park rangers get their goat. Sunday Star Bull. and Ad-
         vertiser, April 28: A-3.
Munro, G. C.
  1955   Make Lanai a hunters' paradise. Honolulu Advertiser,
         May 2 (editorial page).
Telfer, T.
  1968   Feral goat season results—Na Pali and Waimea Canyon,
         Kauai. W-5-R-19, Job 53(19), State of Hawaii, Div. of
         Fish and Game. Honolulu: 4pp., mimeo.
Walker, R. L.
  1968   Big Game Range Survey—Mohihi, Waimea Canyon,
         Island of Kauai. W-5-R-19, Job 55(19), State of Hawaii,
         Div. of Fish and Game. Honolulu: 14pp., mimeo.
Yocom, C. F.
  1967   Ecology of feral goats in Haleakala National Park,
         Maui, Hawaii. Am. Midl. Nat. 77(2): 418–451.

The Mouflon

Ovis musimon

The mouflon sheep was the first mammal to be introduced into the state of Hawaii by the Division of Fish and Game. It was introduced for the purpose of "filling a vacant ecological niche" on the island of Lanai; the motive was, of course, to provide additional hunting on new hunting grounds while at the same time increasing the variety of trophy heads a hunter might seek. At a later date the mouflon was seen as a means of reducing range damage on the unique native forest on Mauna Kea; feral sheep were ravaging the land but could not be exterminated because of the vested interests of a small but politically powerful group of meat hunters who thwarted every effort of the state's biologists to reduce the herd. The idea was conceived of hybridizing the feral sheep with one of their ancient progenitors, the mouflon, and eventually producing an animal that would, by virtue of its social habits, vigor, and temperament, quit damaging the vegetative regrowth so necessary to this unique mountain flora, and unique bird and insect fauna dependent upon it.

After careful and long-range planning, the program was undertaken; during the period when the biologists were experimenting and gathering data on the results of the hybridization (from back-crossing by feral males), seasons were opened on Mauna Kea that were meant to reduce the number of feral rams. Then the entry of mouflon hybrids to the mountain slopes could occur with less competition and consequent greater chance of success. Initially all but a few hunters had agreed to the logic of such a program, and had professed interest in the welfare of plant and animal species other than the sheep, but a small number became alarmed at the reduction and rallied forces to fight the program. On March 13, 1962, legislative instruction (Standing Committee Report No. 75) was given to the Division of Fish and Game that "the mouflon sheep should supplement rather than replace the native Mauna Kea sheep." The experiment was a success, but the program, for reasons politic, had failed. The reader should be apprised that there is no such thing as a "native Mauna Kea sheep" (see chapter on feral sheep).

HISTORY

The mouflon is a true wild sheep from the mountain regions of Corsica and Sardinia and is believed to be one of the original ancestors of many breeds of domestic sheep. Hawaii was one of the first United States areas to have this species released into the wild, the first release occurring on July 30, 1954. Two adult rams, three adult ewes, and five juvenile ewes had been donated by the Honolulu Zoo for the release, which took place on the ridge between Keone and Naupaka gulches on the western slope of Lanai. During the next eight years an additional 35 animals were released. From these 45 animals, the herd has increased to at least 250. It is impossible to get an accurate census because of the rugged terrain from which the mouflon refuse to flush. Twenty-one rams were shot in the first hunting season in 1964, 22 in 1965, and only six in 1966. Females have not been hunted.

In 1958, two adult rams and two adult ewes were introduced into the Na Pali region of Kauai but these animals disappeared in a short time and were never seen again. There is considerable

Feral Sheep

Hybrid

Pure Mouflon

evidence that they were killed by poachers. No further attempts were made to reintroduce animals to that island.

In 1957, Dr. William Graf, professor of wildlife management at San Jose State College, became aware of the Mauna Kea sheep damage problem when he visited Hawaii, and submitted a plan for the hybridization of the existing feral stock with that of the less destructive mouflon. State officials were delighted with the idea and asked the Division of Fish and Game to proceed, gathering breeding stock from where they might. From 1958 until 1962, such mouflon as could be purchased (from any zoo or zoological garden) were kept penned at Pohakuloa on the slope of Mauna Kea and were used as breeding stock. From June 1962 until February 1966, a total of 46 rams and 48 ewes of pure mouflon stock were released on Mauna Kea, as were 33 hybrid rams and 66 hybrid ewes. All releases of hybrid animals were in the Puu Laau area; 16 pure mouflon were released in Puu Laau, and the remaining 78 were released in the Kahinahina section (Walker, 1966).

DESCRIPTION

The great, sweeping yellowish-brown horns of the ram are usually sufficient to distinguish them from the ewes, which are usually hornless. On superior animals the horns sweep up and outward before commencing a curving sweep downward and, eventually, forward. They seldom have the tight curl of the feral sheep and rarely attain the "full curl" of the American bighorn sheep (*Ovis canadensis*).

Rams stand about 26 to 27 inches at the shoulder and ewes are slightly smaller. Rams weigh about 125 pounds when fully grown, with the females slightly less. Both sexes have a generally brownish-tan body color on the upper parts and upper legs, but have a white belly, which color carries down the inner sides of the legs to the "knee"; from there down the leg is whitish. The males exhibit a white saddle patch during the winter months,

One of the mature mouflon rams released on the island of Kauai. John R. Woodworth.

and show a distinctive reddish-black mane of four- or five-inch length covering the neck and throat region. The coat is "hairy" rather than woolly, a character that appears for a while in all newborn sheep with mouflon blood; as these hybrids grow older the woolly coat may overshadow this trait. As Bachman (1964) points out, a hybrid that may have lost whatever mouflon pelage it once had, because of back-crossing with feral sheep, can still be identified by its characteristic horn development, by its much more alert nature and stance, and by its mouflonlike tail.

The mouflons' rump is white and bisected by a short (three to four inch) black tail. Of three one-quarter or less mouflon carcasses checked, all tails were obviously mouflonlike; the feral sheep have tail lengths averaging 10 to 14 inches in length (Bachman, 1965).

DISTRIBUTION

LANAI. In 1961 Walker censused the release area and found that very few animals ranged as far south as the Kaumalapau Highway, and that none had gone beyond Paliamano Gulch to the north (Walker, 1962). Earlier, in 1957 and 1958, several rams were known to have made exploratory trips across the island, and several animals took up temporary residence near the cemetery behind Lanai City but one ram was eventually chased off by dogs, and another was so severely injured by dogs that it had to be destroyed. Sightings were also made of animals on the northern end of the island at Hawaiilanui Gulch, and at the southern end near Manele Bay. These wanderers apparently returned to the main concentration on the western side of the island, since no sightings have been made from these areas in later years.

As of 1968, Walker (pers. comm.) says that a few animals have moved to the south of Kaumalapau Highway, and that the herd has expanded northward to Kaena Point, a linear distance of about eight and one-half miles from the release pen.

Excepting the two rams who lived behind the cemetery at an altitude of about 2,000 feet, the altitudinal range of the mouflon on Lanai varies from sea level to about 1,300 feet. Their eastern boundaries at this altitude are open pineapple flats, which they do not like to enter, but at the northern tip of the island, where pineapple is not grown, it would appear that the population is slowly expanding and moving eastward. In time we may expect to find that the mouflon have circumnavigated the island, occupying all areas except the pineapple fields, the dense mountain forest, and the open plains above the Kaholo Pali on the southwestern edge of the island.

HAWAII. As mentioned earlier, 99 hybrid sheep and 16 pure-blood mouflon were released in the Puu Laau section of the

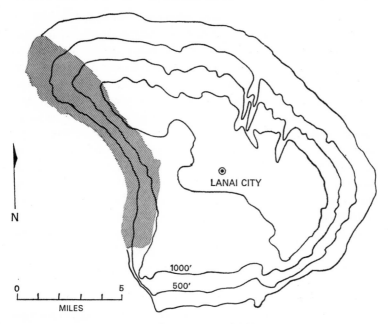

Fig. 6. Distribution of mouflon on Lanai (1968)

Mauna Kea Forest Reserve in 1962. The animals were released
at about the 7,500-foot level of this westernmost section of the
reserve. They remained in the immediate vicinity of the release
site for sometime, with the hybrids almost immediately joining
flocks of feral sheep, and the mouflon initially taking off on
their own for distances of several miles. Bachman (1964) noted
that the mouflon roamed separately, with no flock affiliations,
for about six months before they joined groups of feral sheep
which they still presently attend and, in fact, dominate. This
group of animals has slowly moved northward toward the
Kemole area, and has been observed ranging primarily at an
altitude of nine to ten thousand feet, although some animals
move down to the fenceline at 7,000 feet from time to time.
Bachman (*ibid.*) has also stated that no seasonal movement pat-

tern has been noted; the only movements of any distance appear to be temporary, occasioned by heavy hunting pressure.

Between November 1963 and February 1966, 30 mouflon rams and 48 mouflon ewes were released at the 8,500-foot level in the Kahinahina section on the opposite side of the mountain. These animals remained in the immediate vicinity of the release pen for two months (Bachman, *ibid.*) before beginning to range farther afield. In 1964 several separate groups were seen as far as three miles from the release site, and by 1966 it was evident that they were concentrated in the Puu Kole area, about six miles to the southwest. The vegetative cover in this area is similar to that of the release area, but is somewhat rougher because of greater expanses of open lava fields. It was felt that they may have moved here to take advantage of the protection of these fields, since both man and dog find the jagged ʻaʻa lava slow and painful to traverse, while the mouflon appears unaffected by the rugged terrain.

Several rams took long trips afield; it is not clear whether these were due to curiosity or to being chased by dogs. One ram was seen near Kemole, on the opposite side of the mountain, some two years after release; assuming that it traveled around the contour, rather than directly over the summit, it had wandered about 12 to 14 miles. Another ram, released in June 1965, was captured on the Saddle Road only 13 miles from Hilo, about three months later; it must have traveled at least 12 linear miles through extremely rugged and dense forest. Ewes occasionally move fairly far afield and several observations have been made of ewes and rams keeping company with feral sheep at the 7,000-foot level on Parker Ranch pastureland.

Mouflon hybrids have shown their "hybrid vigor" by expanding their numbers and distribution to an extent not yet evidenced by the pure mouflon. Numbers of these animals have ranged north, almost to the area known as Kanakaleonui, and south to the cinder cones of Kalapeamoa in the Kole section of the mountain, a total distance of about ten miles. They are generally kept from going lower than 8,000 feet by the forest-reserve fence which encircles the mountain, and seldom range above 10,500 feet. It has been noted by hunters that when a mixed flock of animals is "spooked," the feral sheep resort to their usual pattern of heading straight up the slope of Mauna Kea while the mouflon and hybrids move along the contour and disappear into heavy patches of foliage (Bachman, *ibid.*). Generally, mouflon are found throughout the day at lower altitudes feeding among the heavier stands of *māmane* (*Sophora crysophylla*) while the feral sheep tend to browse at the upper treeline. Walker (1966) has noted that, along with their habit of keeping to the lower parts of the forest, the mouflon maintains smaller flock numbers (2 to 23) than the feral sheep, and feels that these two factors substantially lessen the danger of irrevocable damage to the forest.

FOOD HABITS

Strange as it may seem, there have been no food-habit studies made on the mouflon, even after 14 years of residence on Lanai. Biologists on Hawaii can be excused for not collecting this information since most of their experience has been in dealing with penned animals and there was no opportunity to collect enough wild animals to give meaningful data, but there is no excuse for not having examined the stomach contents of the 49 rams taken during the 1964–66 seasons on Lanai.

The only information presently available for Lanai is that animals kept in the release pen at Naupaka Ridge fed on *koa haole* (*Leucaena glauca*), *'ilima* (*Sida fallax*), *klu* (*Acacia farnesiana*), *kiawe* (*Prosopis chilensis*), and "grass" (presumably *pili, Heteropogon contortus,* which is the commonest species in that habitat). Medeiros (1964) noted that considerable *koa haole* was "barked" in the summer of 1963 and theorized that this may have been due to moisture-seeking in this very dry summer (rats were noted barking *kiawe* trees at this same time). It is highly probable that mouflon on Lanai eat about the same plant species as do the axis deer (*Axis axis*), but in different proportions (see axis deer chapter for food list).

The only observations on the Mauna Kea mouflon have been by Bachman (1964) who made the field observation that "mamane appears to be the most important food in their diet as well as small amounts of gosmore (*Hypochaeris radicata*) and various grasses."

REPRODUCTION AND GROWTH

The gestation period of domestic sheep varies between 146 and 161 days and it was assumed that this same period held true for the mouflon; Walker (1960a) confirmed this assumption by observing a hybrid birth happening exactly 150 days after breeding. Either one or two lambs are born after a period of labor lasting about one hour (Walker, 1959).

Walker (*ibid.*) has also recorded that hybrid lambs are "very precocial and were particularly agile in the early morning and late evening. They appeared more playful, more fleet afoot, and more alert than most feral lambs. . . . When captured, the young hybrids displayed unusual strength and endurance. In the three months following their birth, all the lambs grew rapidly, and by June 30 (10 weeks after birth) two of the male hybrids had developed short horn stubs."

There have been insufficient field observations on the mouflon of Lanai to make a definite statement concerning lambing peaks or breeding seasons. Walker (1960a) recorded seeing a newborn lamb in March 1960, but lambs have also been seen in February, April, May, June, and July. In July 1960, Walker (1961) writes of receiving reports of "many ewes . . . seen with new lambs." Rams have been seen attempting to breed ewes in December and January (Walker, 1960a) and one was seen attempting to copulate on April 25 (Walker, 1962). These attempts, if successful, would have produced young in May, June, and late

September. Observations on the captive animals on Mauna Kea are of little value because they were force-bred in an attempt to produce as many hybrids in as short a time as possible. Since the feral sheep appear to be receptive to breeding throughout the year, mouflon rams on Mauna Kea probably breed the feral ewes on a year-round basis.

Male mouflon are believed to be capable of breeding at the age of five months, but because they are not then full grown, and have only very short horns, it is doubtful that many get the opportunity to do so if there is even one adult ram present to challenge them. F-1 generation male hybrids are definitely known to be sexually potent at this age (Walker, 1960b). F-1 female hybrids are known to be fertile at six and one-half months (Walker, *ibid.*) but lambs born to such small, young females often die of malnutrition, since the mother appears to be unable to furnish sufficient nourishing milk.

PREDATION, DISEASE, AND PARASITES

The only predators of any significance to the mouflon are feral dogs and, of course, man. As mentioned earlier, it is believed that poaching accounted for the loss of the four animals introduced to Kauai, and it is certain that other poachers have taken a number of animals from both Lanai and Hawaii. The wild dog (and occasionally, those not so wild) have probably had a greater effect on these two mouflon populations than all the illegal hunting. Packs of dogs have killed an uncounted number of animals on Lanai, making it necessary for Division of Fish and Game personnel to set out lines of "1080" poison stations plus innumerable "coyote getters" (cyanide guns) for several years. These sets apparently were effective since predation appears very low at the time of this writing. Wild dogs have been killing sheep on Mauna Kea for over 100 years and undoubtedly take their toll of mouflon.

No animals are known to have died from parasites or disease

on Lanai, but there was a rather high mortality of mouflon and their hybrid offspring in the breeding pens on Mauna Kea. Much of this mortality can be blamed on crowded conditions within the pens; the many cases of pneumonia (Pasturellosis) were believed due to excessive inhalation of dust, which was impossible to eliminate in the dry climate. From time to time animals suffered from scabies (*Psoroptes equi* var. *ovis*) and enterotoxemia (*Clostridium perfringens,* Type D), while a number have died from either "blackleg" (*Clostridium chauvoei*), malignant edema (*Clostridium septicum*), or a severe worm parasitism of the fourth stomach (abomasum), known as haemochosis (*Haemonchus contortus*). It is most probable that free-ranging mouflon now suffer such other afflictions as are common to sheep in Hawaii (see "Parasites" in the feral sheep chapter).

MOUFLON/FERAL SHEEP RELATIONSHIPS

When the initial scheme of replacing the forest-damaging feral sheep with three-quarter mouflon, one-quarter feral sheep hybrids first got under way, the plan was to produce some 300 hybrids under penned conditions and at the same time regulate Mauna Kea feral sheep hunting so as to eliminate feral rams from the mountain. When this was done, and the hybrids were ready for release, a new season would have been set up whereby any sheep exhibiting feral characteristics was eliminated, and any showing mouflon blood was encouraged. When, because of political pressure, this plan had to be abandoned, the pure mouflon and existing hybrids in the pens were released onto the mountain. A number of interesting observations have been made and are reported:

1. Mouflon do not readily hybridize when both sexes of their species are released together. Although mouflon and feral sheep are frequently seen feeding in the same area, this seems to be the extent of their relationship (Bachman, 1964).

2. When only mouflon rams are released, they soon integrate

and breed with pure feral sheep and hybrids (Bachman, *ibid.*).

3. Mouflon hybrids are harder to approach than feral sheep, thereby rendering it difficult to get close shots. When a flock is alerted, it is always the mouflon or mouflon hybrids that take the lead in running from danger (Bachman, *ibid.*).

4. First generation hybrid lambs (F-1) show at least four different patterns of coloration, one of which is similar to the mouflon pattern (Walker, 1961).

5. Mouflon hybrids of even one-quarter blood, though still showing a woolly coat and varied coloration, are still recognizable by their more sweeping horn configuration, long straight guard hairs on the throat, and an alert nature (Walker, 1966).

6. Second generation ewes do not develop a true hair coat, but still show less of the curly wool character of the F-1 generation; rams, on the other hand, look very much like a mouflon, including exhibition of the saddle patch, but still retain some wool on the dorsal part of the body along the backbone (Walker, pers. comm.).

7. The F-3 generation (seven-eighths mouflon, one-eighth feral sheep) is almost indistinguishable from the wild type, excepting that it is somewhat stockier in appearance, and it exhibits small patches of wool at certain seasons (Walker, *ibid.*).

THE FUTURE

The mouflon can certainly be considered as being established on the island of Lanai, and as noted earlier, will probably continue to expand its range. After further field investigations it will probably come to be recognized as one of the major big game trophy animals in Hawaii, and should be avidly sought by mainland hunters in the future.

The status of the mouflon on Hawaii must be thought of as uncertain; the animal has its enemies among the local sportsmen, who claim that it is too difficult to hunt and that its meat is not as tasty as that of the feral sheep. Some of these hunters would just as soon see the mouflon disappear from the mountain and will probably attempt to thwart any efforts of the state to reduce the feral sheep numbers. If feral rams are not removed in fairly large number, their effect upon the hybridization program will be to submerge, by back-crossing, the positive characters presently being exhibited by mouflon offspring; thus, the future of the mouflon on Mauna Kea is tied irrevocably to that of the feral sheep.

LITERATURE CITED

Bachman, R.

1964   Hybridization of the mouflon (*Ovis musimon*) with the feral sheep (*Ovis aries*). W-5-R-15, Job 51(15), State of Hawaii, Div. of Fish and Game, Honolulu: mimeo.

——

1965   Hybridization of the mouflon (*Ovis musimon*) with the feral sheep (*Ovis aries*). W-5-R-16, Job 51(16), State of Hawaii, Div. of Fish and Game, Honolulu: mimeo.

Medeiros, J. S.

1964   Lanai mouflon survey. W-5-R-15, Job 53, State of Hawaii, Div. of Fish and Game, Honolulu: 2pp., mimeo.

Walker, R. L.

1959   Experimental introduction and hybridization of the European mouflon (*Ovis musimon*). W-5-R-10, Job 51 (10), State of Hawaii, Div. of Fish and Game, Honolulu: 7pp., mimeo.

——

1960a Experimental introduction and hybridization of the European mouflon (*Ovis musimon*). W-5-R-11, Job 51 (11), State of Hawaii, Div. of Fish and Game, Honolulu: mimeo.

——

1960b The hybridization of the mouflon with the Hawaiian feral sheep as a management technique. 40th Ann. Conf.

West'n. Assn. State Fish and Game Comm., Proc.: 148–155.

1961   Experimental introduction and hybridization of the European mouflon (*Ovis musimon*). W-5-R-12, Job 51 (12), State of Hawaii, Div. of Fish and Game, Honolulu: 9pp., mimeo.

1962   Experimental introduction of exotic game birds and mammals. W-5-R-13, Job 50(13), State of Hawaii, Div. of Fish and Game, Honolulu: mimeo.

1966   Hybridization of the mouflon (*Ovis musimon*) with the feral sheep. W-5-R-17, Job 51(17), State of Hawaii, Div. of Fish and Game, Honolulu: mimeo.

The Feral Sheep

Ovis aries

On February 22, 1793, Capt. George Vancouver landed two ewes and a ram at Kealakekua Bay, on the island of Hawaii, as a gift for Kamehameha I.* Since that time, the feral and domestic sheep have probably wrought more changes in the original Hawaiian ecosystem than any other animal, at least on certain areas of Molokai, Lanai, Kahoolawe, and Hawaii. Because of a complete lack of knowledge of the precarious system of checks and balances that go into the make-up of an insular environment such as was originally present, we cannot really blame either the individuals who introduced sheep to the various islands, or the government agencies who allowed these animals to range freely and in ever growing numbers, at least for the first 150 years. During the last two or three decades foresters, biologists, botanists, and conservationists (including many avid hunters) have all been keenly aware of the desperate need to, if not totally eliminate this species from the wild, at least keep their numbers reduced to a point where vegetative reproduction

---

* There is a possibility that Vancouver was not the first to introduce sheep to Hawaii. On page 45 of the 1850 *Transactions of the Royal Agricultural Society*, Vol. 1(1), is the comment that: "Captain Colnet left a ewe and ram on Kauai before the arrival of Vancouver."

can begin to repair the scars of past years. Unfortunately, public apathy and ignorance, combined with specific political pressures by a small number of self-serving and politically powerful hunters, have continually thwarted, or at least hampered, all recent efforts by professional game and range managers to reduce sheep numbers to a proper balance.

The story of sheep in Hawaii can really be little more than reportage of scattered statistics; the assumption has always been made that the life history of the animal was almost exactly that of any domestic sheep (and that the data could be gleaned from any handbook of commercial sheep production), and the ecology has never been studied, partly because of the rugged terrain, and partly due to a lack of available manpower in the agencies charged with the management of this species. Not being a particularly glamorous animal, these "mountain maggots" (as they are called by their detractors) have not excited the curiosity of out-of-state naturalists or ecologists, who might well have obtained grants to study these animals; as a result, management has been mostly of the "count and shoot" nature—count them and, if numbers are high, increase the bag limit; if numbers are low, close the season; count them again next year —a relatively unscientific, but highly effective, technique.

HISTORY

Just 11 months after Vancouver first landed sheep on Hawaii, he returned to Kealakekua Bay and, on January 15, 1794, presented Kamehameha with ten more animals, five rams and five ewes (Henke, 1929). The variety of sheep is unknown.

Kamehameha I put a *kapu* (taboo) on these animals, and they were apparently left to wander where they chose. No further mention of sheep can be found until 1822, when the Reverend Joseph Goodrich, while climbing Mauna Kea, noted: "Very near to the summit, upon one of the peaks I found eight or ten dead sheep; they probably fled up there to seek a refuge from the wild dogs; I have heard that there are many wild dogs, sheep and goats" (Tinker, 1941). Thus we see that in the intervening 28 years, the sheep herds must have increased considerably (perhaps with the unrecorded introduction of greater numbers of sheep); it is just about 40 miles "as the crow flies" from Kealakekua to the summit of Mauna Kea, and there were certainly many additional miles to traverse as the animals passed over the slopes of Mauna Loa and Hualalai.

When the first governmental body was formed, the wild sheep became the joint property of the king and the government, and permission was needed from the government before animals could be killed, captured, or shipped to other islands. From 1822 until 1845 there is a lapse in the records, but we know that in this latter year sheep were present on Kauai (Henke, *op. cit.*). This same year, the first pureblood Merinos were introduced to the islands; it was rapidly becoming evident to the local residents that, since feral sheep could survive so well, there might be money to be made by starting a sheep industry. By 1851, Bishop (1852) estimated that there were at least 3,000 wild sheep on Hawaii, as well as uncounted numbers on Maui, Molokai, and Kauai.

By 1853 Saxon and Southdown breeds were introduced, and in 1862, the emperor of France presented "four picked rams from the Royal flock at Rambouillet to the King of Hawaii" (Henke, *op. cit.*).

Early in 1858, a scouting trip was made to Kahoolawe for the express purpose of evaluating potential sheep pasturage. In a letter (Allen, 1858) to Messrs. Wyllie and Allen, pasturage was considered ample for 20,000 sheep (on an island area of only 28,700 acres), and later this same year, Robert C. Wyllie obtained a 20-year lease for a fee of $505 per year. The venture failed one year later when "scab" (*Psoroptes equi ovis?*) became rampant (Hollingsworth, 1938). The 1859 population is recorded as being 2,075. Presumably most if not all these animals were left to forage for themselves.

A sheep ranch was started on Lanai sometime after 1861, and on April 4, 1864, permission was granted to ship 3,000 sheep from Molokai to Niihau (Henke, *op. cit.*).

Now that all islands had received a supply of "blooded" sheep, ranching was pursued with vigor, and the wild sheep were ignored, except by a few hungry hunters and wild dogs. Between 1879 and 1884, Henke (*ibid.*) records between 101,000 and 121,000 sheep being raised annually, and then shows a continual decline in production until 1928, when he estimated only 25,000 domestic animals left. Lanai is recorded as having had up to 50,000 animals prior to 1910, when the Lanai Company, Ltd., started a switch to cattle raising, and the sheep population on that island dropped from 20,588 in 1911 to 860 in 1920. On Molokai, there were almost 16,000 animals in 1900 (the same year the Tunis sheep was introduced to the islands), about 17,000 in 1907, but only about 200 by 1928; the abandonment of sheep raising on this island was attributed to a combination of sheep and cattle overpasturing and the fact that *kiawe* (*Prosopis chilensis*) thorns on the ground caused too much lameness (Henke, *ibid.*).

From 1928 on, sheep raising in Hawaii has been primarily carried on by Parker Ranch (which went out of commercial sheep production in 1964), and by the Robinson family on Niihau (with a present-day population estimated at 13,000 animals, on this 46,000-acre island).

MAUNA KEA SHEEP

As mentioned earlier, the feral sheep were all but forgotten in the rush to start domestic herds and on the high mountains of Hawaii the herds grew larger and larger. In 1937, there were an estimated 40,000 feral sheep ranging the slopes of the Mauna Kea Forest Reserve; this 80,000-acre reserve encompasses the 13,764-foot-high summit of Mauna Kea and extends down on all slopes to about the 7,000-foot level. Just below this surveyors' boundary was private ranchland, mostly belonging to Parker

Ranch, which itself raised some 30,000 Merino sheep. Feral sheep were also present in uncounted numbers on the lava flat areas of Mount Hualalai and Mauna Loa, as well as the saddle between these two mountains. Foresters had been aware for some years of the tremendous damage that the feral sheep were doing to the native vegetation and in particular to the endemic *māmane* trees (*Sophora chrysophylla*); in some sections there had been no natural reproduction of these trees for years and, as Bryan (1937) noted: "If this state of affairs was allowed to continue it would only be a matter of time before our mountains would be without a protective covering." Up until 1935 the territory had been too poor to finance the building of a 50-mile-long fence around the lower border of the forest reserve, but with the advent of the CCC, work was begun on the fence. This sheep and (supposedly) pig-proof fence took about two years to complete, but in the meantime, the Territorial Division of Forestry, in cooperation with local ranchers (Parker Ranch in particular), undertook the job of shooting or driving sheep off the mountain. As Bryan (1950) records control by shooting, he said: "Men were at one time employed for this purpose and did nothing but shoot goats and sheep. The sheep were formerly so plentiful and easy to shoot that shotguns loaded with buckshot were sometimes used and it was not uncommon for the hunter to kill more than one animal with a single shot."

Driving the animals was a more effective technique and Bryan (1937) tells of a drive conducted in late December 1936, when 3,113 sheep were caught; "Parker Ranch . . . provided 30 cowboys and all riding animals needed. This drive covered an area of between 10 and 12 square miles. . . . The actual drive required only six hours. . . . The actual killing of over 3,000 sheep is quite a problem. It must be done quickly and in a humane manner. Shooting is out of the question on account of the expense and danger to those around. It is not a pleasant job at best but a sharp knife, properly handled, is one good method. The animal is captured by driving small numbers into an inner

Some of the more than 3,000 sheep caught in a one-day drive on Mauna Kea in 1936. Note the heavily browsed and dying *mamane* trees in the background. Archives of Hawaii.

pen, quickly stunned by a sharp blow on the head and then dispatched." It took 25 CCC boys two 13-hour days to kill the sheep. Over 300 carcasses were given to the Salvation Army, and the CCC boys consumed their share, but the majority of carcasses were thrown away; the huge pile of bones from this slaughter can still be seen today at the site of the old pen between Puu Nanaha and Puu Laau.

Other drives were held, shooting continued, and poisoning programs were attempted, but the population still remained high; in the period from 1921 until 1946, 46,765 feral sheep were removed from Mauna Kea alone, and an additional 24,703 were killed on other forest reserve lands (Bryan, 1947). From 1947 thru 1949, over 5,400 more sheep were killed on the "White Mountain," mostly by individual sportsmen. At this time, the Territorial Division of Fish and Game assumed management responsibility for the area, and was shocked to find that a census of the mountain showed only about 200 sheep left. Since the divisions of Forestry and Fish and Game had never contemplated total extermination, but had felt instead that the sheep herd could be kept in balance with vegetative regeneration, the hunting season was immediately closed. This closure stayed in effect until 1953, when another census indicated that there were about 1,000 sheep present, a fivefold increase in three years.

Within two more years this population had doubled and in the years from 1957 through 1960, sheep counts showed almost 3,000 sheep and estimates of the total population approached 4,000. Despite the killing of 7,044 sheep by hunters during this period (Kosaka, 1966), a head count in May 1961, showed 2,418 animals. In this year more sheep were harvested by hunters (2,499) than were counted (2,418), but despite this, 1,835 animals were seen on Mauna Kea in March 1962.

In 1964, Nichols felt that both range and forage conditions were showing improvement on Mauna Kea and that the herd should be kept, through manipulation of hunting seasons and bag limits, at about the 1,300- to 1,500-animal level. Pressures by some hunters did not allow this, and the Mauna Kea herd once again began its upward swing on the cycle. The State Division of Fish and Game constructed six animal exclosures about this time, in an attempt to eventually visually prove to the public the damage done by overstocking. Excerpts from a report (Kosaka, March 1967) show ". . . there is good evidence of mamane sprouting within the exclosure [Puu O Kau]—none on the outside." For the Kaluamakani area he notes: "The area outside of the exclosure is almost denuded of ground cover with no new mamane sprouts. Vegetation within the exclosure is noticeably denser and consists of scattered herbs and grasses, and good sprouting of mamane"; for Puu Kole, "this exclosure shows excellent evidence of recovery with good sprouting of mamane and various annuals. . . . In contrast . . . there is no sprouting of mamane and annuals and [there is] some erosion on the outside." As evidenced by these reports, and the photographs which accompany them, the sheep population is still beyond the mountains' carrying capacity and it is likely that this sad process will continue until some irate faction of Hawaii's citizenry marshals sufficient political backing to successfully overcome the forces which presently dictate their policies to the Department of Land and Natural Resources.

KAHOOLAWE SHEEP

As noted earlier, the first sheep were taken to Kahoolawe in 1858. The next lessee took sheep there again in 1863 and Judd (1916) records that in 1890 the third lessee pastured 12,000 sheep on the island. In 1909 there were 3,200 sheep remaining on the island (Judd, *ibid.*), and because of the damage being done to the island by stock (there were also about 5,000 goats on the island at that time), the government canceled the private lease and designated the Board of Agriculture and Forestry to reseed the land and kill off the remaining stock. Forbes (1913) states that there were still 300 sheep present in 1913 and Judd (*op. cit.*) notes that all but 150 sheep had been eliminated by 1916. The island was withdrawn from forest reserve status again in 1918 (Bryan, 1931) and was leased as a cattle ranch, but sheep were still present. In 1932, Zschokke reviewed past and present conditions on the island and noted that ". . . soil and subsoil to the depth of 15 feet have been blown into the ocean."

No statistics on the sheep are available since 1918, but we do know that attempts were made up until World War II to eliminate both sheep and goats from that island. Tinker (*op. cit.*) thought that the sheep had disappeared from the island by 1939 but noted that ". . . they have left a mark of desolation which will take many years to remove." Unfortunately, there were still a few scattered bands of animals left and, with the coming of the war, at which time the island was turned over to the Department of Defense and used as a practice bombing and shelling range, human access was denied and the sheep population began to increase. Even though Kahoolawe is to this day used as a bombing range, and untold numbers of sheep and goats have been killed by such action, the sheep population has fluctuated from peaks reckoned at 5,000 animals to lows of 200 to 300. In recent years this island has become the private hunting ground for members of various military branches and it is not uncommon for helicopters to return from the island bearing the hindquarters of 30 or 40 sheep and one or two goats.

DESCRIPTION

Mauna Kea sheep, being possessed of the mixed blood of a variety of domesticized breeds, have never really been looked upon as worthy of carefully documented description. The most that can be said for them is that their woolly bodies are of mixed coloration: black, brown, gray, white, and many hues between. Their horns are also either black or yellow-white. Kahoolawe sheep, on the other hand, are mostly white with a few gray animals found from time to time, but all have yellowish-white horns. Rams will sometimes weigh over 100 pounds, but most average 70 or 80 pounds with the ewes being somewhat smaller. Animals that are seen with part wool and part fur coats are hybrid crosses from the mouflon sheep.

BREEDING

Ewes are capable of breeding the first time at an age of about five months; they usually bear only one lamb at this age, but from then on ewes produce one or two offspring twice a year. In late winter or early spring the major lambing peak occurs on Hawaii, but there is a second, smaller peak in late summer; and smaller numbers of newborn lambs can be found every month of the year. No breeding data are available for the Kahoolawe sheep.

PARASITES AND DISEASE

Dr. Joseph Alicata, in his *Parasitic Infections of Man and Animals in Hawaii* (1964), has listed a number of organisms infesting sheep; the reader is referred to pages 86 and 87 of that book for further information. The species list presented below is from page 115 of Dr. Alicata's work.

Name of Parasite	Location	Intermediate Host (if any)
ROUNDWORMS:		
Cooperia punctata	small intestine	
Haemonchus contortus	fourth stomach	
Nematodirus spathiger	small intestine	
Trichostrongylus colubriformis	stomach and small intestine	
TAPEWORMS:		
Moniezia expansa	small intestine	Acarina: species of oribatid mites.
Taenia hydatigena	larval stage attached to liver, mesentery, and omentum	pig, *Sus scrofa*
FLUKES:		
Fasciola sp. (gigantica?)	liver	Gastropoda: *Fossaria ollula*
ARTHROPODS:		
Chrysomyia megacephala	in wounds and external	
Melophagus ovinus	external	
Oestrus ovis	nasal cavities and sinuses of head	
Otobius megnini (larvae and nymphs)	ear canal	
Psoroptes equi ovis	skin	

The mouflon sheep has been found to have suffered from enterotoxemia (*Clostridium perfringens*), malignant edema (*Clos-*

tridium septicum) and "blackleg" (*Clostridium chauvoei*), and it is highly likely that if these diseases were not present in the sheep before the late 1950s, they are now.

THE FUTURE

At this stage of development of game management in Hawaii it is impossible to make any predictions about the future of feral sheep. Even if the Department of Defense were to return Kahoolawe to state jurisdiction, the agreement would probably include a clause noting the vast numbers of live shells scattered over the island, and for that reason would exclude the public until these explosives had been rendered harmless. Since this would require an expenditure of hundreds of thousands of dollars, it is probable that the state will never allow public hunting on the island as a means of reducing or eliminating feral mammals.

The sheep on Mauna Kea and four other nearby game management areas must be kept under some semblance of control if forest regeneration is to take place. The future of the endemic bird known as the *palila* (*Psittirostra bailleui*) hinges upon the abundance and distribution of the *māmane* forests (upon whose seeds it feeds), and there can be no excuse for ever again allowing any Hawaiian bird to become extinct. Citizens of the state must realize the vast scientific interest in this bird (it having been likened along with its relatives to "the Darwinian finches" of the Galapagos Islands), and that the state, through its Division of Fish and Game, is not in the sole business of providing a free butcher shop for its residents.

Certainly there is a place on Mauna Kea for a controlled number of feral sheep; they do provide a rugged and pleasant hunting experience as well as tasty meat, but until such time as professional biologists' opinions are heeded, and the herds kept in control, the sheep situation must be regarded as forceful evidence of the Hawaiian citizens' lack of interest in their own physical landscape.

LITERATURE CITED

Alicata, J. E.
  1964 Parasitic infections of man and animals in Hawaii. Hawaii Agri. Exp. Sta. Tech. Bull. 61: 138pp., illus.
Allen, W. F.
  1858 Letter of May 31 to Messrs. Wyllie and Allen, describing Kahoolawe (Original in Archives of Hawaii). Published in 1938 in: Paradise of the Pacific 50(5): 22, 27.
Bishop, C. R.
  1852 Trans. Roy. Haw'n. Agri. Soc. 1(3): 91.
Bryan, E. H., Jr.
  1931 Kahoolawe, the island of dust. Haw'n. Acad. Sci., Proc. Sixth Ann. Meeting. B. P. Bishop Mus., Spec. Publ. 19: 13–14.
Bryan, L. W.
  1937 Wild sheep in Hawaii. Paradise of the Pacific 49(3): 19, 31.

  ———

  1947 Twenty-five years of forestry work on the island of Hawaii. Hawaiian Planters' Record 51: 1–80.

  ———

  1950 Wild sheep on Mauna Kea Forest Reserve. Paradise of the Pacific 62(12): 112–113, 122.
Forbes, C. N.
  1913 Notes on the flora of Kahoolawe and Molokini. B. P. Bishop Mus., Occas. Pap. 5(3): 3–15.
Henke, L. A.
  1929 A survey of livestock of Hawaii. U. Hawaii Res. Publ. 5: 82pp.
Hollingsworth, L.
  1938 The Kahoolawe boom of 80 years ago. Hono. Star Bull., July 16, Feat. Section: p. 1.

Judd, C. S.
  1916 Kahoolawe. Hawaiian Annual for 1917. Thrum; Honolulu: 117–125.
Kosaka, E.
  1966 Feral sheep survey of the Mauna Kea Game Management Area, W-5-R-17, Job 53(17), State of Hawaii, Div. of Fish and Game, Honolulu: 5pp., mimeo.

  1967 Big game range survey, W-5-R-17, Job 55(17), State of Hawaii, Div. of Fish and Game, Honolulu: 3pp., mimeo.
Nichols, L., Jr.
  1964 Mauna Kea sheep survey, W-5-R-15, Job 53(15), State of Hawaii, Div. of Fish and Game, Honolulu: 6pp., mimeo.
Tinker, S. W.
  1941 Animals of Hawaii (2nd Edit.). Tongg Publ. Co., Honolulu: 190pp.
Wyllie, C.
  1850 Transactions of the Roy. Haw'n. Agri. Soc. 1(1), Gov't. Press, Hono.: 36–49.
Zschokke, T. C.
  1932 The forests of Kahoolawe. U. Hawaii Agri. Ext. Serv., Extension Letter No. 12: 7.

Appendix A

Hawaiian Names of Mammals

ENGLISH	HAWAIIAN
kangaroo (wallaby)	*kanakalū; kanagaru; kanekalu; kanegaru*
bat	*'ōpe'ape'a; pe'a; pe'ape'a*
rat	*'iole.* large rat: *'iole-nui;* water-diving rat: *'iole-po'o-wai*
mouse	*'iole; 'iole li'ili'i*
rabbit	*rabati; 'iole-lapaki*
guinea pig	*'iole-pua'a*
dog	*'ilio*
mongoose	*manakuke; 'iole-manakuke*
cat	*pōpoki; 'owau; 'oau.* Maltese cat: *pōpoki lehu.* tabby cat: *pōpoki pe'elua*
seal	*'ilio-holo-i-kauaua*
horse	*lio*
pig	*pua'a*
deer	*kia* (fr. Eng. dial.)
antelope	*'anekelopa*
cattle	*pipi; pua'a pipi*
water buffalo	*pipi pākē*
goat	*kao; kūnānā; nānā*
sheep	*hipa*

After M. K. Pukui and S. E. Elbert, *English-Hawaiian Dictionary.* Honolulu: U. Hawaii Press, 1964, 188pp.

Appendix B

Gestation Periods and Number of Young at Birth in Hawaiian Mammals

NAME	GESTATION PERIOD	NUMBER OF YOUNG
wallaby	(3–5 weeks)?	1.
Hawaiian bat	?	2, occas. 3–4.
rabbit	28–30 days	3–5, rarely to 10.
rats	21–23 days	3–12, usually 4–7.
house mouse	18–21 days	4–7, rarely to 12.
guinea pig	63–66 days	6–8, rarely to 12.
dog	62–68 days	4–6, rarely 2 to 14.
mongoose	48–50 days	2, rarely 1 to 5.
cat	55–63 days	4–6, rarely to 9.
monk seal	probably about 330 days	1.
horse	11 months	1, sometimes 2.
burro (donkey)	12 months	1.
pig	109–123 days	5–6, rarely to 22.
axis deer	$7\frac{1}{2}$ months	1, very rarely 2.
black-tailed deer	7 months	1–2, rarely 3.
pronghorn	8 months	1–2.
water buffalo	10 months	1–2.
cattle	9 months	1–2, sometimes to 4.
goat	147–161 days	1–2, rarely to 5.
mouflon & sheep	146–161 days (usually 152)	1–2, rarely to 5.

330

Appendix C

Dental Formulae of Hawaiian Mammals

Dental formulae are commonly expressed in one of two ways; in the older technique, all the teeth were numbered, beginning in the foremouth and working back on both sides of the jaw to the molars. The newer technique, and the one used below, is to express for one side of the jaw the upper teeth as numerators and the lower teeth as denominators of fractions. The count is then doubled to reach the total number. The incisors are represented by I, the canines by C, the premolars by P, and the molars by M.

In the case of monk seals, their mode of life has so adapted their tooth structure as to make it impossible to determine whether some of the teeth are premolars or molars; the sum total of these two types are then just called postcanines, and are designated by the letters PC.

	I	C	P	M	TOTAL
wallaby	3/1	0/0	2/2	4/4	32
Hawaiian bat	1/3	1/1	2/2	3/3	32
rabbit	2/1	0/0	3/2	3/3	28
Norway, black, and Hawaiian rats	1/1	0/0	0/0	3/3	16
house mouse	1/1	0/0	0/0	3/3	16
dog	3/3	1/1	4/4	2/3	42
mongoose	3/3	1/1	4/4	2/2	40

cat	3/3	1/1	3/2	1/1	30
monk seal	2/2	1/1	PC 5/5		32
horse	3/3	1/1	3–4/3	3/3	40–42
pig	3/3	1/1	4/4	3/3	44
axis deer	0/3	0/1	3/3	3/3	32
black-tailed deer	all animals listed below are same formula as axis deer				32
pronghorn					32
water buffalo					32
cattle					32
goat					32
mouflon					32
sheep					32

Appendix D

Phylogenetic Classification of Hawaiian Mammals

PHYLUM	Chordata
SUBPHYLUM	Vertebrata
CLASS	Mammalia
SUBCLASS	Theria
INFRACLASS	Metatheria
ORDER	Marsupialia
SUPERFAMILY	Phalangeroidea
FAMILY	Macropodidae
GENUS AND SPECIES	*Petrogale penicillata* (brush-tailed rock wallaby)
INFRACLASS	Eutheria
ORDER	Chiroptera
SUPERFAMILY	Vespertilionoidea
FAMILY	Vespertilionidae
GENUS AND SPECIES	*Lasiurus cinereus semotus* (Hawaiian bat)
ORDER	Lagomorpha
FAMILY	Leporidae
GENUS AND SPECIES	*Oryctolagus cuniculus* (European rabbit)

After Simpson, G. G. 1945. The Principles of Classification and a Classification of Mammals. Bull. Amer. Mus. Nat. Hist. Vol. 85: 350 pp.

ORDER	Rodentia
SUPERFAMILY	Muroidea
FAMILY	Muridae
GENUS AND SPECIES	*Rattus rattus* (black rat) *Rattus norvegicus* (brown rat) *Rattus exulans hawaiiensis* (Hawaiian rat)
GENUS AND SPECIES	*Mus musculus* (house mouse)
SUPERFAMILY	Cavioidea
FAMILY	Caviidae
GENUS AND SPECIES	*Cavia cobaya* (guinea pig)
ORDER	Carnivora
SUPERFAMILY	Canoidea
FAMILY	Canidae
GENUS AND SPECIES	*Canis familiaris* (dog)
SUPERFAMILY	Feloidea
FAMILY	Viverridae
GENUS AND SPECIES	*Herpestes auropunctatus* (small Indian mongoose)
FAMILY	Felidae
GENUS AND SPECIES	*Felis catus* (cat)
SUBORDER	Pinnipedia
FAMILY	Phocidae
GENUS AND SPECIES	*Monachus schauinslandi* (Hawaiian monk seal)
ORDER	Perissodactyla
SUPERFAMILY	Equoidea
FAMILY	Equidae
GENUS AND SPECIES	*Equus caballus* (horse)
GENUS AND SPECIES	*Equus asinus* (donkey)

ORDER	Artiodactyla
SUBORDER	Suiformes
SUPERFAMILY	Suoidea
FAMILY	Suidae
GENUS AND SPECIES	*Sus scrofa*
	(pig)
SUBORDER	Ruminantia
SUPERFAMILY	Cervoidea
FAMILY	Cervidae
SUBFAMILY	Cervinae
GENUS AND SPECIES	*Axis axis*
	(axis deer)
SUBFAMILY	Odocoileinae
GENUS AND SPECIES	*Odocoileus hemionus columbianus*
	(black-tailed deer)
SUPERFAMILY	Bovoidea
FAMILY	Antilocapridae
GENUS AND SPECIES	*Antilocapra americana*
	(pronghorn)
FAMILY	Bovidae
SUBFAMILY	Bovinae
GENUS AND SPECIES	*Bubalus bubalus*
	(water buffalo)
GENUS AND SPECIES	*Bos taurus*
	(cattle)
SUBFAMILY	Caprinae
GENUS AND SPECIES	*Capra hircus*
	(goat)
GENUS AND SPECIES	*Ovis musimon*
	(mouflon)
GENUS AND SPECIES	*Ovis aries*
	(sheep)

Index

Authors listed in the Literature Citations are not necessarily noted in the index. Because the islands of Kauai, Oahu, Molokai, Lanai, Maui, and Hawaii are mentioned many hundred times throughout the text, they are not indicated in the index; all other islands in the archipelago are indexed. Page numbers in boldface refer to entire chapters.